THE INTERNATIONAL DIMENSIONS OF CYBERSPACE LAW

Law of Cyberspace Series

Volume 1

The International Dimensions of Cyberspace Law

DARTMOUTH

UNESCO

Publishing

Aldershot • Burlington USA • Singapore • Sydney

Law of Cyberspace Series, no. 1
Bruno de Padirac, General Editor
This volume edited by Teresa Fuentes-Camacho

© UNESCO, 2000

Published by

Ashgate Publishing Limited
Gower House
Croft Road
Aldershot
Hants GU11 3HR
England

Ashgate Publishing Company
131 Main Street
Burlington
Vermont 05401–5600
USA

Ashgate website: http://www.ashgate.com

Published jointly with the United Nations
Educational, Scientific and Cultural Organization
7, place de Fontenoy, 75352, Paris 07 SP, France

British Library Cataloguing in Publication Data
The International Dimensions of Cyberspace Law.
  (Law of Cyberspace)
  1. Information superhighway—Law and legislation.
  I. Fuentes-Camacho, T.
  341.7'577

Library of Congress Cataloging-in-Publication Data
The international dimensions of cyberspace law/edited by Teresa
  Fuentes-Camacho.
      p.   cm. (Law of Cyberspace series)
    Includes index.
    ISBN 0–7546–2141–3 — ISBN 0–7546–2146–4 (pbk.)
    1. Data transmission systems—Law and legislation.   2. Computer
  networks—Law and legislation.   I. Fuentes-Camacho, T.   II. Series.
  K564.C6I565   2000
  341.7'577—dc21   00–34845

Ashgate   ISBN 0 7546 2141 3 (Hbk)
          ISBN 0 7546 2146 4 (Pbk)
UNESCO ISBN 92–3–103752–8

Typeset by Manton Typesetters, Louth, Lincolnshire, UK.
Printed in Great Britain by MPG Books Ltd, Bodmin, Cornwall.

Contents

Notes on Contributors

Anna Maria Balsano is responsible for intellectual property matters at the Legal Affairs Department of the European Space Agency. An Italian lawyer registered at the Rome Court of Appeal, she is the author of numerous papers on intellectual property and space activities which have been presented at international fora and published in a number of reviews.

Teresa Fuentes-Camacho is a Doctor of Law (PhD) of the University of Paris II, officially recognized in Spain, and is a lawyer at the Madrid Bar Association. She has also been a researcher and Professor of International and European Law. An international civil servant since 1994, she has been responsible for several projects on international legal affairs, particularly in the fields of culture and communication. As a legal officer, she is responsible at UNESCO for the legal aspects of the UNESCO project on the information society.

Gareth Grainger, a lawyer, is Deputy Chairman of the Australian Broadcasting Authority. He is Chairman of the International Council on Young People and Media Research Forum, Chairman of the Communication Network of the Australian National Commission for UNESCO and Vice-Chairman of Commission V of the UNESCO General Conference.

Christina Hultmark is Professor of Commercial Law and Doctor of Law of the University of Gothenburg (Sweden). She is Head of the Swedish Delegation to the UNCITRAL Working Group on Electronic Commerce. She is an expert with UNESCO on the question of cyberspace law and with the International Chamber of Commerce Project on Electronic Commerce, besides being a member of the Co-ordination Group in the Project towards a European Civil Code. She has authored numerous books and papers on contract law and electronic commerce.

Elizabeth Longworth (LLM) is Principal of a law and consultancy firm in Auckland (New Zealand) and an adviser to the New Zealand

Law Commission on electronic commerce. She is a professional mediator and has worked with, or made presentations to, the New Zealand Law Society, UNESCO, ISO, the Australian Broadcasting Authority, the EU Telecommunications Data Protection Working Group and OECD. Co-author of the leading text on New Zealand's privacy law, she has also authored numerous books and papers on information law and policy, legal implications of new technologies, and privacy and alternative dispute resolution.

Bruno de Padirac is a UNESCO civil servant, responsible for the societal aspects of new information and communication technologies. He has been in charge of projects on science and technology policies and ethics, computerized information systems, and management reforms.

Yves Poullet is Dean of, and Professor at, the Faculty of Law, and Director of the Centre for Research on Informatics and Law of the University of Namur (Belgium). He is a member of the Legal Advisory Board of the European Commission and of the Belgian Data Protection Commission. He has been associated many times, as an expert, with the Council of Europe, the European Commission and UNESCO. He sits on the editorial board of a number of legal newspapers specializing in information law.

Pierre Trudel is Professor at the Centre for Research in Public Law, Faculty of Law, University of Montreal (Canada). He is the author of numerous books and papers on cyberspace law, communication law, human rights law, civil law and intellectual property law.

Foreword

The Law of Cyberspace series, under the direction of UNESCO,[*] deals with the legal aspects of the emerging information society and corresponding ethical matters. The Organization's multidisciplinary nature means that the series will be of a far-reaching nature, with studies ranging from national, regional and international law to social and political science, philosophy and ethics, and international relations.

The series is intended to foster pluralist ideas and opinions. The authors are leading academics and professionals who are the principal actors in cyberspace from the public and private sectors all over the world. All are engaged in transdisciplinary reflection and international consultation on the use of the new information and communication technologies to ensure that the emerging information society is more democratic for all. The series is open to the publication of studies and contributions from specialists everywhere at national and international levels.

The intention is to extend the consensus on legal principles, which are the basis of existing international instruments, to alternative ethical values and to reflect this in a universal declaration on cyberspace and human rights. The series is intended for all those whose work relates to philosophy, culture, education, science, technology, industry, politics and the law and who desire to keep informed of cyberspace law developments.

---

[*] Internet site: www.unesco.org/cybersociety.

Preface

The object of *The International Dimensions of Cyberspace Law*, the first volume in UNESCO's Law of Cyberspace series, is to examine the international dimensions of cyberspace law and the timeliness of drawing up the most appropriate international standard instrument for this new environment, exploring ways and means of achieving it and defining the Organization's precise role in this respect.

The framework that UNESCO is helping to develop for the international community, with the participation of all the actors in cyberspace, should be:

- **Ethical**: based on the application to cyberspace of the ethical values and legal principles which lie at the heart of the various international legal instruments, including freedom of expression, universal access to information and knowledge, reliability and harmlessness of information, protection of privacy and personal data, protection of intellectual property, and cultural and linguistic diversity.
- **Flexible and technologically neutral**: taking account of the technological progress and circumstances of each nation and of all categories of actors in cyberspace.
- **Multiform**: comprising complementary educational, legal and technological measures. The core components of the framework would be self-regulation by producers and carriers of information, and the existence of technological tools for protection and empowerment of end users. These two elements should be accompanied and buttressed by a flexible, coherent and stable legal environment comprising harmonized laws and regulations, if necessary at national level, and legal instruments developed by UNESCO and other intergovernmental organizations at international level.
- **Universal**: widely recognized and applied by the main actors in cyberspace, including those in developing countries.

The purpose of this work is to ensure that the emerging information society is more democratic and prosperous for all citizens both now and in the future. We are grateful to the authors who have contributed so generously to this publication and to those within UNESCO who helped bring this project to fruition.

It is to be hoped that the thinking underlying the present volume will help to extend the field of discussion on this vital matter, thereby contributing to the doctrine at the level of international law.

List of Abbreviations

ABA	Australian Broadcasting Authority
ACLU	American Civil Liberties Union
ADR	alternative dispute resolution
APEC	Asia Pacific Economic Council
BT	British Telecom
CDA	Communications Decency Act 1996
CISG	United Nations Convention on Contracts for the International Sale of Goods
COMEST	UNESCO World Commission on the Ethics of Scientific Knowledge and Technology
DNS	domain name system
EC	European Community
ECMS	Electronic Copyright Management Systems
ECSL	European Centre for Space Law
EFF	Electronic Frontier Foundation
EFTA	European Free Trade Association
EPIC	Electronic Privacy Information Center
ESA	European Space Agency
ETSI	European Telecommunication Standards Institute
EU	European Union
GBD	Global Business Dialogue
GII	global information infrastructure
GTPNet	Global Trade Point Network
ICANN	Internet Corporation for Assigned Names and Numbers
ICC	International Chamber of Commerce
ICPA	Internet Consumer Protection Agency
ICT	Information & Communication Technologies
ID	online identity
IGA	intergovernmental agreement
IHPIG	Information Highway Parental Improvement Group
IISL	International Institute of Space Law
ILO	International Labour Organization
IP	Internet Protocol

IP	intellectual property
ISO	International Standards Organization
ISP	Internet service providers
ITC	Independent Television Commission
ITU	International Telecommunication Union
IWGCR	International Working Group on Content Rating
NICT	new information and communication technologies
NPTN	National Public Telecomputing Network
OECD	Organization for Economic Cooperation and Development
PICS	Platform for Internet Content Selection
PKI	public key infrastructure
PKAF	Public Key Authentification Framework
P3P	Platform for Privacy Preferences
RDF	Resource Description Framework
RFC	request for comment
RSAC	Recreational Software Advisory Council
syops	systems operators
UN	United Nations
UNESCO	United Nations Educational, Scientific and Cultural Organization
UNCITRAL	United Nations Commission on International Trade Law
UNCOPUOS	United Nations Committee on the Peaceful Uses of Outer Space
UNCTC	United Nations Centre for Transnational Corporations
UNGA	United Nations General Assembly
USC	United States Code
USSR	Union of Soviet Socialist Republics
VAT	value added tax
WWW	World Wide Web
W3C	World Wide Web Consortium
WIPO	World Intellectual Property Organization
WTO	World Trade Organization

Introduction: UNESCO and the Law of Cyberspace

TERESA FUENTES-CAMACHO

CYBERSPACE

Cyberspace is a new human and technological environment. It involves people from all countries, cultures and languages and of all ages and occupations supplying and demanding information, as well as a worldwide network of computers interconnected by means of telecommunication infrastructures enabling information to be processed and transmitted digitally. Synonyms of the term 'cyberspace' include 'information superhighways' and 'info sphere'.

Interactive and open, this space for expression, information and transaction is potentially accessible to growing numbers of people. Nevertheless, inequalities of access to cyberspace are considerable, and to an even greater degree than for traditional and audiovisual media. Digital information has no stable material form in time and space and circulates in a mainly anonymous and unregulated way. The new information and communication technologies (NICT) operating in cyberspace are used for an infinite number of purposes, for better and for worse, and taking no account of national boundaries, legislations and jurisdictions.

UNESCO'S INVOLVEMENT WITH CYBERSPACE

In conformity with its Constitution, the founding text which dates from 1945, UNESCO is mandated, under Article 1, paragraph 2 (a) and (b), to '[advance] the mutual knowledge and understanding of peoples, through all means of mass communication and to that end recommend such international agreements as may be necessary ... [and to] Give fresh impulse to popular education and to the spread of culture'.

1

What role must UNESCO play, therefore, in order to achieve an international agreement on cyberspace? How can the Organization ensure the promotion and protection of human rights and fundamental freedoms in cyberspace in the domains of education, science and culture?

Under its mission in respect of traditional and audiovisual media and global digital networks, UNESCO has a mandate to guarantee freedom of expression and the right to information. For this reason, the Organization promotes the application of human rights and fundamental freedoms in the media and works to reduce the gap between those who have information and scientific knowledge and those who are excluded. Since its foundation, its activities have been concerned with all means of mass communications, from traditional media (books and the press) to audiovisual media (film, television and optical media) and, more recently, cyberspace (global digital networks). In view of the particular characteristics of cyberspace, the Organization has a unique role to play in societal and technological terms.

UNESCO'S ROLE AS A CATALYST FOR CYBERSPACE

The progressive development of international law in the electronic age is one of the principal responsibilities of the United Nations system. With the close of the United Nations Decade for International Law, the new environment of cyberspace has become an important domain for the exercise of these responsibilities.

UNESCO is qualified to study the issues arising from the interaction of the societal and technological aspects of cyberspace at global level, being the sole specialized agency of the United Nations system to have multidisciplinary competence, fulfil an ethical mission and enjoy the advantage of global intergovernmental coverage. By reason of its multidisciplinary competence in the fields of education, human and natural science (particularly philosophy, psychology, sociology and law), culture and communication (particularly information and communication technologies), UNESCO is particularly well placed to undertake and promote transdisciplinary research on the ethical, legal and societal issues of cyberspace. All institutions concerned by the impact of cyberspace in their domains of competence should definitely conduct this research in concert – particularly the Council of Europe, EU, OECD, ITU, UNCITRAL, WIPO and the WTO.

According to its ethical mission, UNESCO's role is one of complementing the dimension introduced by electronic commerce. Its mandate to advance the 'mutual knowledge and understanding of peoples' means that the Organization must define the ethical values intended to inspire the future information society so that it may be democratic both for all those living today and for future generations. Reaching a consensus on such values requires the participation of the philosophical, political, cultural, educational, legal, religious, scientific and technological communities which are the traditional partners of the Organization. Independent persons from these communities make up UNESCO's World Commission on the Ethics of Scientific Knowledge and Technology (COMEST). In addition, the participation of the industry and the private sector, which are the main actors in electronic commerce, is essential and has been underlined by Resolution 36 adopted by the General Conference of UNESCO at its 29th session (hereafter, 29 C/Resolution 36).

By reason of its intergovernmental coverage and the multicultural membership of its partners, institutional or otherwise, UNESCO is a window on the world; hence it is qualified to contribute to ethical reflection and the development of a universal legal framework for cyberspace, which could be accepted and respected by all the actors working in this international environment.

In short, UNESCO has a constitutional mandate specifically relating to freedom of expression, universal access to information and the development of communication.

UNESCO'S WORK IN THE DOMAIN OF ETHICS AND CYBERSPACE LAW

UNESCO's strategy for cyberspace is based on a transdisciplinary reflection involving all domains of knowledge, as well as international concerted action involving all the actors in cyberspace. This strategy is being developed along two complementary lines – one societal and the other technological. It consists of:

- promoting transdisciplinary reflection and concerted international action on the ethical, legal and societal issues of the emerging information society, so that it may be more democratic and prosperous, and remain an environment where the rule of law prevails
- ensuring that the NICT are more readily accessible to all, and more effectively used for the development of education, science, culture and communication.

UNESCO is proceeding with the following tasks relating to the law and ethics of cyberspace:

- promoting or establishing permanent observatories, information exchange centres and Internet discussion groups on the ethical, legal and sociocultural issues of the new information and communication technologies used in cyberspace, the aim being to disseminate information on codes of conduct, national laws and regulations, international law, and policies and institutions that are active in the domain of cyberspace law and ethics

•   encouraging and conducting transdisciplinary research on the ethical and legal aspects of the information society, particularly on freedom of expression, universal access, intellectual property and fair use, protection of privacy, personal data security, violence, crime, pornography, paedophilia and racism on the Internet, the rights of the child, cultural pluralism, multilingualism and, in general terms, the application of human rights and fundamental freedoms in cyberspace

•   collaborating with member states, international institutions and organizations, inside or outside the United Nations system, as well as the private sector. This collaboration aims to reach a consensus on the ethical values and legal principles to be promoted in cyberspace. It also involves examining the expediency of, and the ways and means for, the gradual establishment of a flexible ethical and legal framework that will apply globally to cyberspace and be universally recognized.

The Task Force on Cyberspace Law and Ethics is mandated within the Secretariat of UNESCO to perform or coordinate the above-mentioned tasks. COMEST, for its part, advises the Organization on the various ethical questions posed by the information society.

SOME POSITIONS OF PRINCIPLE

The increasing development of NICT has led to some confusion with regard to broad legal questions. The technological revolution, which is so stimulating for all humankind, necessitates a thorough examination and consolidation of traditional legal concepts and values, while imposing new legal requirements (*ius novum*). In the new situation created by cyberspace, UNESCO must adopt certain positions of principle in accordance with its Constitution.

Technological Neutrality in the Domain of Informatics, Telecommunications and Multimedia

UNESCO must promote and use the NICT to facilitate freedom of expression, the dissemination of information, access to knowledge, scientific research, the conservation and development of the cultural heritage, and prosperity for all. While science aspires to know reality, in the interests of objective truth, technology, for its part concerned with utilitarian efficiency, aims to take action on reality at a given time and place. Technology is incorporated in intellectual works, as well as in processes and products generally distributed by industrial and commercial concerns for commercial gain. Unlike science, technology is not neutral either in cultural or economic terms. By reason of UNESCO's intergovernmental composition, global competence and universality of ideal, and bearing in mind its intellectual and ethical mission, the Organization has to respect the general principle of technological neutrality when it examines the ethical, legal, educational, scientific, social and cultural issues of cyberspace, or promotes a particular NICT or uses it through a specific proprietary work or industrial process or product. This implies that the Organization recommends its member states or partners to respect this principle when using a particular technology to fulfil a given function at a particular time. It is absolutely not within the competence of the Organization to recommend any particular proprietary work or commercially available industrial process or product to its member states. Unless specifically requested by a member state as part of an expert mission, the Organization must not publicly promote or criticize:

- any particular computer software, whether or not provided free of charge, which is developed by a publishing house or independent software developer, or
- any particular hardware branded and marketed by the computing, telecommunication or multimedia industries.

Privacy and Electronic Commerce

There exists a serious risk that electronic commerce might compromise human rights and the fundamental freedoms, which are universal, inalienable and indivisible. Since 1996 the most advanced countries in economic and technological terms (particularly in respect of NICT) are adopting legal guidelines and rules for electronic commerce from the point of view of trade law within interregional and international bodies. Such guidelines and rules are intended to protect human rights and fundamental freedoms. In particular, privacy protection and intellectual property rights have been the subject of attention on the part of organizations such as the Council of Europe and the OECD. They should correspond to the interests, or meet the needs, of the least developed countries and also complement or form part of the universal framework for cyberspace.

Freedom of Expression and Control of Illegal or Harmful Material

Cyberspace must be a free and safe environment. Freedom of expression is one of the fundamental freedoms upheld by UNESCO, one of whose mandates is to 'promote the free flow of ideas by word and image'. The campaign against illegal and harmful content to certain vulnerable groups and individuals is also part of the Organization's programme. This campaign cannot justify any form of censorship and must be achieved through educating all the actors in cyberspace, self-regulation by information producers and providers, and the provision of technical means of selection and filtering for end users to adapt to their own ethical values.

Common Good, Intellectual Property and Public Domain

Cyberspace must serve the common good which requires both the protection of intellectual property (Article 27 of the Universal Declaration of Human Rights) and the free flow of information (ibid., Article 19) in cyberspace. UNESCO must promote the protection of intellectual property in cyberspace, as it has done in the traditional and audiovisual media, for such protection contributes towards universal access to information and knowledge by encouraging creativity and the distribution of intellectual works. However, it must also encourage the protection, extension and accessibility of public information in the interests of democracy and universal participation in public affairs and culture at national and international levels. Such information of a public nature generally includes works on which the copyright has expired and which therefore come into the public domain. It also consists of information produced by the public sector, including national local authorities and administrations of all kinds, and information relating to the common heritage of mankind, particularly cultural and scientific. This public information may be accessible, whether or not free of charge. UNESCO should ensure that the cost of information, whether public or private property, remains affordable and reasonable, to prevent costs creating a barrier to universal access of information in cyberspace. UNESCO therefore has to promote the principle of universal access in cyberspace, in the interest of all – authors and public – without erecting any barriers, public or private, and protect the balance between the private interests of individuals or businesses (such as the right of authors to fair remuneration) and the general interest of society (such as the promotion of creativity or the conversion of information into knowledge) – a balance which constitutes the common good to which cyberspace must contribute.

Towards a Universal Framework for Cyberspace

In cooperation with qualified experts from all regions of the world and competent international organizations UNESCO has studied this complex issue since 1995. Within its interdisciplinary project on the ethical, legal and societal challenges of the information society, the Organization has raised the question of the need for an international agreement on cyberspace, expressed as a framework in the broad meaning of the term, and built on a general consensus. In 1997 its supreme body, the General Conference, 'convinced that UNESCO should be the organization of the United Nations system to take the intellectual lead in this area', recognized 'the urgent importance of establishing a framework relating to cyberspace at the international level by formulating a body of educational, scientific and cultural principles', and stressed that 'full consideration should be devoted to all relevant aspects' (see 29 C/Resolution 36).

The authors of this publication are all internationally recognized experts in cyberspace law. They have worked closely with the UNESCO Task Force on Cyberspace Law and Ethics to study the various and complex legal issues raised by this new environment. They have attended different meetings on the subject organized or sponsored by UNESCO and which have contributed to the formulation of a body of international principles. These appear in the Report of the Experts Meeting on Cyberspace Law (Monte-Carlo, Principality of Monaco, 29–30 September 1998) given in the Annex to the this publication. Thanks to their expertise and knowledge, the following chapters should contribute in a meaningful way to international dialogue and reflection under the auspices of UNESCO.

1 The Possibilities for a Legal Framework for Cyberspace – including a New Zealand Perspective

ELIZABETH LONGWORTH

INTRODUCTION

The complexity and diversity of the legal, ethical and societal issues raised by the global information infrastructure and the emerging information society has prompted UNESCO[1] to question whether there is a need for a new international agreement – a 'cyberspace law', to be expressed as a framework and built on an underlying consensus – to address these issues. Most countries, including New Zealand, agreed that a careful study of the issues was required before any decision should be taken. This chapter was prepared as a contribution to the ensuing dialogue.

The Creation of a New Political Economy through Cyberspace

The UNESCO brief for this paper was to consider the desirability, feasibility and difficulties of establishing a legal framework for cyberspace. The significance of addressing future developments in 'cyberspace law' is apparent if we look at the wider context. Don Tapscott in *The Digital Economy* describes humanity as being 'at the dawn of an Age of Networked Intelligence – an age that is giving birth to a new economy, a new politics, and a new society'.[2]

The Internet will be the critical medium for the transformation predicted by Tapscott. The need to examine the role of the law and regulation is obvious in a world where there is 'the potential for severe social stratification, unprecedented invasion of privacy and other rights, structural unemployment, and massive social dislocation and conflict'.[3]

The desirability and feasibility of 'establishing cyberspace law' will come down to the decisions and actions (whether conscious, passive or by omission) within the various hierarchies of the Internet and by the numerous agencies worldwide that are currently considering the impact of this new technology within their own spheres of influence.

The task for this chapter is to provide a better understanding of just what is possible within the design parameters of 'cyberspace law'. It should also suggest a methodology by which any suggestion of 'regulation' of the Internet, and its impacts, could be analysed.

Desirability and Feasibility: From whose Perspective?

Any discussion which focuses on the prerequisites to developing 'an international cyberspace law' must first clarify its assumptions. From which perspective is the desirability and feasibility of such an outcome to be viewed? What do we mean by a 'cyberspace law'? Is it an international law in the conventional sense or a macro-strategy for all laws touching on, and touched by, the advent of the Internet? What are the mechanisms for implementing a cyberspace law? Who and what institutions would make the rules and enforce them (irrespective of their content)? At the abstract level, who is to be governed? Who will be the 'cyberpolice'?[4] And even if such a complex topic could be distilled into these few issues, why should cyberspace be regulated?

The Paradigm Shift away from Substantive Centralized Legal Models

The scope and complexity of the concept of cyberspace law and the pervasiveness of its influence on nations, economies and societies mean that much of the commentary on this topic moves straight to issues of substantive law. It has proved relatively easy for commentators to consider the adaptation of existing and discrete laws to the electronic systems within the global networked environment. It is far more difficult to devise a strategy which assumes a unified global approach to law design and which is capable of responding to the dynamic relationships within cyberspace.

For this reason there is plenty of commentary on specific aspects of laws in cyberspace: for example, intellectual property (copyright) issues; the liability of systems operators; the growth of electronic commerce; surveillance and the privacy invasive potential of Internet technologies; the undermining of sovereign control (tax havens); the opportunity for criminal and anti-social behaviours (pornography and paedophile rings) to go unchecked; encryption and law enforcement rights to intercept communications; and the value of freedom of speech versus censorship.

Much of the discussion on the possibilities of international cyberspace law is based on conventional legal paradigms: for example, matrices of rights and duties; centralized sources of law; defining legal outcomes in physical terms; and being constrained by the physical parameters of geography, location and the ability to fix an event or activity at a point in time.

David Post[5] explains that the focus on the substantive content of legal rules is known as 'legal centralism'. This is where the inquiry focuses on alternative sets of substantive laws, on the assumption that there is some law-making body in a position to choose the optimal set. He observes a difficulty in that the global network is proving 'relatively resistant to centralised control'. The reasons for this are explored in this chapter.

The concepts of cyberspace demand a reassessment of how we create and apply law. In his analysis of *Law in a Digital World*, Ethan Katsh talks about the law as journeying in new directions and to new places, to being displayed on screen rather than on paper, and as posing significant challenges to traditional legal practices and concepts. These include:

> … an unfamiliar and rapidly changing information environment … where the value of information increases more when it moves than when it is put away for safekeeping and is guarded. To a world of flexible spaces, of new relationships, and of greater possibilities for individual and group communication. To a place where law faces new meanings and new expectations.[6]

A macro-analysis of the legal implications of cyberspace is justified, even if Tapscott's prediction on the 'Age of Networked Intelligence' is only partly true. The role of the Internet has been likened to 'the revolutionary media of the past' and is seen as 'central to this quiet and radical reallocation of political and economic power – the creation of a new political economy. The I-Way is the technological enabling mechanism.'[7]

The Focus on the Process of Design and Law-making

This chapter will suggest that a credible discussion of the possibilities of a legal framework for cyberspace must follow a process-based analysis. The method assumes that the question of a cyberspace law is essentially a design issue, necessitating an understanding of how and why laws are made. The significance of this approach is illustrated by Katsh, as he explains the way in which law is employed as both a tool and a symbol:

> Law is a process that we hope will shape behaviour, settle disputes, secure rights and protect liberties, even achieve justice. It is a social force with many components, something that touches many other institutions and, in turn, is influenced by them. It is a set of rules and doctrines, an institution that embodies cultural values and traditions, and it is also a profession. It can, of course, be much less than this by preserving injustice, violating principle, and denying the realization of rights.[8]

The methodology of the following analysis begins with a consideration of the characteristics of cyberspace. What is peculiar to activities on, and the nature of, the Internet which impact on the development of law? How do the architecture, network protocols and worldwide access to the global information infrastructure impact on the design of the legal infrastructure which has already emerged or will evolve? The description of these particular characteristics will identify critical design parameters. These constraints and opportunities modify and influence the development of a legal framework for cyberspace.

There are also various law-making processes that are highly relevant to the emerging 'landscape' of cyberspace law. These include applicable regulatory models, an understanding of how control is exerted within a networked environment, the effect of competition and the analogy of customary law. It is also important to consider the reasons why laws are made, and their inherent values and policy objectives.

Any analysis of a legal framework must also address the difficulties of dispute resolution in cyberspace. In particular, the issues of jurisdiction, choice of law and enforcement pose significant constraints on the evolution of a cyberspace law. This discussion considers the merits of existing legal structures, such as international law, by treaty and forum. The possibilities of adapting private law, especially contractual arbitration, are explained, along with the potential to develop certain alternative dispute resolution models.

What emerges from the discussion is a clear outline of a legal framework for cyberspace. The existing infrastructure has been identified. The desirability and feasibility of developing certain components have been addressed. The framework is illustrated by reference to the New Zealand experience and perspective.

In order to conceptualize such a complex topic and diverse issues, the chapter is structured into three principal sections, as follows:

1.   The Characteristics of Cyberspace and the Processes which Influence Law-making
2.   Dispute Resolution in Cyberspace, and
3.   The Emerging Legal Framework for Cyberspace.

A Synthesis to Identify Relevant Themes or Principles

There are a number of key authors and other sources who have influenced the approach taken in this chapter; they include David Johnson, Ethan Katsh, Lawrence Lessig, Darrell Menthe, Henry Perritt and David Post. I have drawn on their work because of their philosophical and jurisprudential focus on the dynamics and evolution of regulatory controls in cyberspace. The following discussion, therefore, is a synthesis of many views into themes and principles that are distinct possibilities for a legal framework. All these are worth pursuing in terms of future directions and, from a New Zealand perspective, are consistent with that country's approach to regulation and governance.

THE CHARACTERISTICS OF CYBERSPACE AND THE PROCESSES WHICH INFLUENCE LAW-MAKING

What is Cyberspace?

What is meant by references to 'cyberspace'? This popular term was originally coined to describe 'the emerging digital world'.[9] It conveyed the experience of a new environment and dimension, as being the inverse of physical reality; cyberspace is thought of as an 'alternative' reality where the computer controls sensory stimuli. It is now a common expression used to describe the complexities of the phenomenon created by a global network of computers that use the telecommunications infrastructure to transmit electronic messages.[10] It encompasses various components, including the system of 'node' computers and web servers scattered throughout the world, and intermediaries such as systems operators and service providers.

There are many interchangeable terms in use for the same concept, including the World Wide Web, the Global Information Infrastructure

(GII) and the I-Way. These arise out of the convergence of computer and telecommunications technologies manifested by the communications network or structure known as the Internet.

The Internet is described as 'self-healing' (an example being the ability to remail messages).[11] The reason for this is that the computers (comprising the Internet) are interconnected in such a way that transmissions can be rerouted around inoperable or congested parts of the network. The messages are also broken into packets, rather than being forwarded as a single data stream, for transmission. Each packet may take a different route and will still be received and reassembled at the computer of destination.[12] The data is transmitted around the Internet using 'hundreds of switching computers and dozens of telephone networks'.[13] It is a global network comprising many individual networks.

There are a number of intermediaries operating on the Internet, providing the services of transmission, routing and receipt of messages. These are known as Internet service providers (ISPs) and systems operators (sysops). The network protocols established by these operators, and between networks, will play a key role in the 'regulation'of the Internet.

The visual representation of information on the Internet is made available through web pages within web sites. The World Wide Web is accessible by the identifiers of domain names and site addresses, and through the use of search engines. The domain names are allocated by a centrally coordinated system of registries under the auspices of the recently established Internet Corporation for Assigned Names and Numbers (ICANN). Incorporated in October 1998, ICANN is a non-profit corporation, responsible for administering the Internet Protocol (IP) number system, the Domain Name System (DNS), and related Internet protocols.

The increasing popularity and uptake of the Internet is dramatic, with the statistics changing hourly. The rate of subscription to online services is dynamic. It is also sufficiently new technology (in terms of its increasing globalization, capacity and interconnectivity) to justify its description as a 'phenomenon'.

Characteristics of Cyberspace which Impact on Legal Design

No Geographic Limitations

What are the relevant characteristics of cyberspace which impact on legal design? The most significant defining characteristic of the digital frontier is the irrelevance of geographic boundaries. Cyberspace is about cross-border electronic communications. It is not localized.

The significance lies in the comment that 'the Internet is not merely multi-jurisdictional, it is almost a-jurisdictional'.[14]

Conventionally, territorial borders have delineated areas within which different sets of legal rules apply.[15] Henry Perritt explains that 'the close relationship between state power and judicial authority historically led to a localization of judicial authority'.[16] The advent of the Internet, with its global communications, challenges the practice of applying laws based on physical and geographic boundaries. There is a 'lack of congruence between cyberspace's global, transnational character and the national geographic limitations on the courts ... '.[17]

The consequences, summarized from David Post, may be presented briefly. The ability to impose sanctions on law violators is fundamentally constrained by the need for physical proximity and physical control. This is not an absolute constraint because there are mechanisms whereby individual sovereigns can impose their rules on those not physically present within the jurisdiction; however, these mechanisms entail additional enforcement costs in terms of the direct costs of projecting sovereign power extraterritorially and the costs of coordinating and harmonizing the legal regimes of competing sovereigns.[18]

Johnson and Post describe the shift in presumption (away from territorial constraints) as follows:

> While these electronic communications play havoc with geographic boundaries, a new boundary, made up of the screens and passwords that separate the virtual world from the 'real world' of atoms, emerges. This new boundary defines a distinct Cyberspace that needs and can create new law and legal institutions of its own. Territorially-based law-making and law-enforcing authorities find this new environment deeply threatening.[19]

These commentators predict that

> Separated from doctrine tied to territorial jurisdiction, new rules will emerge, in a variety of online spaces, to govern a wide range of new phenomena that have no clear parallel in the nonvirtual world. These new rules will play the role of law by defining legal personhood and property, resolving disputes, and crystallizing a collective conversation about core values.[20]

Anonymity in Cyberspace

There are other features of cyberspace that undermine the traditional development and application of the law. The Internet allows users to remain anonymous. Its very nature enables mobility; a user may source its information activities anywhere in the world. The origins of a message can be disguised. The user can create a cyber-identity or profile which is very different from real or physical identity. In effect, it is possible to use these techniques to 'create havens to avoid legal responsibility'.[21] Examples where this trend is already apparent are found in the areas of intellectual property infringement, defamation, pornography, taxation of cross-border transactions and information warfare activities.

Ability to Escape Controls

There is another angle on the mobility of users, in terms of the multitude of diverse sites on the Internet and the choices available to users as to who they visit or communicate with. It is possible for those who are subject to various rules or controls to change jurisdictions to find a more favourable set of rules. As David Post explains, 'The Internet allows a relatively easy change of jurisdiction, or "exit", from any given controller, leading to the unprecedented – and unpredictable – situation of a "free market" in rule sets.'[22]

The effectiveness of a sanction, imposed by a top-down or centralized authority, is:

> ... an inverse function of the ease with which the lower-order controllers can 'exit' from the regime defined by those laws – by evading detection of rule-violating behaviour, evading the State-imposed sanctions for such violations, or somehow withdrawing from the rule-making jurisdiction of the State as controller.[23]

Structural Hierarchies and Zones

The Internet is three-dimensional in structure, with its hierarchical system of domain name registries and asymmetrical proliferation of intermediaries (such as sysops and certification authorities) controlling the gateways, network protocols and web servers. It also comprises 'zones', by which the architecture enables or prevents access to or the distribution of certain goods and services.[24]

These structural features of cyberspace are of vital importance to the construction of a future legal framework because the operational structure and architecture of the Internet is responsible for the emergence of 'polycentric' or 'decentralised, emergent' law[25] (discussed below). These theories can be extrapolated from a factual analysis of the characteristics of cyberspace. For example, David Post argues that 'There may well be no principle more important for understanding rule-making in cyberspace than that of distinguishing between the Internet as a whole and the individual networks that are its component members'. It is the interplay between these 'that will prove to be of fundamental importance in determining the efficacy with which State law can be imposed on individual network communities'.[26]

Interactive, Dynamic Nature

The interactive and dynamic nature of communicating in cyberspace is another characteristic which is very significant in terms of its impact on the creation and maintenance of cyber-relationships. Interactive electronic documents operate on different assumptions from those printed on paper in that they lack discrete qualities (in time and space). The focus, for electronic information, is on the present and the process of change whereas paper-based information emphasizes the past and reinforces the historic intention of the parties. The speed of electronic updating, and the emphasis on interactive communication, mean that change will become the norm, rather than the stability of, and reliance on, print documents. Ethan Katsh explains the significance of this revolutionary change in information transactions as follows:

> ... as new forms of communication are employed, new concerns will arise and the focus on the past will be less emphasized. Process and dispute solving and re-establishing relationships may, for example, prove to be valued much more than determining what was intended at the time some contract was formed.[27]

In this way, the nature of the relationships within cyberspace will influence the development of cyberspace law. For example, if the interactive dynamic nature of the communication results in the parties to a relationship looking forwards, not backwards, then the corollary is a greater interest in alternative dispute resolution. If the emphasis is on maintaining and improving the current relationship, then this should impact on the way cyberspace parties manage their contracts and resolve their conflicts.

Electronic Linkages

There are other implications for the cyberspace legal framework. The electronic contract, as a dynamic and hypertextual document, can link parties and information in a way that is not feasible with paper. It can monitor relationships and respond to, and inform, parties of changing events, as well as fulfil the more traditional function of specifying obligations and conditions of performance. 'The electronic contract, in other words, connects the parties to each other and, if desired, to other people and to other sources of information in ways that are difficult to imagine with paper.'[28]

One of the cumulative effects of this new contractual environment – along with the Internet architecture, hyperlinks, speed and disregard for distance – is to encourage self-regulatory controls or behaviour. This in turn will promote the use of private law as a significant component of the cyberspace legal infrastructure.

Impact on Legal Design

The impact of these cyberspace characteristics as parameters (both constraints and opportunities) on the design of future law can be summarized by the comments of Johnson and Post:

> Cyberspace radically undermines the relationship between legally significant (online) phenomena and physical location. The rise of the global computer network is destroying the link between geographical location and: (1) the power of local governments to assert control over online behaviour; (2) the effects of online behaviour on individuals or things; (3) the legitimacy of the efforts of the local sovereign to enforce rules applicable to global phenomena; and (4) the ability of physical location to give notice of which sets of rules to apply.[29]

This means that cyberspace has certain characteristics or features which will serve to define what is possible in the way of a legal framework. The Internet 'radically subverts the system of rule-making based on borders between physical spaces' or any claim that it should 'be governed by territorially defined rules'.[30] The hierarchies and architecture of the Internet (its networks within a network) are already decentralized and multidimensional. The nature of the communications on the Internet encourage a self-regulatory and proactive approach to managing relationships. Users have huge flexibility and mobility on the Internet; they can evade controls and sanctions. Conventional enforcement mechanisms outside a governing jurisdiction have corresponding costs.

The model of centralized governance or authority (described as 'top-down') is not feasible, given these unique characteristics of the Internet. These very same features make it more probable that the legal framework will be heavily reliant on collective action involving the voluntary acceptance of standards or technical protocols. This acceptance may translate into an uptake of the more formal model of private law, including (possibly) alternative dispute resolution mechanisms. The emergence of decentralized decision-making could well provide the most coherent, comprehensive and recognizable form of governance in cyberspace. This is what Johnson and Post call 'decentralised, emergent' law.[31]

This thesis is supported by other analyses of how laws are made. For example, the following discussion (pp.23–35) considers the governance models which are a consequence of applying the concepts of regulation by 'code', economic and competition theories of control, and customary law. Implicit in this discussion are the reasons why laws are thought necessary in the first place – in other words, the objectives of law-making. How can public values and interests be reflected, or the 'greater good' be recognized?

Reasons or Need for Law

The Objectives of Law-making

Since the objectives of law-making are an exceedingly complex topic, this chapter addresses the question only to the extent necessary to place the following discussion in context and, in particular, the role of cyberspace 'controllers' in, and the reflection of values (through the Internet architecture and activities) within, the cyberspace law-making process.

At the most general level, law-making is driven by many different imperatives. Where law is seen as a control or regulation of behaviour or activity, it exists to impose a constraint of some kind, to operate as an incentive or to reflect a policy of a higher authority. The concepts of control and influence feature heavily in the following analysis of law-making in cyberspace.

Another way of discovering why laws evolve is to focus on substantive law. The substance or content of each law is designed to reflect a value, to protect specific interests or stakeholders, to order interactions or relationships in a certain way or to uphold a right or principle.

There are, of course, many other reasons and theories. Some may prefer to see the objectives of law-making defined by reference to the fundamental activities of the law. These have been described as 'accommodating conflicting claims, defining property rights, establishing rules to guide conduct, enforcing those rules, and resolving disputes'.[32]

Legitimacy and Authority for Law

The significance of this issue, when considering the future legal framework for cyberspace, is that the reasons for law-making go to the heart of questions as to the legitimacy of, and appropriate authority for, the law. This raises a number of further issues.

For example, if the emerging norm (or virtual reality) for cyberspace is a structure which is no longer controllable by a top-down centralized authority (having, instead, decentralized projects and global self-regulation), how can such a legal structure be reconciled with the original imperatives of each substantive law? One solution might be to focus on the purpose of the law-making process rather than the purpose of the content of substantive law. It is then possible to justify a decentralized governance model where 'The basic purpose of law is to maximize individual rational choice, and to minimize the role of power or force enjoyed by the few, in determining outcomes'.[33]

Another aspect of the same difficulty is the notion that legitimacy relies on being sourced to some form of sovereign authority. This in turn may draw on constitutional principles and institutions to imbue it with that authority. In a democratic constitutional model this authority would derive from institutions which represent 'the collective voice' of their constituents. In a democratic environment, the notion of legitimacy implies the 'consent of the governed', where those who are subject to the laws have a role in their formulation.[34] If governance on the Internet equates to controls exerted through architectural design infrastructure (such as domain name hierarchies) and technical specifications, how will it be possible to ensure that the 'collective voice' and 'consent of the governed' is somehow reflected in the regulated outcomes in cyberspace?

Can self-regulation – such as a decentralized private law framework for cyberspace – be sufficient 'authority' for that form of law-making? While in areas of commerce the notion of regulation through consensus may be acceptable, what of other traditional paper-based activities that migrate to become online services? A common response is that Internet users make an active choice to enter cyberspace and there is, therefore, a consensual element to interaction. There are two aspects to this. The first is that, by exercising rational choices and because of the availability of exit options on the Internet, the users are playing a role in the formulation of the applicable rules; this is legitimacy through the consent of the governed in cyberspace. The second aspect of the decision to enter (participate in) cyberspace is that Internet users are a sufficient 'collective voice' and it is not necessary to reflect other broader-based societal values or interests. However, the accessibility of cyberspace to all cultures and ages, and the proliferation of information and services which are increasingly only available through this medium, mean that the consensual argument is becoming more tenuous. Arguably, that Internet use no longer reflects some kind of 'closed shop' for an elite group of informed and consenting participants. As this change occurs, the question of how to reflect values and to protect interests enters a new phase.

I return to this issue when discussing 'The interrelationship between law-making and values' (p.25) in the context of how we know that a particular value, which is imposed through regulation by architectural controls of the Internet ('code'), is the right one. In this way, the debate over projecting values (and the other imperatives for law-making) is intrinsically linked to the discussion of the levels of awareness in cyberspace. Control through architecture (and therefore influence over law-making objectives) is far more insidious if users are unaware of how their choices, behaviours and the values by which they wish to live can be modified in this way.

Reflecting Values and the Greater Good

What of the need for overt recognition of a value or interest in cyberspace law? Again, the unique characteristics of cyberspace will constrain what can be achieved through legal objectives, as well as how the legal framework can evolve. The characteristics of cyberspace include its ability, as a medium, to communicate a diverse range of views and activities. Users can move between environments and adopt cyber-profiles or personae. These features could pre-empt any successful attempts by nations or sovereign authorities to impose their own view as to which values, rights and policies should prevail in a global cyberspace community.

At the level of actual interaction and disputes on the Internet, the problem of how to reflect the 'greater good', in term of values, has been described as follows:

> The central problem for the regulation of the net is not how to enforce widely agreed upon rules but, rather, how to define what we mean by wrongdoing. What is infringement? or defamation? or a privacy invasion? or unacceptably obscene? The net creates many different phenomena requiring the development of new rules. Is it wrong to send large volumes of unsolicited commercial email? What notice should be given before a host system writes a cookie file to my hard disk? Under what circumstances is it wrong to 'cache' a web page?[35]

The answer is provided by the authors of these questions, Johnson and Post. Again, guidance lies in the defining characteristics of the Internet (already discussed):

> The great virtue of the net is that it allows multiple, incompatible resolutions of such policy questions – by giving those who disagree about the resolution of any particular question the means to avoid contact with one another ... and to filter out messages from non-congenial areas.[36]

Johnson and Post define the problem of collective action as the selection of means by which individuals coordinate and order their interactions to achieve what they believe is a greater good.[37] They argue that the new decentralized processes of the Internet may address this issue in ways that are very different from conventional law-making or traditional ways of enforcing behavioural norms:

> Cyberspace is not being conditioned on any required promises to comply with (or to require users to comply with) specific laws or behavioural standards. That has, to be sure, left sysops free to impose their own rules on end users. But the diversity of differing venues on the net, and the ability of users to decide where to visit (and where not to visit) and with whom to communicate, has tended both to keep sysop tyranny in check and to limit the adverse impact of wrongdoing by individual users.[38]

The Internet and Freedom of Expression

It is possible for the actual architecture and design of the information technology to manifest values. The significance of this, in terms of legal design, for the emerging legal framework for cyberspace is explained on page 25. For now, the point can be illustrated by a macro-view of the Internet; its advent manifests a key value of public international law. In the New Zealand High Court decision of *Oggi*,[39] the judge commented that the Internet has 'the effect of promoting a major principle [Article 19] of the International Covenant of Economic, Social and Cultural Rights to which New Zealand and many other states are party'. This is the value-based consensus, reflected in international convention and enshrined in national law (such as in New Zealand), which recognizes the freedom of expression.

Other Pressures and Influences

There are a number of pressures which can be expected to influence views on the desirability of regulating cyberspace. For example, as the Internet develops and becomes more complex and interconnected with other technologies comprising the global information infrastructure (GII), there will be corresponding demands for reliability. We can expect less tolerance for data packets which are misrouted or errors in the translation of electronic addresses. There are certain activities which will be regarded as undesirable, involving information warfare. Disseminating computer viruses through software code will be regarded as unacceptable activiety. Those who use the Internet for electronic commerce will want to be sure that their interests are protected through encryption and other safeguards.

We have previously discussed the connection between the decentralized design of the Internet and the implications of this characteristic for the ability of a sovereign to enforce its rules extraterritorially. The cost of pursuing enforcement against persons or entities not physically located within the jurisdiction, and the drain on time and financial resources in pursuing the harmonization of substantive laws between governments, are in themselves significant constraints on law-making.

All these pressures will focus attention on the need for some form of governance. As we will see later, conventional models will be of limited assistance. The ultimate legal framework or infrastructure will comprise many elements. The dominant theme will be those models which accommodate decentralized and self-regulatory initiatives. The ultimate framework can be expected to include actual features of the Internet, such as its 'self-healing' nature and the availability of the technology itself to be used as a sanction or deterrent for certain activities – for example, electronic copyright management systems. This will operate as a constraint on activities which are perceived as 'wrongdoing' or will serve to impose a behavioural norm.

Regulatory Models of Direct Law, Norms, Market and Code

The Four Structures of Control

In order to postulate on future cyberspace law, it is important to understand the structures of control – that is, the applicable regulatory models. Lawrence Lessig describes how behaviour is regulated by four types of constraints:[40] direct law; social norms; the market; and 'code'.

The first constraint, the direct effect of the law, is where a particular behaviour will suffer a sanction or penalty if it violates a directive under that law.[41] The examples given by Lessig of how the law regulates behaviour in cyberspace include copyright, defamation and obscenity laws.[42] Irrespective of the difficulties of enforcement, there are substantive laws which can be invoked to impose a sanction in response to an infringement of a corresponding right.

The second constraint consists of social norms. These regulate behaviour by threatening an adverse consequence or punishment to be imposed by society or the community. Norms influence in a decentralized manner, rather than being enforced by a centralized authority, such as government.[43] Users within the cyberspace community will respond, through the technology, to discourage certain behaviours. In other words, understandings and 'netiquette' (customs and etiquette on the Internet) will impose norms by constraining certain cyberspace activities through the threat of decentralized sanctions.[44]

It is well recognized, especially in the New Zealand (deregulated) economy, that markets regulate: they constrain both individual and collective behaviour.[45] Pricing structures such as access charges to certain information on the Web and to Internet services, as well as factors such as congestion, influence the choices that cyberspace consumers make and are all examples of cyberspace market regulation.

Finally, Lessig describes the constraints of architecture or nature – what he calls the constraints of 'real space code'. The analogy, in cyberspace terms, are the features of Internet architecture, its software, network protocols or 'code'. These constrain by imposing conditions on the way in which users can operate online. Lessig gives numerous examples of this type of regulation through 'code': the requirement of an access password; the ability to participate anonymously or to have a number of e-mail identities; the availability of encryption options; filtering and censorship mechanisms; and systems designed to prevent copyright infringement. Lessig emphasizes that these features, selected by the code-writers, constrain behaviour and the range of possible activities on the Internet.

When discussing the four regulatory models, Lessig highlights two qualities which further the understanding of the nature of regulatory constraints. These are of strategic importance because, before deciding which type of regulatory constraint should apply, the lawmaker must understand how these constraints are susceptible to change.[46] The first concept is 'directness or immediacy of the constraint at issue': a more direct constraint is more effective in terms of its ability to exert control.[47] The second concept is 'plasticity'. Lessig explains that 'plasticity describes the ease with which a particular constraint can be changed'.[48]

Regulating Cyberspace through 'Code'

The significance of regulation by code is that it is possible to attribute certain values to the way code influences choices. Lessig explains that there is a 'relationship between the values imbedded in a particular cyberspace place (its architecture), and the code that makes those values possible'.[49] He illustrates this by reference to the rules of various online services. For example, a service may stipulate that participants in a discussion group must have only one cyber-identity and that this must be the user's true (real space) identity. While, in one sense, this may constrain users in what they feel free to discuss, it also manifests a value where 'individuals are tied to their real space reputation; where that reputation is used, in a sense, to moderate or control the conversation of that space'.[50]

Some services offer blocking features. Such software is designed to enable a user to block access of a subsidiary screen name. This is not only a parental control feature, it also says something about the values embedded in that code. It gives parents the 'power of code' to control what might otherwise only be achieved by threats (a process akin to regulation through law) or by educative norms.[51] Other software, which does not offer blocking features or which encourages chat rooms, irrespective of identity or profiles, reflects a value of openness and freedom of speech. The use of tracking devices, embedded in a computer chip, have been criticized for not respecting the privacy value. The software technology which prevents downloading of electronic text is adopting a position on the use of intellectual property which may not recognize the balance within most copyright regimes – that is, between constraints on copying and exceptions such as 'fair use'.

Lessig concludes that the software (or code-writers) are in effect defining the constraints that apply to the users of these services and technologies. Therefore, 'different code architectures express different values'.[52] 'Code in cyberspace can more easily substitute for law, or norms. Code can more subtly control and discipline behavior. Code is a richer alternative to these other forms of constraint.'[53]

In other words, if Lessig is correct and the legal framework is dominated by regulation through code, this leaves the question of whether or not the 'right' values are being projected through code unaddressed. Lessig describes the problem as follows:

> Once it is plain that code can replace law, the pedigree of the codewriters becomes central. Code in essence becomes an alternative sovereign – since it is in essence an alternative structure of regulation. But who authors the sovereign authority? And with what legitimacy?[54]

The Interrelationship between Law-making and Values

A significant issue in the development of a cyberspace framework therefore is the values inherent in each rule-set and their reflection within the legal structures. It seems reasonable, from the preceding analysis, to expect far greater reliance on the role of contracts as one of the methods of decentralized governance within cyberspace. It is thus appropriate to distinguish at this point between the situation where there is clearly a binding agreement, or contract, established by the parties within a relationship on the Internet (whether between users or sysops), and other circumstances where we can identify the influence of regulation by code. An example of the latter category might be an operating constraint imposed on a user by a network protocol of an online service or a domain name registry requirement.

Lessig[55] argues that it is incorrect to assume that 'code' equates to contract. While they may be structurally similar, law by contract (as opposed to code) has a number of other critical components in order to constitute a binding agreement enforceable through the courts.

The most important distinction, argues Lessig, is that with every agreement 'there is a judgment made by the enforcer about whether this obligation should be enforced'.[56] The courts must take into account the various doctrines reflected in the law of contract, such as public policy interests, frustration, mistake, misrepresentation, fair trading practices, restitution, estoppel and other principles of equity. In other words, the contract comprises a mix of public values – manifest in the public policy exceptions and other applicable statutory requirements – and private obligations.[57]

The concern in the context of code operating as regulation (or law) is: 'When the code enforces agreements, or when the code carries out a self-imposed constraint, these public values are not necessarily weighed into the mix … . The codewriter operates free of the implicit limitations of contract law.'[58] If law-making, and its enforcement, involve a degree of 'due process' in assimilating and reflecting public values (in the sense that contract law is 'public' law[59]), what is the significance of *de facto* regulation by the structures imposed through code? We should not assume that the 'invisible hand of codewriters'[60] will be liberal: the development of filtering and copyright management software indicates otherwise.

Government Intervention through Legislation of Code

The inability to control cyberspace and its participants through top-down centralized law-making has been quite threatening for many governments.[61] The initial response was to debate the pros and cons of legislative intervention from the presumption that national legislation for cyberspace was feasible. There is now a far better understanding of the phenomenon of cyberspace and the inherent characteristics which undermine attempts to regulate it through territorially-based centralized law-making. Despite this, there may still be room for a limited degree of legislative intervention in the cyberspace legal framework.

In his discussion on the US environment, Lessig provides a number of examples within the telecommunications industry where direct law (such as the Digital Telephony Act), designed to have an indirect effect on some other activity (namely, law enforcement) has been enacted. This is what Lessig describes as an example of law regulating code; in this case, Congress enacted a law requiring telephone companies to select a network architecture that facilitates wire-tapping (and therefore reduces the constraints that the code or architecture might otherwise have imposed on law enforcement).[62] This is an example of legislative intervention to modify the implied values within the architecture or code. There are many other examples, such as Germany's Teleservices Data Protection Act 1997 which addresses the need for systemic data protection measures in the design and selection of technical devices.[63]

The significance is that, if it is felt that a particular value or policy should be pursued, through law-making, in cyberspace, it may be possible – depending on the way in which value or policy translates within the architecture or code of the Internet – to fall back on legislative intervention to reflect these public values or policies. These objectives would have to be achieved by imposing constraints on the actual design or operation of a specific architecture or network protocol. This component of the cyberspace legal framework will be of limited application, but it still exists as an avenue of regulation.

Control of the Internet through Competition

The law-making process for cyberspace, and predictions as to the key components of a legal framework, can be analysed in other terms – for example, under competition theory. David Post in his article, 'Anarchy, State, and the Internet: An Essay on Law-Making in Cyberspace'[64] focuses on who will make and enforce the rules which will govern cyberspace. He rephrases these questions as, 'How does the competition among these controllers proceed? What are the "controller-selecting rules" that determine which controllers' rules take precedence in the event of conflict?'[65]

Network Protocols as Primary Rule-maker

As in the preceding discussion, Post analyses the characteristics of the Internet and identifies the unique role of network protocols. He states that 'the person or entity in a position to dictate the content of these network protocols is, in the first instance at least, a primary "rule-maker" in regard to the behavior on the network'. They have a competitive advantage over other controllers, 'by virtue of their ability to control entry onto the network by excluding behavior that is inconsistent with the message entry rules'.[66]

There are many intermediaries within the Internet, whether in the form of network or service providers or operators of contents servers and search engines. Given the control that some of these intermediaries have, and their subtle role in creating the 'rule-sets' discussed previously, there may be a tendency to look to these intermediaries to accept responsibility for the activities carried out on their network and to expect them to intercede in resolving disputes. This may take the form of banishing a user, removing controversial material or blocking the dissemination of a file. An example is the Australian proposal[67] to regulate the carriage of highly offensive or illegal content over the Internet, to be administered by the Australian Broadcasting Authority (ABA). Under this proposal, an online service provider could be required to remove material which does not meet the Australian classification standards.

It is not only the control over entry to the network which is significant, but also the potential to control message content through the technical network specifications. For example, some sysops can impose rules regarding permissible or prohibited network behaviours or activities. In New Zealand a number of ISPs have entered into the Internet Service Provider Code of Practice (June 1999). Post concludes that organizations such as these will potentially be the locus for much of the substantive rule-making in cyberspace, due to their advantageous position in 'the competition for rule-making precedence'.[68]

Controller Hierarchies

It is apparent, from the earlier discussion on the characteristics of cyberspace, that the 'structures' of the Internet (vertical and asymmetrical) will impact on the legal framework. It is possible for a network organization (sysop/ISP/registry) to impose conditions on the users and other contracting parties that are controlled by the nature of the vertical hierarchy. However, when it comes to government attempting to apply the same type of control, the effectiveness is undermined by the very nature of the Internet which enables users or 'lower order controllers' to exit from this sphere of influence or jurisdiction and to begin operating from somewhere else within cyberspace. As noted by Post, if the network functions as a gatekeeper for users in cyberspace, it is to be expected that governments may attempt 'to impose coercive sanctions on network administrators (and thereby on the network rules) in order to implement their own [government's] particular preferred set of rules on behaviour in this environment'.[69] The Australian proposal to control the hosting of proscribed offensive material includes legislative sanctions for breach of a code of practice or an ABA-imposed standard.

The Internet as an Exit Strategy

The ability to exit is a form of control. A significant feature of the architecture is that it 'was designed without a centralised control mechanism or any single location through which all internet work must travel'. This means that 'all network nodes are effectively equipotent, each equally capable of performing the key internetwork message routing functions'.[70]

Post explains the implications of this design feature in terms of the Internet being an 'exit strategy' for individual network rule-makers, by allowing one to exit by evading detection and to withdraw from jurisdictional control:

> Decentralisation implies that the costs of monitoring behaviour are substantially higher, and rule-violative behaviour substantially more difficult to detect, than would be the case under a centralised internetwork design ... Should a particular network rule-set be incompatible with the law of sovereign x, the network rule-set itself can, with relative ease, be transferred elsewhere on the internetwork, outside of the sovereign's jurisdictional boundaries.[71]

Post concludes, most significantly, that while 'each individual network can be constrained from "above" in regard to the rule-sets it can or cannot adopt, the aggregate range of such rule-sets in cyberspace will be far less susceptible to such control'.[72] He uses the analogy of a 'market for rules' in which competitive forces between networks will result in the users' preferences being reflected both in the choices available and in the design of the rules for accessing or operating within the particular network.

Customary Law in Cyberspace

Post's conclusions lead to the same question as that posed by Lessig: namely, what is the legitimacy of this form of rule-making? Cyberspace, on the above analysis, can be viewed as an unregulated market, reflecting the values and preferences of: those who control the design of the network protocols and technical specifications; the users who choose to access certain networks and be governed by their inherent controls or rule-sets; or those who exercise their 'exit strategy' (just another form of control). These law-making processes therefore raise a number of issues as to the authority and legitimacy of such outcomes. For this reason, it is relevant to explore the notion of customary law.

One of the common themes to emerge from the literature on cyberspace law is the analogy between the decentralized, self-regulatory model and the historical development of medieval customary law known as 'merchant law' (*lex mercatoria*). Post describes this as representing 'an example of unregulated and unconstrained rule-making in the absence of State control'.[73]

The Analogy of Merchant Law

Historically, in the Middle Ages, disputes were resolved at the local level, the focus being the feudal law relating to land claims. Jurisdictional problems arose with the growth of trade and the need to find a way to resolve disputes other than by reference to local law. They needed to reflect a common recognition of certain rules (reflecting the reality of cross-border trade), but in a way which was independent of any particular sovereignty.

The merchant law is seen as one of the models of customary law. This 'law' was based on customs that had a sufficient degree of recognition and acceptance to elevate that custom to binding authority. Customary law has been described as coming from a period:

> ... when legal theorists didn't much care to trace law to its source. Law could be recognised as normative, and authoritative, without locating the ultimate agent responsible for this normativity. Custom, whatever its source and however it had been transformed, could bind.[74]

The Need for a Source of Authority

During the twentieth century the notion of customary law as a source of authority has been challenged by the theory of 'positivism' which 'drives the jurist to locate the source of law in a sovereign before that law can be recognised as authoritative'.[75] One view is that the source of authority for upholding custom does originate with a sovereign if that custom or law is then enforced through the courts. This in turn raises a debate as to the appropriate role of the courts in interpreting and applying the common law, as opposed to actually creating law.

In response to this need to source any legal authority to an underlying generative or sovereign authority, the proponents of customary law began to rely on the concept of consent. This was reflected by the rise of contract as the mechanism to record consent and become the source of authority in law.[76] This is also illustrated by public international law which recognizes a number of sources, including international custom – which is evidence of a general practice accepted as law – and international conventions which are often a codification of customary law rather than an attempt to create new rules. The treaty process, especially multilateral negotiations, illustrates 'the formulation of a broad consensus, and this consensus is often expressed in customary international norms'.[77]

The significance of the discussion on customary law is that the advent of cyberspace may force an acceptance of 'rich customary authority not grounded in the actions of any particular sovereign ... . Cyberspace may become a model for understanding again how there could be authority without a law giver.'[78] The practice of issuing a RFC (request for comment) on the Internet is seen by many libertarian users as a source of 'customary' cyberspace law.

Grounding in Conventional Law

However, the positivist premise is not abandoned. In order to work within the current legal culture, Goldsmith and Lessig[79] make the point that any system, such as a legal framework for cyberspace, that wishes to establish itself as an enforceable system of authority must recognize that an authority for a law of cyberspace still needs to be grounded directly in the 'law of real space' – that is, in a current and recognized conventional system of law. Such a requirement is quite compatible with our previous conclusions: that cyberspace will see a growth in private law by virtue of its reliance on self-regulating relationships, its decentralized nature, and the significance of rule-making by code and the presence of various controllers within the network hierarchies.

The Internet can be seen as a 'technology for contracting'.[80] It is through this mechanism that it is possible to construct a system of law comprising self-imposed obligations which are enforceable through a legal system. This should satisfy the positivist requirement of a founding or originating authority because, as Goldsmith and Lessig explain, 'The authority for an obligation comes from it being self-imposed; its significance comes through its enforceability'.[81]

In this way, we separate the issues surrounding the law-making process and the authority for law in cyberspace from a different matter – namely, the efficacy of a cyberspace legal system. The latter issue focuses on the difficulties with jurisdiction and enforceability (see the discussion in 'Dispute resolution in Cyberspace' (p.35).

Issues arising out of Decentralized Rule-making

Regardless of which analysis is applied to the characteristics and the new environment of cyberspace, the consensus is that an uncoordinated, decentralized system of rule-making will emerge within cyberspace. As will be discussed later, this will not be exclusive of all other law-making models. The ultimate framework will comprise a number of components, even if decentralized self-regulation by 'private actors' will predominate. What, then, are some of the concerns arising out of the cyberspace law-making process? The following issues are summarized from Johnson and Post's web publication, *And How Shall the Net be Governed?*[82]

Reflecting Collective Values

In the earlier discussion on the reasons for, or objectives of, law-making, the issue arose as to how to reflect collective values or the 'pursuit of the public good' within cyberspace. It is possible for behavioural norms and sanctions on unacceptable activities to be imposed, and for netiquette and consensus (custom) to emerge, through a number of features. This is a consequence of the ability to regulate the Internet through code (architecture and technical specifications), combined with the freedom of choice of many rule-sets available through sysops and other intermediaries.

The Need for Authentication

The organizations working on the implications of the GII are currently grappling with a very significant feature of the future legal infrastructure. This is the development of authentication mechanisms, such as digital signatures and certification registries, within the Public Key Infrastructure (PKI) (discussed under 'The emerging legal framework for cyberspace' (p.47). As these mechanisms evolve – and it will be an evolutionary process as 'new releases' supersede unstable or discredited versions[83] – it should be possible to address a significant issue: namely, the need to be able to link a user's electronic identity to the true (non-virtual or real space) identity of an individual or organization. This authentication facility will be a very significant development in the growth of private law, particularly in the use of contracts for global electronic commerce.

Finding Optimal Rule-sets

One of the reasons why this chapter has explored the economic and competitive theory of control within cyberspace is because these ideas influence perceptions of the law-making process. For example, Johnson and Post[84] point out the lack of objective criteria by which to measure whether any particular rule-set is optimal. (This is in the context of whether or not decentralized private decision-making can be relied on to produce outcomes which are either in accord with the collective definition of the public good or else anticipate the outcome that would have been proposed by conventional sovereign law-making.) They argue that decentralized decision-making – as opposed to uniform rules across the Internet on each topic – 'is the most cost-effective and accurate means of reflecting the real preferences of participants on the net with regard to the structure of electronic federalism'.[85]

They also introduce the concept of 'net leverage', referring to:

> The option and burden of identifying connections to avoid, or users to banish, or specific messages to filter, can be spread across the entire base of net users, as sysops and users decide unilaterally whether or not to rely on the recommendations of others.[86]

Contrast this with the costs of projecting a specific view of each law onto a centralized global policy-making process. The time and resources to negotiate and ratify international treaties support the above view of the efficiencies and economies of the decentralized model.

Government Intervention to Protect Vital Interests

What are the chances of existing governments (sovereign authorities) attempting to intervene to outlaw certain activities or to protect what they perceive to be the vital interests of their constituencies? It is recognized that this temptation will always exist. Much will depend on the quality of self-governance that emerges from the experience of living with cyberspace.

As a more direct response on this issue, a number of authors turn to the doctrine of 'comity'. This is expressed as follows:

> A state may not exercise jurisdiction to prescribe law with respect to a person or activity having connections with another state when the exercise of such jurisdiction is unreasonable ... '. [In the context of conflict of laws] ... 'each state has an obligation to evaluate its own as well as the other state's interest in exercising jurisdiction and should defer to the other state if that state's interest is clearly greater.[87]

The significance to the cyberspace framework is that:

> ... comity reflects the view that those who care more deeply about and better understand the disputed activity should determine the outcomes ... . This doctrine does not disable territorial sovereigns from protecting the interests of those individuals located within their spheres of control, but it calls upon them to exercise a significant degree of restraint when doing so.[88]

The precedent effect of the doctrine of comity has also been applied to other concepts of self-regulation – in particular, to the importance of learning from the practice of delegated authorities. This is where industries or organizations have been empowered by their governments with rule-making functions and the protection of their vital interests. The convergence and precedent effect of these doctrines are important to the rule-making process for cyberspace:

> Comity and delegation represent the wise conservation of governmental resources and allocate decisions to those who most fully understand the special needs and characteristics of a particular 'sphere' of being. Although Cyberspace represents a new sphere that cuts across national boundaries, the fundamental principle remains. If the sysops and users who collectively inhabit and control a particular area of the

Net want to establish special rules to govern conduct there, and if that rule-set does not fundamentally impinge upon the vital interests of others who never visit this new space, then the law of sovereigns in the physical world should defer to this new form of self-government.[89]

Attempts to control online behaviour, such as by overly aggressive regulation, could force affected users to conduct their activities so that they are outside the jurisdiction – or 'offshore'. This has been described as 'regulatory arbitrage' and could operate 'to disconnect the local territory from the new, valuable global trade'.[90]

Maximizing Individual Choice

The consensual adoption of standards of behaviour as law raises a serious objection that such standards are merely ethics or custom. Furthermore, the decentralized emergent model of governance destroys 'traditional notions of equality before the law'. Johnson and Post deal with these arguments in terms of the purpose or objectives of law-making – namely, as being to maximize individual rational choice and to minimize the role of power or force enjoyed by the few in determining outcomes. They explain that:

> Because the net allows easy movement among differing spaces, and also allows easy (online) separation of people who don't agree on basic groundrules, it can afford NOT to be consistent. Its inconsistency gives all users an equal right to create or select the rule sets they find most empowering. This new emergent law of the net can thus maximise individual, well informed, choice without failing to give clear prospective guidance regarding applicable rules (for any particular online space).[91]

Negative Impacts should not determine the Model

Finally, under the heading 'The Net Needs a Good Foreign Policy', Johnson and Post point out a related concern to the above discussion on the reasons for government intervention. Certain online activities can have demonstrable and unacceptable negative impacts on people in the real world who never elected to participate in cyberspace. The possibilities of these types of 'negative externalities' do not equate to preferring a particular governance model over another: 'The mere possibility of negative externalities cannot itself, in the abstract, answer the question of net governance.'[92]

Again, the necessity for nations, if sufficiently motivated, to take concerted action to protect vital security and other interests is not precluded by the decentralized governance model. The possibility of international treaty or action in extreme cases forms part of the legal framework for cyberspace, even if in practice it is rarely invoked, would face numerous impediments and may have inherent limitations.

DISPUTE RESOLUTION IN CYBERSPACE

The Problem of Jurisdiction and Enforcement

The issues of which jurisdiction (choice of law and enforcement mechanism) should apply to cyberspace has been the most significant constraint on the evolution of cyberspace law. The conventional application of conflict of laws doctrines to the unique characteristics of cyberspace poses immediate feasibility problems. Although there continue to be instances of sovereign nations attempting to control Internet users within their geographic jurisdiction, the assumption when developing a legal framework for cyberspace must be that:

> The non-geographic character of the net makes it very difficult to apply current, territorially-based rules to activities online … . Local sovereigns may have a monopoly on the lawful use of physical force, but they cannot control online actions whose physical location is irrelevant or cannot even be established.[93]

However, these difficulties in determining and applying jurisdiction in the context of Internet claims or actions are not insurmountable; they require a multilateral approach. The issue of jurisdiction should be tackled separately from the question of how the Internet should be governed. This is not to deny the close relationship between these issues; but the difficulties with jurisdiction and enforcement impact primarily on the efficacy of the law, rather than on its legitimacy.

As has already been discussed (and will be illustrated in the next main section), it is possible to identify an emerging governance model for cyberspace and to distinguish the various components in the resulting legal framework. The Internet is not anarchic. It is currently regulated, albeit not in the conventional or traditional sense; the underlying presumption of laws having to be based on geographic boundaries is displaced by the demands of cyberspace.

The difficulties encountered when trying to apply domestic (local) jurisdiction or territorially-based laws to the cyberspace environment can be illustrated by the following scenarios. In any Internet communication there are numerous participants or 'actors'. Given the transnational nature of the communications, it will prove exceedingly difficult to determine which jurisdiction should apply. For example, in any interaction in cyberspace there is an uploader (of information), a downloader, the potential to access or view information, a server containing the web page files, the routing of data in packets through nodes around the world, the practice of constituent parts of a web page (such as images) being called up from other servers, links from the web page to other pages from elsewhere in cyberspace, and the intervention of sysops.[94]

Each of these actors and activities may be 'located' in different jurisdictions. It will be the norm, rather than the exception, that these participants are unknown to each other, as opposed to being seen as senders and recipients in a predetermined relationship. The question, therefore, is which country's substantive legal rules should apply to message content or other information or activities accessed via the Internet? Whose courts should have the jurisdiction to adjudicate civil disputes and prosecute crimes?

There have been attempts by states to prescribe the laws that will apply to online activities. Minnesota, in the United States, was one of the first to attempt a general exercise of jurisdiction.[95] However, the effect of its rule was to make all cyberspace subject to Minnesota law and this has been soundly criticized for having ignored the presumption against extraterritoriality in the application of US law:[96] 'The Court looked no further than its own state's long-arm statute in finding *in personam* jurisdiction without considering issues of federalism, comity, or international law, that is, without considering whether jurisdiction to prescribe existed or not.'[97]

Rules on Conflict of Laws

The choice of law (jurisdiction to prescribe) will be highly significant in the context of cyberspace and the growth of private law. Although a forum may have personal jurisdiction and venue, the choice of law rules may require that the dispute be heard under the substantive law of another jurisdiction. Each country has its own private international law (forming part of its national or domestic law). These variances between countries are what distinguish each body of private international law from public international law. Despite these differences, there have been many initiatives to harmonize this area of law. Many jurisdictions pursue common objectives and are influenced by the doctrine of comity and the need to respect the civil justice systems of other countries.[98]

The New Zealand Approach

In the New Zealand context, a dispute over an international transaction on the Internet raises the following issues:

- Can the court exercise jurisdiction to deal with the case under its own law (known as the law of the forum or *lex fori*)?
- Will the court exercise jurisdiction?
- Which law should apply to the resolution of the dispute? (Parties to a contract may choose the governing law to apply to the contract.)
- How can the judgment be enforced?[99]

US doctrines of Judicial Power

The laws of each country or state may vary in terms of the tests within each one of the above categories. In the context of North American law, Henry Perritt[100] describes the overlapping doctrines of judicial power to decide a dispute over substantive rules as being: personal jurisdiction (over persons and organizations); notice by arrest, service of process or otherwise; choice of law or the jurisdiction to prescribe the applicable law; venue; and the ability to have a judgment recognized and then enforced.

As Henry Perritt explains, a tort claim:

> ... requires determining the state with the most significant relationship to the occurrence and the parties, including consideration of the place where the injury occurred, the place of the conduct causing the injury, the domicile, residence, nationality, place of incorporation and place of business of the parties and the place where any relationship between the parties is centred. Contracts cases are adjudicated according to the law chosen by the parties or, in the absence of any such chosen law, by the law of the state which has the most significant relationship to the transactions and the parties with respect to a particular issue. The most significant relationship in contract cases is determined based on the place of contracting, the place of negotiation of the contract, the place of performance, the location of the subject matter of the contract, and the domicile, residence, nationality, place of incorporation and place of business of the parties.[101]

The concept of 'place' and territoriality dominate in the above choice of law rules. Clearly, the presumptions of physical location and proximity (by linking territoriality to geographical borders) is fundamentally challenged by the global characteristics of cyberspace. Despite these characteristics, it still needs to be remembered that 'the GII may span geographic boundaries, but its human actors are present in some traditional jurisdiction, and the hardware, software and financial assets used to operate each part of the GII are located in some traditional jurisdiction'.[102]

The outcome of a successful court action is usually a judgment which is enforced by executing against property owned by the judgment debtor. In the criminal law, judgment ordinarily requires the physical custody or presence of the defendant because personal jurisdiction in criminal cases is universally based on physical presence. The formal process of extradition (in order to obtain custody of a defendant located in another jurisdiction) is an example of an international uniform approach to procedural rules.

The Matrix of International Law

The situation is confused even further by the matrix of international law which has a bearing on the jurisdiction and enforcement issue. For example, in the context of the international sale of goods there is a governing convention (the United Nations Convention on Contracts for the International Sale of Goods, April 1980 or CISG) which affects jurisdiction. This may apply to international traders who are in different contracting states (under the Convention) and have not excluded the application of the Convention to the contract. Similarly, in the European Union, the adoption of two Conventions (Brussels and Lugano) has modified the conflict of laws rules.

Creating a Distinct Jurisdiction of Cyberspace

The difficulties in determining issues of choice of law and jurisdiction have led to two suggestions on how to approach this issue within cyberspace. The first is that, for the purposes of jurisdictional analysis, cyberspace should be treated as a fourth international space (the others being Antarctica, outer space and the high seas). The jurisdiction to prescribe the choice of law would derive from nationality, not territoriality.[103] The other approach also involves a recognition of the unique characteristics of cyberspace and a call to treat cyberspace as a distinct 'place', by recognizing a legally significant border between cyberspace and the non-virtual 'real world'.[104]

Rather than focusing on where an activity occurred in a geographical world, the proponents of this approach ask:

> What rules are best suited to the often unique characteristics of this new place and the expectations of those who are engaged in various activities there? What mechanisms exist or need to be developed to determine the content of those rules and the mechanisms by which

they can be enforced? Answers to these questions will permit the development of rules better suited to the new phenomena in question, more likely to be made by those who understand and participate in those phenomena, and more likely to be enforced by means that the new global communications media make available and effective.[105]

The significance of this design approach is that an online user would no longer need to determine which territorially-based authority might apply to the particular activity. Rather, the issue would be one of deciding whether or not the user has crossed the boundary into cyberspace. This assumes that the electronic boundary can be perceived and that crossing over is a meaningful act. It would be essential to be able to determine the point at which the user is operating within cyberspace because the cyberspace laws pertaining to a particular activity could well be different from those which apply to a manual or paper-based activity. Of course, such an outcome runs counter to the philosophy that law reform should be neutral; a party to a transaction should not acquire greater rights or a competitive advantage due only to the fact that it occurs in cyberspace.

The underlying objectives of each of these substantive laws (in each jurisdiction) would need to be reassessed in the light of the unique characteristics of cyberspace. To illustrate, Johnson and Post discuss the strategy surrounding copyright and the shift away from exclusive property rights to control the reproduction and distribution of works, to giving away information at no charge:

> ... as a means of building up reputational capital that can subsequently be converted into income (for example by means of the sale of services). ... A profound shift of this kind in regard to authorial incentives fundamentally alters the applicable balance between the costs and benefits of copyright protection in Cyberspace, calling for a reappraisal of long standing principles. So, too, do other unique characteristics of Cyberspace severely challenge traditional copyright concepts. ... Treating Cyberspace as a distinct location allows for the development of new forms of intellectual property law, applicable only on the Net, that would properly focus attention on these unique characteristics of this new, distinct place while preserving doctrines that apply to works embodied in physical collections (like books) or displayed in legally significant physical places (like theatres).[106]

The cumulative effect of such modifications to substantive law, and the corresponding change in incentives, is to resist attempts, based on territorially local claims, to restrict online transactions which have no bearing on the vital and localized interests of the territorial government.[107]

Such is the dynamism of the Internet that other trends are already emerging that undermine the above arguments in respect of copyright laws. The use of electronic copyright management systems, combined with the power of sophisticated search engines, provide the means to prevent copying of electronic text and to track infringements on a global scale. If anything, technology which could reinforce substantive laws on copyright is emerging. However, this still leaves the problem of jurisdiction and enforcement.

The theory of international spaces, with its focus on nationality as a guiding principle to resolve conflict of laws, and the re-evaluation of key areas of substantive law are not mutually exclusive in the ultimate cyberspace legal framework. The focus on substantive law can take place at the national (local) level. It can also be the subject of harmonization initiatives between countries and even international conventions or protocols (such as already exist in some of the key areas concerning intellectual property). The concept of a recognition of electronic boundaries and an online 'place' would mean that jurisdictional disputes would still have to be resolved under conventional laws until an alternative universal approach is developed. For example, nations could apply the same methodology and restructure their local laws on jurisdiction to reflect an agreed principle adopted at the international level, such as the nationality principle or some other uniform approach.

The Use of International Treaties and Conventions

A common model for governance of cyberspace, which has its analogies in public international law, is to address these challenges (including conflict of laws) by creating a uniform cyberspace law using the international treaty process. There are a number of difficulties with this approach. The most obvious is that international treaty negotiation and ratification is painstakingly slow, whereas the technologies of the Internet are dynamic and constantly evolving. This speed of change would require any uniform international approach to be based on principles which recognize this characteristic. For example, any uniform law would need to be 'technology neutral': it would have to be drafted so that it is not just reacting to existing technology but is expressed in such a way as to meet technological advances. The underlying principles and the drafting of the UNCITRAL Model Law on Electronic Commerce illustrate this approach.

Another requirement would be a two-tiered approach to international treaty negotiation, the first requiring international consensus on the guiding principles for cyberspace – that is, treaties – and the second focusing on the substantive content of the treaty. There would still be questions about the scope of any cyberspace treaty. For example, would it focus on specific activities which it is globally agreed are unacceptable? Would it deal with the harmonization of the jurisdictional problems? Or would the treaty be limited to specific areas of substantive law, such as intellectual property? Before embarking on treaty negotiation, the participating countries would need to consider the possibility that a minority will disagree with either the values to be upheld or the interests to be protected by international law, let alone the possible sanctions. In the absence of unanimous agreement, users will always be able to escape sanctions by moving their online presence 'offshore'.

These are the sorts of concern which emerged from the early discussions on UNESCO's enquiry into the need, or otherwise, for some form of international 'instrument' on cyberspace law. However, subsequent work by UNESCO on developing a set of 'cyberspace principles' (discussed in 'The emerging legal framework for cyberspace' (p.47)) can be seen as part of that first step towards building an international consensus on cyberspace issues which are of universal interest.

The role of custom and codification of consensus in public international law provides processes and methodologies suitable for adaptation to a cyberspace framework. However, law-makers should not rely on the use of treaties as a governance model because:

> ... even if some core principles for the governance of the net could be agreed upon by treaty, such an agreement would almost certainly take the form of a high level document written with a fair degree of generality. But the devil is the details ... . The bottleneck characteristics of any centralized law-making machinery – and the natural frailties of law-making processes based on writing authoritative texts – makes centralized systems unsuitable for tackling a diverse, rapidly changing, large scale set of problems like those posed by the net.[108]

It is anticipated that there will be moves towards multilateral international agreements to deal with specific aspects of cyberspace. Although, this will not be the predominant form of governance on the Internet, it will still have an albeit limited role to play.

Establishing an International Organization for Cyberspace

One question often posed is whether there is some international organization which could establish and implement rules to govern cyberspace. Again, the logistics and constitutional difficulties attaching to such a proposal prevent it from being a viable governance model.

Various organizations will, however, have a critical role to play in setting standards and guidelines and perhaps even providing redress in the cyberspace framework. However, this is different from being the centralized authority for rule-making on the Internet. The continued involvement of the United Nations is vital, especially given its leadership role as the originator of numerous international conventions which operate as constraints and which have become the foundation of international laws. In this respect, UNESCO's work, particularly the dialogue on 'cyberspace principles' (discussed later), is most timely. There is also the OECD's work on the GII, under which it has developed guidelines in the areas of data protection[109] and encryption.[110]

The establishment of a new international organization would bring its own problems: for example, what would be the source of its authority to 'govern'? Given the characteristics of the Internet, how could it prevent competing rules being adopted within cyberspace? To whom would the organization be accountable? Whose values would it represent? Would it be vulnerable to being 'captured' by a particular sovereign or interest group? How would it protect unpopular minorities? At the time of writing, some of these questions are being asked of ICANN in US Congressional Hearings.[111] The issues under scrutiny include: the adequacy of ICANN's constitutional foundation, such as membership structures; the role of ICANN as an implementer and manager (of domains), as opposed to global 'governance' or policy-making; and the involvement of WIPO (World Intellectual Property Organization) in assisting ICANN to define its role.

In the context of a global cyberspace agency:

> It is not easy to set up an appropriate balance of powers within a new organization with quasi-governmental powers when the participants and constituents come from geographic places that have widely divergent views regarding democratic institutions, centralized authority and even 'fairness' itself. And, even if we could write a 'bill of rights' for the net and create a judiciary branch capable of interpreting it, such mechanisms would deal only with the most fundamental problems – hardly supplying an appropriate source for the myriad decisions that must be made, somehow, everyday regarding whether some particular online behavior is or is not permitted in the context in which it occurs.[112]

This is not to dismiss the important role of a number of international organizations (whether ICANN or other international fora) in the cyberspace framework. It is more likely, however, that their significance will be in respect of a particular task or responsibility, as was originally intended for ICANN (and its predecessors).

The Role of an International Court

It is worth exploring to see whether any public international courts exist, or could be established, for the purpose of dispute resolution in cyberspace. Examples are an extension of the International Court of Justice (international arbitration jurisdiction) or the establishment of an International Criminal Court under the auspices of the United Nations. At a 1998 Conference in Rome, reputedly 100 countries voted in favour of establishing a permanent international criminal court.

Again, the same issue arises as to the scope of such a court's jurisdiction: what types of disputes could be brought before an international criminal court? The ratification of the proposal will allow independent prosecutors to investigate genocide, crimes against humanity and war crimes. It is to be expected that there will be the usual anxiety over the perception of loss of sovereignty if certain activities can be referred to an international court. In fact, this was given as the reason why certain influential countries have been reluctant to endorse the proposal.

The various participants within cyberspace have different interests and a different perception of what activity should be the subject of legal control. For example, Henry Perritt[113] points out that intermediaries, such as sysops, almost always prefer to minimize the legal control of their activities and could be expected to oppose initiatives to develop a new international forum or other machinery to force legal obligations against participants in cyberspace. This commentator goes on to predict that: 'The only group with significant political power likely to favor the establishment of new machinery are content originators interested in reducing the incidence of intellectual property infringement.'[114]

Despite the questions over the role and jurisdiction of an international criminal court, there may still be a role for some kind of 'residual jurisdiction by international criminal institutions'.[115] The current proposal for an international criminal court is focused on crimes against humanity, rather than issues of cyberspace jurisdiction. However, the possibility of this forum being developed into a dispute resolution mechanism should be embodied in the future legal framework for cyberspace.

Private Law and Arbitration

We have noted that the decentralized rule-making which is evolving in cyberspace will result in greater reliance on private law. This creates an opportunity for the parties to a cyberspace relationship to formalize the applicable dispute resolution processes. For example, parties could invoke the law of contract or, alternatively the 'controllers' could set terms and conditions of access and use this opportunity to prescribe the choice of law governing the contract or relationship.

There are strong conventional precedents for the resolution of civil disputes in the form of arbitration – a legal process where a binding decision is made by the arbitrator appointed under the procedures within the (private law) agreement previously entered into by the disputing parties. The decision to arbitrate is based on a valid agreement. There are also jurisdictions in which, when a dispute arises, national law provides a process for parties to agree to submit it to arbitration. The question of whether or not the dispute falls within the scope of a valid arbitration agreement is a matter of 'substantive arbitrability' and is for the regular courts to decide. If the arbitration submission is upheld, the parties are obliged to comply with the ultimate award of the arbitrators.

The use of arbitration as a dispute resolution model is directly applicable to cyberspace. It is possible, through contractual arbitration, for parties to agree in advance on the class of disputes and the procedural rules for submission to an arbitration forum. Given the problems with cyberspace jurisdiction discussed above, it is important for the choice of law to be resolved within an agreement to arbitrate prior to the dispute arising. The parties can choose their forum and governing law (for enforceability by the courts of the chosen jurisdiction) or else refer to the rules of procedure of specific organizations which promote arbitration. Examples of these are the International Chamber of Commerce (ICC) and the United Nations Commission on International Trade Law (UNCITRAL).[116]

The agreement (or clause to that effect) on the submission to arbitration could become a condition of access to the Internet by those controllers (whether ISPs or others) who are in a position to dictate the dispute resolution model. At the international level, enforcement can be facilitated by the use of treaties. For example, the New York Convention on the Recognition and Enforcement of Arbitral Awards obliges the national courts of signatory countries to recognize and enforce arbitration agreements and awards.[117]

Online Mediation and other Forms of ADR

In the same way as arbitration has evolved, there is an opportunity for alternative dispute resolution (ADR) models to be adapted to online disputes. For example, a wide range of methods has come into existence for resolving conflict in 'real space', ranging from facilitated negotiation to mediation, 'med-arb', the use of experts and arbitration. The latter technique (arbitration) involves a third party with the power to impose decisions or to make an arbitration award. At the other end of the spectrum there are a number of alternatives, the most common being mediation. This involves a disciplined procedure, facilitated by an independent third party, the most significant difference being that the mediator's authority is consensual. The mediator assists the parties to recognize each other's needs and to identify options for resolution, but has no power to give a view on an outcome nor to impose a decision.

The cyberspace arbitration analogy is directly applicable to mediation. At present, mediation is being conducted in 'real space' using formal agreements to mediate (which provide for both procedure and jurisdiction). Where a mediation culminates in an agreement, the terms are recorded in a settlement agreement between the disputing parties. Although recognition of mediation by the courts is relatively recent, there is sufficient experience to regard the agreement to mediate (as with an arbitration clause) and the settlement agreement (as with an arbitration award) as generally enforceable by the courts.

As ADR techniques gain credibility in the real world, we can predict greater acceptance of these models for the resolution of online disputes. Many of these mechanisms develop skills and expertise for conflict management which are more appropriate to the autonomous and consensual nature of interaction on the Internet. This is consistent with a need to build a mindset which does not breed dependence, given the peculiar nature of the emerging and decentralized legal structures within cyberspace. It would be worthwhile encouraging recognition of this form of dispute resolution as a valid, but not mutually exclusive, model within the international treaty framework.

As ADR gains acceptance (such as through the two projects discussed below), there would be value in having a convention, analogous to the international arbitration environment, which recognizes the autonomy of disputing parties to decide in advance on their dispute resolution rules, forum and governing law. Such a convention should make it possible for this form of private law to be adjudicated and enforced by the signatory nations without being undermined by the ability of disputants to exit a cyberspace zone (network protocol or service) and escape the sanction of being held to its obligations.

The Virtual Magistrate Project

There are currently a number of online dispute resolution pilot projects. These are at different stages of development and are experiencing varying degrees of success. Some have been established to address very specific concerns. For example, the World Intellectual

Property Organisation (WIPO) Online Dispute Resolution Process, implemented on 1 January 2000, is concerned with challenges to domain name registration. It is not appropriate to summarize these pioneering initiatives. However, it is interesting to refer to one of the earliest pilots because the original discussion papers on its web site illustrated the system design issues which must be addressed in order to develop a successful online process.

The possibilities of online dispute resolution were tested by the Virtual Magistrate Project, announced publicly on 4 March 1996.[118]

This project sought to establish a virtual dispute resolution activity, drawing on an arbitration model. It was to be supported by the American Arbitration Association, which would administer the Project, review cases or complaints for their suitability and then assign them to a Magistrate for a decision.

The goals for the Virtual Magistrate were originally described as:

> Establish the feasibility of using online dispute resolution for disputes that originate online. Provide system operators with informed and neutral judgments on appropriate responses to complaints about allegedly wrongful postings. Provide users and others with a rapid, low cost, and readily accessible remedy for complaints about online postings. Lay the groundwork for a self-sustaining, online dispute resolution system as a feature of contracts between system operators and users and content suppliers (and others concerned with wrongful postings). Help to define the reasonable duties of a system operator confronted with a complaint. Explore the possibility of using the Virtual Magistrate Project to resolve other disputes related to computer networks. Develop a formal governing structure for an on-going Virtual Magistrate operation.[119]

The merit of the Virtual Magistrate is that it was an early attempt by the Internet community to police itself. It illustrated the many issues, which impact on the development and evolution of online dispute resolution. These included ways of encouraging ISPs and other intermediaries to use the process, for example the Virtual Magistrate, such as by translating this into some form of defence or shield from liability; how to ensure that the decision-making process is transparent versus the value of confidentiality in attracting disputants; and whether a submission must be by consent or can it be imposed as a condition of access or online service.

Online Ombuds Office Project

Another concept that is being explored as an ADR model is the use of ombudsmen to inquire into online disputes. Historically, the role of an ombudsperson is that of a 'watchdog' to monitor any arbitrary or administratively unfair government and bureaucratic authority. The Online Ombuds Office Project, established within the Massachusetts Centre for Information Technology and Dispute Resolution, was intended as a pilot[120] for the adaptation of conventional dispute resolution techniques to the particular challenges of the Internet environment. It offers mediation services and is developing tools and resources for online ADR.

Future ADR in Cyberspace

Adapting the negotiation and ADR intervention process to the 'fluidity and malleability' of the Internet poses significant challenges. Despite this, the use of private law adjudication mechanisms could play a significant role in addressing the problems of conflict of laws in cyberspace. The use of ADR is directly applicable to the cyberspace legal framework. It is also consistent, as a conflict management technique, with the type of proactive contract management encouraged by the dynamic and interactive nature of cyberspace relationships. This does not, by any means, resolve all jurisdictional and enforcement issues, but the results should be sufficiently pervasive – given the opportunities for rule-making by the numerous controllers within cyberspace – to support the dominant governance model of decentralized emergent law. The opportunity and possibilities exist to develop workable dispute resolution mechanisms in cyberspace.

THE EMERGING LEGAL FRAMEWORK FOR CYBERSPACE

Possibilities and Opportunities within the Framework

Having identified the design parameters and law-making processes which influence the development of a legal framework for cyberspace, and having considered the nature of specific difficulties (such as problems with jurisdiction and enforcement), the remaining sections of this chapter attempt to synthesize the components of the emerging legal framework.

In some respects, the legal framework is a fledgling development; there are gaps to fill, blurred outlines requiring sharper focus, and certain parts which demonstrate a process of continuous evolution. In other respects, the framework is well established, although this may not be reflected in the corresponding levels of awareness of those affected by cyberspace. Clearly, there is no single strand called 'cyberspace law'. Cyberspace, in terms of its breadth, its layers and hierarchies, is multidimensional and therefore demands a corresponding degree of sophistication in terms of legal design and policy response.

The following discussion will describe the possibilities and opportunities in respect of each component of the framework, summarize particular challenges, identify guiding philosophies and principles for future analysis, and comment on any future trends or initiatives.

After considering the influences at work, and the various theories concerning the nature of regulation and control, what is the composition of the emerging legal framework for cyberspace? What are the possibilities in terms of the desirability and feasibility of its components? As the Internet has evolved, so has a decentralized model for governance; it is likely to be an integral component of the legal framework and, as such, to predominate in cyberspace for the foreseeable future. This model does not exclude other opportunities for influence by sovereign authorities or governments. Although some of these law-making processes and methods of exerting control may not achieve their aims, or have other consequences, they still have their place within the legal framework. In terms of legal infrastructure (which is a more tangible notion than a framework), there are two systems or structures which are expected to play a significant role in the future. These are the domain name registries and the growing industry of certification authorities (within the public key infrastructure (PKI)).

Predominant Governance Model

The governance model for cyberspace that is most likely to dominate within the ultimate legal framework is the emergence of decentralized decision- or rule-making (referred to earlier as self-governance or self-regulation). Specifically:

> De facto rules may emerge as a result of the complex interplay of individual decisions by domain name and IP address registries (regarding what conditions to impose on possession of an online address), by sysops (regarding what local rules to adopt, what filters to install, what users to allow to sign on, and with which other systems to connect) and by users (regarding which personal filters to install and which systems to patronize).[121]

This model reflects the design parameters which are a consequence of the unique characteristics of cyberspace. It is polycentric, in the sense of there being many individual networks within networks; hence the 'complex interplay of individual decisions' between the various participants in cyberspace. The Internet has been described as hierarchical with a number of vertical controllers. It is also asymmetrical, with 'gatekeepers' in a position to control access to various zones.

Cyberspace is dynamic and interactive and, within it, change is the norm. It has already evolved from being a very open and free environment with a libertarian philosophy to being far more structured and controlled. This metamorphosis has occurred without:

> ... governmental mandate ... or ... anything like a centralised process of decision. ... It is moving, that is, from a relatively unzoned place to a universe that is extraordinarily well zoned. The architecture of cyberspace – the software that constitutes it – is becoming quite quickly far better at facilitating discriminations in access and distribution than any equivalent technologies in real space.[122]

Another consequence of the technological and architectural design features of cyberspace is the opportunity for direct control or regulation by code (architecture). The network protocols and the technical specifications for the Internet can influence the decisions and activities of its participants. Once the opportunity to exert direct influence, via the code-writers and sysops, is recognized, there will be an avenue for rule-making using the regulatory models of direct law, market forces and behavioural norms. For the most part, control via code is operating in a self-regulatory fashion. There have been, however, instances of legislative intervention. While this may serve to operate at a localized level where a government may dictate the nature of the online service to be provided by sysops within that country, this rule-making process will suffer from the same impediments and challenges as any other centralized top-down decision-making process which tries to impose its values and policies on a global basis. It will also be possible to apply indirect influence on rule-sets determined by code, by market forces (and users' exit strategies), by education and by awareness, which develops a consensus on appropriate standards of behaviour within cyberspace.

A self-regulating or self-governing model means that there will be a high degree of reliance on private law. The hierarchies and zones of the Internet provide opportunities for various 'controllers' to exert control. This can be translated into the imposition of conditions of access or use. There should be an increase in the use of contracts to govern relationships and activities. The corollary will be the growth in adjudication mechanisms – whether arbitration, mediation or some hybrid – to ensure that the contractual relationships are enforceable through conventional jurisdictional rules. ADR procedures could have a significant role to play in the legal framework.

The governance model also recognizes the role of customary law. The growth of custom and netiquette will influence norms of behaviour and allow for the imposition of (decentralized) sanctions. The consensus which underlies the emergence of a custom or practice on the Internet may, in some circumstances, develop into a contractual obligation.

There are also economic drivers behind the emergence of a decentralized governance model which relies heavily on private law. There is global interest, at both user and government level, in facilitating the growth of electronic commerce which uses the Internet as its medium. This is prompting national and industry reviews of the need to harmonize laws and remove impediments to electronic commerce. While certain legislative initiatives at the national level can be expected – for example, statutory recognition of electronic signatures – it is generally well recognized that electronic commerce will be heavily reliant on the use of private law and adjudication. It is also assumed that this reliance will be supported by some form of international rationalization of the domestic laws on choice of law and jurisdiction and by recourse to any applicable international conventions which have the effect of developing uniform laws governing the various participants in an electronic commerce transaction.

While the technology of the Internet poses challenges for lawmakers, it may also offer a solution. Although, as previously discussed, it is not feasible to try to channel or direct such a dynamic, ubiquitous and pervasive technology on a global scale, the Internet has also been described as 'turning out to be an organism with some remarkable inbuilt features which are designed to ensure its own survival'.[123] The earlier discussion on the characteristics of cyberspace identified the ability to remail messages as an example of a 'self-healing' feature. The mobility of users and the options presented through 'exit' strategies give participants the opportunity to exercise choice and therefore exert a degree of market influence. This is a very important feature, with implications for the shaping of acceptable standards of behaviour and activity on the Internet.

The accessibility of the technology, the multiplicity of zones within cyberspace and the difficulties of imposing top-down centralized control make it possible to reflect the diversity of cyberspace cultures. This is extremely significant in the context of arguments over legitimacy and authority which require a broad base of consensus if the evolving rule-sets in cyberspace are to be a genuine reflection of the 'consent of the governed' and the 'collective voice' of the cyberspace communities. The ability of the technology to reflect diversity is therefore very significant to the legitimacy of a self-governance model.

Opportunities for Conventional Forms of Influence

The predominance of the decentralized decision-making model of governance is not mutually exclusive of other opportunities for influence, or conventional legal systems, within the framework. The following are all components of the emerging framework, even if some will have minimal effect on a global scale, have not yet been invoked, or else remain a distant possibility.

Substantive law will have an important role to play – particularly where a dispute over substantive law proves amenable to local or national jurisdiction and is enforceable. Not all cases will face a conflict of laws. There will be situations in which the courts can attach responsibility to a particular organization or location of a human actor or an asset. Furthermore, there are many instances where substantive law is governed by the international law of treaty. In the intellectual property arena, for example, it is expected that content originators will continue to keep the enforceability of international laws under review.

International consensus can be codified into international conventions and ratified at the national or state level. Examples are the UNCITRAL model laws on electronic commerce, proposals on cross-border insolvency, and the OECD's current work on developing consumer protection guidelines for Internet users. These harmonization initiatives will become increasingly important in the cyberspace framework. The UNESCO work on cyberspace principles is a fledgling development towards building an international consensus.

We have already discussed how, in some areas, sovereign authorities – that is, governments – are attempting to exert control by legislating for or against certain choices or values to be reflected within the Internet network protocols or architecture. There are natural constraints on this type of intervention, due to the disparate, decentralized and numerous intermediaries in cyberspace. However, since the technology makes it possible for many of these to escape controls imposed by one or another jurisdiction, only some sysops or ISPs could be subject to this form of control. Nevertheless, in limited circumstances, this form of intervention may be feasible, although its desirability is debatable, depending on its consequences (refer back to the discussion in 'Reasons or need for law' (p.19) about the objectives of law-making, and how certain types of intervention force an activity to move 'offshore'). There are other limitations in that legislative intervention, by influencing code, is most feasible for industries which have a recognizable infrastructure and control over their industrial activity because of their monopoly over, and ability to influence, the values and interests reflected in the design and specifications of the Internet. The telecommunications industry is a good example of this.

The situation may arise where governments believe that their vital interests are threatened and there is sufficient motivation for concerted action at the international level. This would occur through either the treaty negotiation process, the development of an international convention or within some other forum such as the United Nations. While this form of top-down authority is feasible, its efficacy as a governance model is questionable for the reasons already discussed – in particular, the time it takes to develop consensus, the limited scope or coverage of international treaties, the debate over whose values should dominate (for example, some countries prioritize freedom of choice and expression whereas others focus on their perception of stability and security), and the concern of some countries over the perceived loss of sovereign control.

Governments can also exert influence on a sphere of activity, a sector or an industry. In New Zealand much of the energy on developing policy in response to cyberspace is concentrated in vertical industry structures. For example, New Zealand initiatives have focused on electronic commerce through the Asia Pacific Economic Council (APEC) and the World Trade Organization, and on the OECD's initiatives to develop guidelines on cryptography and consumer protection.

Finally, a number of organizations and international fora have a role to play in the emerging framework. The United Nations has sponsored many initiatives to develop uniform approaches to the law. The International Standards Organization (ISO) and the International Chamber of Commerce (ICC) are influential in developing standards and international conventions or cooperation. UNESCO is broadening the debate with its consideration of social, legal and ethical issues of the GII. The expertise and work to date of these organizations could be utilized to address specific tasks or challenges that arise out of the existing framework. In other words, they could provide the tools and mechanisms to tackle specific issues and promote harmonization of laws on specific topics, such as those which are currently the subject of substantive laws at the local or national level.

The current proposal to establish an international criminal court may evolve, in the future, in a way which makes it appropriate to extend its jurisdiction. It could possibly address Internet activities which the cyberspace community are unable to tackle through the self-governance model, although these activities would have to be deemed sufficiently serious to warrant the application of an international criminal jurisdiction. However, while this is a feasible move, some nations will undoubtedly question its desirability. Of course, the behaviour would have to be serious enought to warrant referral to such a court, and it is possible that certain information warfare activities could develop, which would be regarded at the collective (international) level as being sufficiently threatening. All this presupposes support from each nation to ensure that the activity complained of cannot escape sanction by hiding behind the jurisdictional or conflict of laws issue. These laws would have to be harmonized and rationalized to ensure the proper functioning of the court.

When considered against the volume of interactions on the Internet, the above conventional forms of authority (national legislation and international treaties, conventions and organizations) are examples of either indirect influence by sovereign authorities or else would have minimal impact at the global level. Although these examples of top-down decision-making may be feasible components of a future legal framework, their significance will be limited by the degree to which they can be enforced and can influence the future evolution of cyberspace decision-making.

Domain Name Registries

The domain name registries are a significant component of the current and future legal infrastructure for cyberspace. As the 'dispensers of virtual addresses' (the essence of online identity) they 'stand at the border checkpoint between the virtual and the nonvirtual world, and the contract pursuant to which one receives a domain name or other on-line ID can potentially serve as the means … by which the most basic rights and obligations of all Cyberspace participants can be specified.'[124] Following an initial flurry of litigation questioning the obligations and responsibilities of these registries, there are still many economic and policy questions surrounding their authority and operation which have not yet been answered. What is the scope of their authority to operate? Can they impose prerequisites to domain name registration, such as minimum requirements or conditions on the domain name or 'passport to netizenship'?[125]

As mentioned earlier, the debate over the role of the governing registry body (ICANN) is at a critical stage. ICANN's role is often referred to in governance terms, attracting the criticism that it should restrict its focus to management of the Domain Name System, and not purport to make global policy. Despite the language of 'governance' (in discussions on ICANN's powers), this organization is just one of the structures within the cyberspace framework – albeit a very important component, given the potential for the ICANN's decisions to have far-reaching effects on access to cyberspace.

Certification Authorities

The ability of the Internet to facilitate the growth of global electronic commerce will have implications for the cyberspace legal infrastructure. In particular, concerns over security and the need for protection through encryption have resulted in the development of a public key infrastructure (PKI), also known as the Public Key Authentication Framework (PKAF). This involves the establishment of certification authorities, suitably empowered to assign and administer the encryption keys which, in turn, enable secure participation in a transaction over the Internet. Various nations are at different stages of development in terms of their legal recognition of the needs of electronic commerce. For example, a number of countries have been reviewing their laws for compatibility with the PKI, including the need for the legal recognition of electronic (digital) signatures and the use of certification authorities. The certification authority industry, whether in the form of the Global Trade Point Programme[126] or various other government and private sector projects to implement public key technology, will create opportunities for the growth of private law in cyberspace in the form of access terms and conditions.

Conclusion

The possibilities for a legal framework for cyberspace are many and varied. The predominant theme or governance model, which best suits the unique characteristics of cyberspace (and is, indeed, a product of its evolution), is the decentralized self-regulatory form of decision-making. One of the consequences of this governance model will be to elevate the significance of, and reliance on, the adaptation of private law and adjudication to resolve disputes in cyberspace. There are many other opportunities for conventional forms of influence, including top-down centralized law-making, based on international conventions. However, whether at the national level or internationally, these law-making processes and mechanisms will have a limited role to play in cyberspace.

   The framework itself has a recognizable legal infrastructure. The key components are the architecture of the Internet, including the many intermediaries (whether code-writers, ISPs or otherwise) and the domain name registries. The future certification authorities will also play a critical structural role because of their ability to exert control over access to, and participation in, the many zones of cyberspace.

Issues to be addressed from the Framework

A number of issues arise out of the legal framework for cyberspace, which pose specific difficulties for its future development. A number of them require a certain amount of education or awareness-building.

The numerous challenges for law-makers, when designing appropriate legal responses to the developments of cyberspace, have already been discussed in this chapter. The following summary highlights some of the more significant issues.

Awareness of the Public Interest and Inherent Values

One of the issues – on which there needs to be far more education – is the problem of how to reflect public interest or values within the rule-making processes in cyberspace. The first point is the need to recognize that the technology of cyberspace – Internet architecture, network protocols and code – is not necessarily passive or benign. There is an opportunity for code-writers and other intermediaries – who stand as gatekeepers to the zones of cyberspace – to exert subtle influence over the norms of behaviour and to control through rule-sets.

One of the advantages of minimal intervention in cyberspace is that this philosophy would encourage a diversity of participants and reflect the pluralism of cyberspace cultures. One possible consequence might be the avoidance of 'colonialism' on the Internet, where one sovereign authority tries to extend its governance to those outside its territorial jurisdiction. Minimal intervention also prevents arguments as to whose values or public interests should prevail.

The linkage between notions of 'collective voice' and 'the consent of the governed' has already been discussed (see pp.19–21) in the context of the legitimacy of, and authority for, self-governance in cyberspace.

The other aspect of the concern over reflecting public values is that self-regulation through custom and Internet rule-sets does not necessarily equate to the conventional role and significance of the law of contract. The doctrines of contract and equity have developed in such a way that the courts can exert a moderating influence on the outcomes of contractual disputes by introducing notions of public policy exceptions. In other words, conventional contract law has a public law aspect which may become obscured when relying on the self-regulatory private law of contracting in cyberspace.

There is a danger of failing to recognize the power and influence of the regulatory forces already in existence in the cyberspace legal framework. The law-makers and the cyber-community need to appreciate how these can impact on the values, interests, incentives and controls being projected through the rule-sets that are a consequence of the interplay between the many participants in cyberspace.

The Speed of Change

The assumptions which underlie discussions on legal developments and the Internet must be constantly reviewed on account of the speed of change in cyberspace, the 'plasticity' of the controls, and the dynamic and interactive nature of the networked environment. In a conventional (real space) environment, it is always very difficult for the law to keep pace with technological change. This is exacerbated in cyberspace because of the defining characteristics of the Internet and the paradigm shift in governance. The Internet has already evolved into an environment that has far more zones and controls compared to the open and freely accessible environment of its infancy. Obviously, any legal response, within a cyberspace framework, should be technology-neutral.

Jurisdiction and Enforcement

The jurisdictional and conflict of laws issues pose serious constraints on the development of a legal framework, and these must be addressed by parallel or concurrent initiatives. For example, the substantive laws need to be reviewed and then adapted to reflect the new environment of cyberspace. This is the path of least resistance because it is a process which is already well underway within each sector or industry at both international and local/national levels.

At the same time, law-makers should find ways to encourage the use of existing or conventional laws as a means of 'grounding' a cyberspace relationship in 'real space' laws. Linkages between cyberspace interactions and existing judicial systems must be found. For example, the decentralized governance model will rely heavily on the development of private law and adjudication mechanisms, such as arbitration. In this way, conventional law – such as arbitration – can be used to enforce cyberspace rule-sets.

It is also possible to adapt these conventional laws to reflect the dynamics of the cyberspace framework, while still relying on conventional means of enforcement. The most powerful example of this trend is the use of mechanisms which draw on arbitration and mediation models to resolve online disputes and this trend is illustrated in the earlier discussion on the Virtual Magistrate Project and the Online Ombuds Office Project. These ADR mechanisms empower the cyber-participants in a way which is consistent with the self-governance model. Being able to address the choice of law issue and other jurisdictional procedures as part of the relationship rules in cyberspace, they therefore have recourse through conventional enforcement systems such as international arbitration or national/local courts.

Despite the problems with the international treaty and convention process, there are opportunities for nations to cooperate on the question of cyberspace jurisdiction and to harmonize their national laws with other countries or with an appropriate international convention. This is the current situation in respect of the United Nations Convention on Contracts for the International Sale of Goods (CISG) and the impact of the Lugano, Brussels and Hague Conventions on jurisdictional issues arising within signatory countries, all of which currently impact on cyberspace dispute resolution. As the Internet evolves, and nations learn from their experiences in living within cyberspace, opportunities arise to rationalize the approaches to conflict of laws through international cooperation.

If, over time, the specific difficulties in determining jurisdictional issues cannot be resolved in a cost-efficient manner, there may be sufficient incentive for a concerted recognition of a separate notion of cyberspace jurisdiction (as discussed on pp.38–40). Again, sovereign authorities would need to be convinced that they would lose no sovereign control, since the dispute would otherwise have been outside their specific jurisdiction. Meanwhile, the difficulties with jurisdiction and enforcement do not determine the particular governance model, nor questions of legitimacy and authority for the emerging model, but involve the efficacy and global application of the particular form of decision-making in cyberspace.

Conclusion

All of the above issues need to be kept in perspective:

> If the net is allowed to develop a responsible self-regulatory structure, by means of decentralised, emergent law-making, and if this new mechanism proves up to the task of building a productive and non-predatory order, then all concerned will have saved the larger resources that might otherwise have been spent trying, perhaps without similar success, to impose rules from a centralised source.[127]

Guiding Principles

There are a number of themes, philosophies and principles emerging from the many responses to cyberspace. Consequently, the following 'pot-pourri' contains diverse views which nevertheless are worth reproducing, given the numerous global initiatives on the implications of 'cyberspace law' and the need to promote greater understanding of current and potential legal issues.

Economic and Logistical Realities

There is no doubt that the perceptions surrounding a legal design meeting the demands of cyberspace are influenced by the prevailing philosophies of the law-maker or sovereign authority. In the New Zealand context, this can be illustrated by the perceived disadvantages of, and reaction against, overt 'regulation' which is seen as too interventionist. This philosophy is driven by a recognition of the economic needs of commerce to trade and compete in a fair market, without incurring unnecessary costs, while still protecting business assets, resources and certain other interests. It is implicit that commerce or business benefits from consistency and predictability – the prerequisites to assessing and managing risk.[128] There is, therefore, a guiding principle in the sense of the need to recognize the logistical and economic realities of the conventional legal system and its disincentives. For example: 'Experience to date indicates that self regulation combined with entrepreneurial ingenuity and the technology are fostering the ongoing development of the Internet.'[129] If this statement is correct, then it is possible that effective self-regulation is likely to become a competitive asset for those businesses which regard safeguarding their reputation and credibility in an electronic environment as critical to their survival.

Again, using the New Zealand example, there are a number of principles that can be distilled from the underlying economic philosophy. For example:

> If government intervention is required to maintain certainty for business and consumers, it should consist of simple and predictable regulation that is technology neutral and is able to respond to the pace of change in the electronic movement … . Industry and governments need to work together to identify which policies require change, addition, or elimination to facilitate electronic commerce: any regulatory approach should be minimal, globally consistent and independent of specific technologies. The same basic tenet holds: new regulations should not be imposed merely because commerce is being conducted electronically.[130]

Law-makers must keep the unique characteristics of cyberspace uppermost in their minds. A number of principles will flow from this recognition. For example, an attempt to project centralized law-making at a global level would be extremely time- and resource-intensive because the Internet is its own free market of rule-sets. For this reason, the decentralized model is seen as a more economic and efficient method of decision-making. The inefficiency and cost of continual conflict resolution will impact on, and give incentives to, consensual approaches at the national level. The principle of 'comity' in international law will have an economic imperative.

The Need for Flexibility and Pragmatism

It is important to be somewhat pragmatic and flexible when translating the demands of cyberspace into a legal framework. For example, it would be easy to dismiss the analogies of customary law as lacking authority (see the earlier discussion on 'positivism' on pp.30–1). However, the legitimacy of a governance model within the legal framework relies on the very high volume of participants in the cyberspace community, the mobility to exit a zone, the ability to reflect the diversity of views and cultures in cyberspace, a viable range of choices, the accessibility of information, and the growing awareness of the way in which the Internet is controlled and of its inherent biases. These forces combine to produce a degree of consensus and custom from which can be derived notions of legitimacy and authority.

The New Zealand viewpoint recognizes the reality that top-down centralized law-making, dependent on territorial or geographic boundaries, will not work in the context of cyberspace. Such a model is of limited application at an international level since sovereign authorities may, for example, try to direct law through treaties and conventions. Nevertheless, it should be recognized that conventional models are constrained in terms of their effectiveness by their lack of responsiveness and because they defy the very nature of the Internet.

Collective Conversation on Values

Before attempting to control by direct law, each nation should have an idea of what its values are, while recognizing, at the same time, that values shift over time and are never absolute. This is another reason why the evolutionary process of law design, using the shifting and evolving nature of the Internet, may result in better outcomes than top-down approaches. At the global level there is still a need for a crystallizing collective conversation on core values through the medium of the Internet and for our understanding to evolve over time as our experience with cyberspace deepens. This is not necessarily incompatible with the following suggestion.

Another theme is the need to rethink existing paradigms on 'the greater good'. The technology allows for diversity, migration between zones, the filtering of content and user deterrents against unacceptable activities or unacceptable use of the Internet. In this way, the Internet allows for multiple, incompatible resolutions of policy questions. This has a positive effect in that it protects diversity, allows for cultural differences and avoids fear of monopoly, based on the assertion that one country's law is better than another's, or that one value should be promoted over another.

The UNESCO Cyberspace Principles

The development of a collective understanding on values will be greatly assisted by international organizations, such as UNESCO, taking the lead in creating awareness of the critical issues. The ensuing dialogue can build an international consensus, to be reflected in the harmonized domestic laws of member states, and could also facilitate greater international cooperation on cyberspace issues. To illustrate, the *Report of the Experts' Meeting on Cyberspace Law*[131] proposed that UNESCO promote two key principles:

1. **Communication Principle**: The right of communication is a fundamental human right.
2. **Participation Principle**: Every citizen should have the right to meaningful participation in the information society.

These key principles embody the concept of every person's right to access the new environment of cyberspace, and in particular:

3. **Universal Principle**: States should promote universal services where, to the extent possible given the different national and regional circumstances and resources, the new media shall be accessible at community level by all individuals, on a non-discriminatory basis regardless of geographic location.
4. **Multiculturalism and Multilingualism Principle**: States and users should promote cultural and linguistic diversity in cyberspace by the promotion of regional and local participation in Internet activities, information collection, and new information services.
5. **Ethics Principle**: States and users should promote efforts, at the local and international levels, to develop ethical guidelines for participation in the new cyberspace environment.
6. **Education Principle**: All persons should have a right to appropriate education in order to read, write and work in cyberspace. There should be specific initiatives to educate parents, children, teachers and other Internet users on the implications of their participation in cyberspace and on how to maximize the opportunities presented by the new media.
7. **Free Expression Principle**: States should promote the right to free expression and the right to receive information regardless of frontiers.
8. **Privacy and Encryption Principles**: The fundamental right of individuals to privacy, including secrecy of communications and protection of personal data, should be respected in national law

and in the implementation and use of technical methods as well as private legal remedies and other self-regulatory measures.

9. **Access to Information Principle**: Public bodies should have an affirmative responsibility to make public information widely available on the Internet and to ensure the accuracy and timeliness of the information. This information could include government information, information concerning cultural heritage, and archival and historical information. The traditional balance between the rights of authors and limitations on these rights, including the free use of ideas in published works, should be maintained in cyberspace in the interests of the public and of the authors. States should preserve and expand the public domain in cyberspace.

10. **Training Principle**: Job training in electronic media should be encouraged to enable people to communicate in the new media and to create new opportunities in employment.

11. **International Cooperation Principle**: States shall cooperate at an international level and seek to harmonize national law to resolve jurisdictional or conflict of laws differences.

The importance of this work has been underlined throughout this chapter, particularly its usefulness in stimulating global dialogue on 'collective values' for cyberspace, and possibly in providing a building-block for an international consensus on the 'rules' of accessing and operating within the Internet.

Relationship Management

The Internet may well impact on the way in which relationships are managed, due to the dynamic nature of interaction through this medium. This will influence the willingness of parties to resort to ADR techniques in order to preserve and re-establish relationships in a proactive and positive manner rather than be inward-looking and focused on past intentions. In real space, such trends would be interpreted as a healthy development for those affected by conflict or disputes.

A Word of Caution

The overriding theme of this chapter cautions against ill-considered interventions in law-making for cyberspace. Unless there is some specific interest which demands regulation or protection, or unless there is some identifiable gain from the imposition of direct law, then the guiding principle should be to observe how cyberspace is evolving before assuming that intervention is necessary. The point has been made that, on a global level, we have not yet resolved what should be the prevailing values to be reflected in cyberspace. Although the UNESCO Cyberspace Principles provide a useful 'template' on which to commence this discussion, it would be presumptuous to interpret these Principles as a distillation of all the potential desirable values. It is far too early to argue that the self-governance model will result in 'predatory and unproductive' behaviour on the Internet. Conversely, neither should we assume that its inherent biases or values will align with our own. In the absence of a strong justification, law-makers should be cautious about actively trying to develop the existing legal framework in a particular direction to the exclusion of another (even if this were possible, given the freedom of choice existing between the zones of the Internet).

CONCLUSION: FUTURE TRENDS AND INITIATIVES

The emerging legal framework is multidimensional. Therefore, despite the predominant governance model (of decentralized decision-making), it is still appropriate for nations to continue their existing efforts to harmonize national laws and to build consensus in the form of international dialogue and conventions.

This chapter has already identified the importance of global 'awareness-building' through the numerous worldwide initiatives that are focusing on the implications of the Internet for particular activities and industries. This resembles delegation of policy-making on a massive scale and is probably the most effective way to pervasively tackle issues of substantive law.

The cumulative effect of these consultations will identify cross-linkages, open dialogue and establish working parties who will draw on world expertise. Such activities must foster international cooperation. Consequently, rather than seeing cyberspace as the cause of greater conflict between nations (as distinct from a 'marketplace of conflict'), cyberspace could have a unifying and consensual effect – despite the loss of sovereign control, the paradigm shifts, the growth of Internet litigation and the disquiet in those government circles that are used to top-down regulation. The cooperative effect will be particularly evident at the lower echelons of the hierarchies, as illustrated by the development of private law and the use of contract. Within the hierarchies, we will see associations or zones through shared values and interests, as users and providers exercise their freedom of choice. At government level, harmonization initiatives and international conventions will necessitate closer ties and cooperation. Each nation will need to join others in the international community, around the discussion table, where there is a shared interest in cooperating to uphold mutual values or interests. There will be a growing trend to facilitate harmonization and a greater recognition of the global need for consistency and uniform approaches. Again, this trend can coexist with the decentralized emergent law of cyberspace; it is not mutually exclusive.

The need for awareness of and informed debate on, the *de facto* regulatory nature of cyberspace cannot be overemphasized. It is possible that the Internet will develop in such a way that the values inherent in the architecture and code are not consistent with so-called public values. Again, it may be possible to develop a consensus on certain (high-level) global values or interests to be protected. The UNESCO Cyberspace Principles are an example of this process. Otherwise, the safeguard may lie in the preservation of diversity and freedom of choice within the zones and hierarchies of the Internet.

The legal framework must always reflect the design parameters derived from the unique characteristics of cyberspace. Far greater awareness of the law-making processes applicable to cyberspace and the way control is exerted within that environment is needed. Conventional sources of law and methods of influence – through international law, existing judicial power and the adaptation of these conventional systems – are significant components of the emerging legal framework. But, for the time being we need to experience and understand living with the framework where the predominant governance model is that of self-regulation and private law, supported by international cooperation whether in the form of harmonization of national law or international treaties.

As noted in the introduction to this chapter, the Internet is the technological medium for a 'radical reallocation of political and economic power'. It follows that such a force will be inherently threatening to sovereign authorities and will provoke an immediate tendency to try to resist the self-governing forces of cyberspace and focus on means of exerting centralized control. We need to resist the temptation to assume that the only possible response is one of intervention, because the impact of cyberspace on resulting legal frameworks is far more subtle than that. The legal response should continue to be guided by the design parameters which are a product of the unique characteristics of cyberspace. The developments in cyberspace law should be expressed in terms of frameworks or mosaics, comprising many different components. Although these may serve different objectives or ends, and are a reflection of global diversity, there are encouraging signs that the challenges posed by cyberspace could facilitate more cooperative, harmonized relationships among nations. It is possible for the Internet to have a unifying effect, as governments, operators and users recognize their mutual difficulties and commonality of interest.

ACKNOWLEDGEMENTS

Contributions, suggestions and other assistance from the following are gratefully acknowledged: the Communications Sub-Commission of the New Zealand National Commission of UNESCO; Pat McCabe, Convenor of the afore-mentioned Communications Sub-Commission, New Zealand; The Hon. Justice W. D. Baragwanath, President of the New Zealand Law Commission; Paul Heath, QC, Barrister and Law Commissioner, Hamilton, New Zealand; Jim Higgins, Director, The Networking Edge Limited, Wellington, New Zealand; Graham Greenleaf, Associate Professor of Law, University of New South Wales, Sydney, Australia; Ministry of Commerce; Reg Hammond, Manager, IT Policy Group, Wellington, New Zealand; and Colleen McCabe, researcher and personal assistant, Longworth Associates, New Zealand.

NOTES

1   UNESCO Working Document for Experts' Meeting on Cyberspace Law, prepared by the Secretariat for the Meeting in Monte Carlo, Principality of Monaco, 29–30 September 1998, reference CII-98/CONF-601.2
2   D. Tapscott, *The Digital Economy, Promise and Peril in the Networked Intelligence*, New York, McGraw-Hill, 1996, p.2.
3   Ibid.
4   In discussion with Paul Heath QC, Barrister, New Zealand.
5   D.G. Post, 'Anarchy, State and the Internet: An Essay on Law-Making in Cyberspace', *Journal of Online Law*, 1995, art. 3, p.2.
6   E.M. Katsh, *Law in a Digital World*, Oxford: Oxford University Press, 1995, p.4.
7   Tapscott, *The Digital Economy*, op. cit., p.308.
8   Katsh, *Law in a Digital World*, op. cit., p.4.
9   See ibid., citing science fiction writer, William Gibson, in his novel *Neuromancer*.
10 J. Higgins, *Net Profit – How to Use the Internet to Improve Your Business*, Auckland, New Zealand: Penguin Books Ltd, 1997, p.21.
11 Ibid., p.15.
12 *Oggi Advertising Limited* v. *The Internet Society of New Zealand Incorporated et al.*, CP147/98, New Zealand High Court.
13 See Higgins, *Net Profit*, op. cit., p.21.
14 See Post 'Anarchy, State, and the Internet', op. cit., p.15.
15 D.R. Johnson and D.G. Post, *Law and Borders: The Rise of Law in Cyberspace*, http://www.cli.org/X0025_LBFIN. html,1996, p.2.
16 Henry H. Perritt jr, *Jurisdiction in Cyberspace: The Role of Intermediaries*, http://www.law.vill.edu/harvard/article/harv96k.htm, p.1.
17 Ibid., p.1.
18 Post 'Anarchy, State, and the Internet', op. cit., p.14.
19 Johnson and Post, *Law and Borders*, op. cit., p.1.
20 Ibid., p.1.
21 See Perritt, *Jurisdiction in Cyberspace*, op. cit., p.2.
22 See Post 'Anarchy, State, and the Internet', op. cit., p.1.
23 Ibid., p. 12.

24 L. Lessig, *Reading the Constitution in Cyberspace*, <http://einstein.ssz.com/
    austin-cpunks/text/crypto.lessig.const.html>, p.9.
25 D.R. Johnson and D.G. Post, *And How Shall the Net Be Governed? A Meditation
    on the Relative Virtues of Decentralized, Emergent Law*, (draft) http://www.cli.org/
    emdraft.html, 1996, p.4.
26 See Post 'Anarchy, State, and the Internet', op. cit., p.13.
27 See Katsh, *Law in a Digital World*, op. cit., p.123.
28 Ibid., p.125.
29 See Johnson and Post, *Law and Borders*, op. cit., p.3.
30 Ibid.
31 Johnson and Post, *And How Shall the Net be Governed*, op. cit., p.4.
32 Johnson and Post, *Law and Borders*, op. cit., p.16.
33 Ibid., p.9.
34 Ibid., p.2.
35 Johnson and Post, *And How Shall the Net be Governed*, op. cit., p.8.
36 Ibid.
37 Ibid., p.1.
38 Ibid., p.3.
39 *Oggi Advertising Limited*, op. cit.
40 L. Lessig, 'The Law of the Horse: What Cyberlaw Might Teach', *Stanford Law
    Review* Working Paper, http://stlr.stanford.edu/STLR/Workingpapers/97
    Lessig 1/article.htm, 1997, p.3.
41 Ibid., p.3, para. 13.
42 Ibid., p.10, para. 50.
43 Ibid., p.3, para. 14.
44 Ibid., p.10, para. 51. Lessig gives the following examples: 'talk about demo-
    cratic politics in the alt.knitting newsgroup, and you open yourself to a flaming;
    "spoof" someone's identity in a MUD, and you might find yourself "toaded";
    talk too much in a discussion list, and you are likely to be placed on a
    common bozo filter.'
45 Ibid., p.3, para. 15.
46 Ibid., p.5, paras 27 and 28.
47 Ibid., p.4, paras 19 and 20.
48 Ibid., p.5, para. 25.
49 Ibid., p.11, para. 54.
50 Ibid., p.13, para. 68.
51 Ibid., p.12, para. 62.
52 Ibid., p.14, para. 74.
53 Ibid., p.14, para. 74.
54 Ibid., p. 14, para. 76.
55 Ibid., p.2.
56 Ibid., p.16, para. 89.
57 Ibid.
58 Ibid., p.16, para. 90.
59 Ibid., p.17, para. 94.
60 Ibid., p.28, para. 179.
61 See Johnson and Post, *Law and Borders*, op. cit., pp.3 and 4, for examples of
    attempts by governments to prevent or regulate cross-border information
    flows.
62 See Lessig, 'The Law of the House', op. cit., p.18, para. 108, p.19, para. 109.
63 G. Greenleaf, *An Endnote on Regulating Cyberspace: Architecture vs Law?*, http:
    //www.austlii.edu.au/au/other/unswlj/thematic:1998:vol21no2/greenleaf.
    html, 1998.
64 Post, 'Anarchy, State, and the Internet', op. cit.

65   See ibid., para. 11. Post discusses five types of controllers as being the actor, the person acted upon, non-hierarchically organized social forces, hierarchically organized non-governmental organizations and governments. See also para. 8.

66   Ibid., para. 16.

67   Senator Richard Alston, Minister of Communications, Information Technology and the Arts, Australia, *Media Release*, 19 March 1999.

68   Post, 'Anarchy, State, and the Internet', op. cit., para. 26.

69   Ibid., para. 31.

70   Ibid., para. 38.

71   Ibid., paras 39 and 40.

72   Ibid., para. 42.

73   Ibid., p.17, fn. 5.

74   J. Goldsmith and L. Lessig, *Grounding the Virtual Magistrate*, <http:// www.law.vill.edu/ncair/disres/groundvm.htm>, p.2.

75   Ibid.

76   Ibid.

77   D. Menthe, 'Jurisdiction in Cyberspace: A Theory of International Spaces', *Michigan Telecommunications and Technology Law Review*, **3**(4), 23 April 1998.

78   Goldsmith and Lessig, *Grounding the Virtual Magistrate*, op. cit., p.2.

79   Ibid.

80   Ibid.

81   Ibid., p.3.

82   Op. cit.

83   S. Orlowski, *Privacy and Emerging Information Technology Evaluation: Opportunities and Key Issues*, Melbourne, Australian Attorney-General's Department, Information and Security Law Division, 1998.

84   Johnson and Post, *And How Shall the Net be Governed*, op. cit., p.8.

85   Ibid.

86   Ibid.

87   See Johnson and Post, *Law and Borders*, op. cit., p.12, citing the principles set out in the Restatement (Third) of Foreign Relations Law of the United States, Section 403.

88   Ibid.

89   Ibid.

90   See Johnson and Post, *Law and Borders*, op. cit., p.4, citing Michael Froomkin for the description of 'regulatory arbitrage'.

91   Ibid., p.9.

92   Post, 'Anarchy, State, and the Internet', op. cit.

93   Johnson and Post, *And How Shall the Internet be Governed*, op. cit., p.4.

94   See Menthe, 'Jurisdiction in Cyberspace', op. cit.

95   See ibid., paras 19–20, citing Minnesota's Attorney-General, Hubert Humphrey III, Memorandum stating: 'Persons outside of Minnesota who transmit information via the internet knowing that information will be disseminated in Minnesota are subject to jurisdiction in Minnesota courts for violations of state, criminal and civil laws.' He cites the Minnesota courts as having upheld the rationale and finding personal jurisdiction based merely on the fact that information placed on the Internet was downloadable in Minnesota.

96   Ibid., para. 23.

97   Ibid., para. 25.

98   New Zealand Law Commission Report on Electronic Commerce, *Conflict of Laws*, Wellington, New Zealand, 1998, ch. 6.

99   See ibid.

100   Perritt, *Jurisdiction in Cyberspace*, op. cit., p.2.

101   Ibid., p.5.
102   Ibid., p.3.
103   See Menthe, 'Jurisdiction in Cyberspace', op. cit., para. 59.
104   See Johnson and Post, *Law and Borders*, op. cit., p.6.
105   Ibid.
106   Ibid., pp.9 and 10.
107   Ibid., p.13.
108   Johnson and Post, *And How Shall the Net be Governed*, op. cit., p.5.
109   OECD Guidelines Governing the Protection of Privacy and Transborder Flows of Personal Data (1980).
110   OECD Cryptography Policy Guidelines, adopted 1997.
111   ICANN, http://www.icann.com/index.html.
112   Johnson and Post, *And How Shall the Net be Governed*, op. cit., p.6.
113   Perritt, *Jurisdiction in Cyberspace*, op. cit., p.12.
114   Ibid., p.13.
115   Ibid.
116   Ibid., p.11.
117   See Goldsmith and Lessig, *Grounding the Virtual Magistrate*, op. cit., p.6.
118   R. Gellman, *A Brief History of the Virtual Magistrate Project: The Early Months*, http://www.law.vill.edu/ncair/disres/gellman.htm, 1996.
119   Ibid., p.2.
120   *The Online Ombuds Office*, http://aaron.sbs.umass.edu/center/ombuds/default.htm.
121   Post and Johnson, *And How Shall the Net be Governed?*, op. cit., p.3.
122   Ibid., p.10.
123   Perritt, *Jurisdiction in Cyberspace*, op. cit., p.16.
124   Johnson and Post, *And How Shall the Net be Governed?*, op. cit., p.2.
125   Ibid.
126   The United Nations Global Trade Point Network (GTPNet) was launched in 1994, under the auspices of the United Nations, to set up a global system of trade points or hubs which enable traders to interact securely, using the Internet.
127   Johnson and Post, *And How Shall the Net be Governed?*, op. cit., p.4.
128   R. Hammond, 'Electronic Commerce: Role of Government and the Private Sector', paper presented at APEC meeting, 1998.
129   See note 126.
130   See note 126.
131   UNESCO, *Report of the Experts' Meeting on Cyberspace Law*, Monte Carlo, Principality of Monaco, 29–30 September 1998, CII-98/CONF.601/CLD.1.

BIBLIOGRAPHY

Baragwanath, Hon. Justice (1998), 'The Function of the High Court Judges Today and Judicial Appointments', New Zealand Bar Association Address, Christchurch, New Zealand.
Bennett, C. (1997), *Prospects for an International Standard for the Protection of Personal Information*, Report to the Standards Council of Canada, Ottawa, Canada: Standards Council of Canada, http://www.cous.uvic.ca/poli/bennett/research/ISO.htm.
Berkman Center for Internet and Society at Harvard Law School (n.d.), 'Open Governance – Exploring the New Governance BCIS and ICANN', paper, http://cyber.harvard.edu/projects/governance.html.

Burnett, R. (1994), *The Law of International Business Transactions*, Australia: The Federation Press.

Clarke, R. (1995), 'Information Technology and Cyberspace: Their Impact on Rights and Liberties', address to the 'New Rights' Seminar Series of the Victorian Council for Civil Liberties, http://www.anu.edu.au/people/Roger.Clarke/II/VicCCL.html.

Cronin, M. and Jew, B. (1997), *Governance of Internet – What Jurisdiction?*, paper to the New Zealand Institute of Public Administration (Inc.), Wellington, New Zealand.

Dunning, N. (1997), 'Freedom of Information: Privacy v. Injury to the Public Good', speech to New Zealand Institute of Public Administration (Inc.) of Governance of Internet, Wellington, New Zealand.

Gellman, R. (1996), *A Brief History of the Virtual Magistrate Project: The Early Months*, http://www,vill.edu/ncair/disres/gellman.htm.

Goldsmith, J. and Lessig, L., *Grounding the Virtual Magistrate*, http://www.law.vill.edu/ncair/disres/groundvm.htm.

Grainger, G. (1999), 'Co-regulation and International Co-operation: Australia's Approach to Online Content Regulation', paper presented to the Asia-Pacific Internet Conference, Bali, Indonesia.

Greenleaf, G. (1996), 'Privacy – Lost in Cyberspace?', paper to Information Privacy Conference, IIR Conference, Sydney, Australia.

Greenleaf, G. (1998), *An Endnote on Regulating Cyberspace: Architecture vs Law*, paper on web site, http://www.austlii.edu.au/au/other/unswlj/thematic/1998/vol21no2/greenleaf.html.

Hammond, R. (1998), *Electronic Commerce – Role of Government and the Private Sector*, paper for an APEC Meeting, Wellington, New Zealand: Ministry of Commerce.

Heath, P. (1997), *Electronic Commerce: Report on Seminar in Melbourne*, 30–31 October 1997, Wellington, New Zealand.

Hettinga, R. (1997), *Carts, Horses, Other Dromedaries, and the Needle's Eye of Economics ...* , http://www.shipwright.com.

Higgins, J. (1997), *Net Profit: How to Use the Internet to Improve Your Business*, Auckland, New Zealand: Penguin Books (New Zealand) Ltd.

ICANN, http://www.icann.com/index.html.

'Internet Public Key Infrastructure', *Infosec Bulletin*, 1996.

Internet Society of New Zealand (1999), *Internet Service Provider Code of Practice*, http://www.isocnz.org.nz/code.htm.

Johnson, D.R. and Post, D.G. (1996), *And How Shall the Net Be Governed? A Meditation on the Relative Virtues of Decentralized, Emergent Law*, http://www.cli.org/emdraft.html.

Johnson, D.R. and Post, D.G. (1996), *Law And Borders: The Rise of Law in Cyberspace*, http://www.cli.org/x0025_LBFIN.html.

Katsh, E.M. (1995), *Law in a Digital World*, Oxford: Oxford University Press.

Katsh, E.M. (1996), *The Online Ombuds Office: Adapting Dispute Resolution to Cyberspace*, University of Massachussets, Department of Legal Studies, paper to National Conference on Online Dispute Resolution, http://www.law.vill.edu/ncair/disres/katsh.htm.

Kirby, Hon. Justice M. (n.d.), 'International Dimensions of Cyberspace: Law Protection of Privacy and Human Rights in the Digital Age', address to UNESCO.

Koppenol-Laforce, M., Dokter, D., Meijer, G.J. and Smeele, F.G.M. (1996), *International Contracts, Aspects of Jurisdiction, Arbitration and Private International Law*, London: Sweet & Maxwell.

Lessig, L. (n.d.), *Reading the Constitution in Cyberspace*, http://einstein.ssz.com/austin-cpunks/text/crypto.lessig.const.html.

Lessig, L. (1997), 'The Law of the Horse: What Cyberlaw Might Teach', *Stanford Law Review*, Working paper, http://stlr.standford.edu/STLR/Workingpapers/ 97Lessig1/article.htm.

Lessig, L. (1999), 'Animal Farm Revisited', *Back Talk Web Magazine*, http:// www.cio.com/archive/webbusiness/060199_backtalk_content.html.

Lessig, L. (1999), *Open Code and Open Societies: Values of Internet Governance*, paper, Computers, Freedom & Privacy 1999, http://www.cfp99.org/program/papers/ lessig.htm.

Menthe, D. (1998), 'Jurisdiction in Cyberspace: A Theory of International Spaces', *Michigan Telecommunications and Technology Law Review*, 3(4), 23 April, http:// www.law.umich.edu/mttlr/volfour/menthe.html.

Ministerial Council for the Information Economy (Australia) (1998), *Building the Information Economy: A Progress Report on the Enabling Legal and Regulatory Framework*, Canberra, Australia: National Office for the Information Economy.

Ministry of Consumer Affairs (New Zealand) (1998), *Draft Recommendation of the Council Concerning Guidelines for Consumer Protection in the Context of Electronic Commerce*, paper for an APEC Meeting, DSTI/CP(98)4, Wellington, New Zealand: Ministry of Consumer Affairs.

New Zealand Law Commission (1998), *Electronic Commerce Report*, Wellington, New Zealand: New Zealand Law Commission.

Oggi Advertising Limited v. *The Internet Society of New Zealand Incorporated et al.*, CP147/98. New Zealand High Court.

Online Ombuds Office, Center for Information Technology and Dispute Resolution, University of Massachusetts, http://aaron.sbs.umass.edu/center/ombuds/ default.htm.

Orlowski, S. (1998), *Privacy and Emerging Information Technology Evaluation Opportunities and Key Issues*, paper, Canberra, Australia.

Perritt, Henry H., jr (1996), *Electronic Dispute Resolution*, paper, http:// www.law.vill.edu/ncair/disres/PERRITT.HTM.

Perritt, Henry H., jr (1996), *Jurisdiction in Cyberspace: The Role of Intermediaries*, paper, Harvard University, Kennedy School of Government, http://www. law.vill.edu/harvard/article/harv96k.htm.

Post, D.G. (1995), 'Anarchy, State, and the Internet: An Essay on Law-Making in Cyberspace', *Journal of Online Law*, Article 3.

Post, D.G. (1996), *Dispute Resolution in Cyberspace: Engineering a Virtual Magistrate System*, Working Paper no. 2, Cyberspace Law Institute, http://www.law.vill.edu/ ncair/disres/DGP2.HTM.

State Government of Victoria, Department of State Development (1998), *Promoting Electronic Business: The Electronic Commerce Framework Bill*, discussion paper, Victoria, Australia: Multimedia Victoria 21, Department of State Development, State Government of Australia, July.

Tapscott, D. (1996), *The Digital Economy, Promise and Peril in the Age of Networked Intelligence*, New York: McGraw-Hill.

UNESCO (1999), *Report of the Experts Meeting on Cyberspace Law*, (CII/USP/ECY/ 99/01, CII-98/CONF.601/CLD.1.) Monte Carlo, Monaco, 29–30 September 1998.

UNESCO (1999), 'Experts Meeting on Cyberspace Law: Working Document', (CII/ USP/ECY/99/01, CII-98/CONF-601.2.)

UNESCO (1999), 'Reinforcement and Co-ordination of UNESCO's Activities Relating to Cyberspace and Establishment of a World Panel on Communication and Information, Memorandum – DG/Note/99/7.

Virtual Magistrate (1996), *The Virtual Magistrate Project Basic Rules*, http:// www.law.vill.edu/ncair/disres/DGP2.HTM.

Wright, H. (1996), 'Law, Convergence and Communicative Values on the Net', *Journal of Law and Information Science*, 7(1).

2 Freedom of Expression and Regulation of Information in Cyberspace: Issues concerning Potential International Cooperation Principles[1]

GARETH GRAINGER

INTRODUCTION

The explosion in the use of the Internet has precipitated a vigorous debate in Asia, Australia, Europe and North America about whether and how such services can or should be regulated. The failure of the US Communications Decency Act has found that country's Congress and Executive searching for different solutions. The UNESCO General Conference in Paris in 1997 considered the possibility of an international treaty or legal framework on cyberspace. Dr Martin Bangemann, the European Commission's Telecommunications Commissioner, is now advocating an International Agreement on a wide range of communications issues with content aspects.

In 1997 the Organization for Economic Cooperation and Development (OECD) debated the possibility of some form of international agreement on online services. Within the European Commission these issues have been canvassed in major discussion papers such as 'Protection of Minors from Harmful Content on the Internet' and 'Protection of Minors and Human Dignity in Audio-visual and Information Services', and an action plan has been announced. The

Australian Broadcasting Authority's well received 1996 *Report on Investigation into Content of On-line Services* advocated substantially self-regulatory schemes for such services within Australia. However, it seems clear that national schemes of self-regulation will not work effectively unless they are part of a broader scheme of self-regulation in key content-generating countries.

It is important to recognize, at every stage of this discussion, that online services, including the Internet, represent outstanding opportunities and advantages for the twenty-first century. It is important for those of us who are working in this field to recognize that part of our role is to help engender a sense of public confidence in such services by ensuring that to the extent necessary, and no more, appropriate safeguards are easily available and readily understandable to those who invite the Internet into their home or office.

While there can never be 100 per cent guarantees, outstanding progress has recently been made in identifying appropriate structures for industry self-regulation with the minimum appropriate level of government intervention. The development of technology to permit content labelling and the early growth of complaint hotlines in a number of countries has helped provide the ingredients for self-regulatory schemes.

Much of the discussion has been at an international level and has focused on the need for international cooperation. This chapter explores at least some of the major developments in the area of national and international cooperative measures for effective online industry self-regulation and considers some possible international principles for cyberspace. It focuses on the dilemmas that face those who seek to balance the principle of freedom of expression against the right of people to be protected from illegal or harmful material.

CYBERSPACE: THE NATURE OF THE ONLINE ENVIRONMENT

The Origins of Cyberspace

'Cyberspace' is the term William Gibson coined in his 1984 science fiction novel *Neuromancer* for the realm of communications networks that are accessed through computers, of which the outstanding example is the Internet. The alternative descriptor for this is 'online,' relating the form of communications to its mode of transmission by telecommunication lines.

The Internet consists of a network of computer networks that span the world. It was developed in the 1960s by the United States for military purposes, and was designed as a decentralized communications system that could survive damage to any one part of the network. Decentralization remains an important characteristic of the Internet's culture and technology.

By the 1970s academics had begun to use the Internet as the computer networks that had emerged in universities were first linked with networks in other academic institutions, and then also to the Internet. Over the next decade an increasing number of individuals connected to the Internet and the number of users continued to increase exponentially.

Content accessible on the Internet is stored in thousands of linked computers and is available equally by and from governments, corporations, interest groups, institutions and individuals from anywhere around the world. This content is provided either free of charge or for a fee.

The online environment is now a rapidly expanding international medium in which literally millions of users are providing and accessing content on a daily basis. For this reason, the Internet offers an unprecedented variety and quantity of content that is continually changing as new content is created, and existing content is updated, deleted and/or moved around computers located all over the world. Part of the reason for the growth in Internet usage flows from the relatively low costs of participation relative to other media. The necessary equipment comprises a computer, a modem and access to a telephone line, the cost of which, while not insignificant, is within the reach of many individuals and organizations.

An important feature of the online environment is that, although content can be accessed from any computer connected to the network, it may be actually stored on a number of different computers or 'servers' which need not be in the same jurisdiction as the person accessing the material.

It is also important to note that the Internet did not depend on commercial incentives for its original growth. Rather, it has developed essentially from a desire to share and obtain information, entertainment and communication. Many Internet users view themselves as part of an 'Internet community'. As no single entity controls the operation of the Internet or the material available on it, it is impossible to determine at any one time what exactly the Internet looks like, its size or the quality or quantity of content available.

One of the most important features of the Internet is that it enables any person with access to it to create their own material and make this available to others, wherever they may be located. This means that the Internet has enormous potential as a means to increase the diversity of information and views that are expressed by, and accessible to, users around the world.

There are other online systems as well as the Internet. France, for example, has a very widespread online system, known as Minitel, which is in daily use throughout that country.

The Development of Online Content Filter and Rating Systems

By the 1990s concerns about problematic content on online services had prompted the development of a range of content filter software and rating systems including, in 1996, the widely supported Platform for Internet Content Selection (PICS) which was developed by the World Wide Web Consortium (W3C), itself founded in 1994 to develop common protocols for the World Wide Web's evolution and ensure its interoperability.[2] PICS is a set of technical specifications that help software rating services to work together and was originally conceived in response to US government concerns about Internet content, and following controversy over the Communications Decency Act. The PICS protocol can support a variety of ratings and labelling systems so they can be tailored to the needs of each user. Flexibility will be the critical feature of any system of content rating to enable it to embrace the enormous range of cultural perspectives on censorship.

Organizations in several countries established labelling schemes, which conformed to the PICS standards, designed for use by parents and schools. Many of these were based in North America. They included the Recreational Software Advisory Council labelling scheme for the Internet (RSACi),[3] Safesurf,[4] Cyber Patrol[5] and SurfWatch.[6]

The RSACi rating system addresses the level of violence, sex, nudity and language on a web site. The content is given a rating between 0 and 4 on each of these topics. The label operates as a classification of the content on an Internet site rather than making a judgement about its appropriateness for any given audience or purpose, and gives users the ultimate choice about what material they wish to see. Such an approach has advantages over those filtering programs that operate on a keyword basis to exclude offensive material as, inevitably, a significant amount of useful, inoffensive content is also blocked. Its major disadvantage is that it is limited to rating functions, rather than more general information. Consequently, it is not adapted to perform more complex information retrieval searches. Safesurf, Cyber Patrol[7] and Net Nanny[8] are examples of filtering software that can operate with PICS and RSACi protocols.

An open labelling platform allows content providers, and teachers and parents, to apply tailored ratings to online content. This preserves the full diversity of the Internet for adults who wish to use it while allowing latitude to moderate it for children. However, there are also serious concerns about the amount of benign material that is excluded by filtering. In December 1997 the Electronic Privacy Information Center (EPIC), trialled a recently released 'Family Search' filtering program,[9] produced jointly as an initiative of Net Shepherd and AltaVista.[10] EPIC reported that, in every case, the filtering program excluded more than 90 per cent of sites which were returned by searches without restriction. Many of the sites excluded contained valuable, relevant and harmless material. The search terms tested were those considered to be relevant to the education or interest of young persons such as 'Boy Scouts of America' and 'Thomas Edison'.

As an extension of the PICS initiatives, in 1997 W3C created the 'Metadata Activity' which includes the Resource Description Framework (RDF) Working Group.[11] RDF is a protocol for the description of Internet content based on a set of 15 'categories' of information, known as the 'Dublin Core'.[12] It continues in the PICS tradition of creating data sets about web pages that may be searched rather than having to scan the contents of pages themselves. In this sense, it is termed 'metadata' or data about data.

The Dublin Core does not seek to deal with controversial content but aims to describe aspects of content such as authorship, publishers, date and source in a similar way to that developed by library catalogues. It does not aim to protect children from harmful content but rather to facilitate more effective searching.[13] Filtering out obscene content is just one potential use but it has been designed to perform more complex retrieval tasks, such as search engine data collection and searching digital library collections.[14] It has not yet been widely touted as an alternative to those schemes that eliminate content on the basis of its controversialness alone.

The categories of information were selected at a series of workshops held in Dublin, Ohio, from as early as 1995. These drew together professionals from diverse, but related, fields of computer science, librarianship, online information services, abstracting and indexing, imaging and geospatial data, and museum and archive control. The aim was not centred on restricting the availability of online content but rather on advancing the development of methods, standards and protocols to locate, describe, organize and access network information resources. The 15 'labels' that emerged were as follows:

Content	**Intellectual Property**	**Instantiation**
Title	Creator	Date
Subject	Publisher	Type
Description	Contributor	Format
Source	Rights	Identifier
Language		
Relation		
Coverage		

Within each of these fields a standard dictionary of terms can evolve to apply to all Web content. Importantly, it allows different application communities to define the 'metadata' property set that best serves their needs. Since it is not restricted to controversial content, such as language, sex and violence,[15] it may be possible to overcome the problems in existing content filtering and labelling schemes identified by EPIC as outlined above. However, the Dublin Core has not yet been widely touted as an alternative to those schemes that eliminate content on the basis of controversial content alone.[16]

The development of these capacities has provided the basis on which proposals for some form of regulation of content in online services developed during the 1990s.

LEGAL AND POLICY DEVELOPMENTS IN THE UNITED STATES REGARDING REGULATION OF CYBERSPACE CONTENT

The exponential growth in usage of online services in the United States during the late 1980s and early 1990s led to demands for Internet operations to be regulated.

The Communications Decency Act 1996

One of the most important policy and legislative responses to the development of the Internet was the introduction by the US government of the Communications Decency Act 1996 (CDA) in early 1996.

Section 502 of the CDA amended sections 223(a) and (d) of Title 47 of the United States Code (USC). Those provisions prohibited the making of obscene or 'indecent' material and its transmission to a minor by means of a telecommunications device, and the use of an interactive computer service to send or display 'patently offensive' material to minors. The provisions also prohibited a person from knowingly permitting a telecommunications facility under that person's control to be used to commit these offences.[17]

The US District Court Decision in the CDA Case

In *American Civil Liberties Union* v. *Janet Reno, Attorney-General of the United States; American Library Association, Inc.* v. *United States Department of Justice* (the 'CDA Case'), a large number of organizations and individuals challenged the CDA on the basis that the provisions of section 502, referred to above, were unconstitutional.[18] Two provisions of the CDA, seeking to protect minors from harmful material on the Internet, were challenged in this case. The first provision, described as the 'indecent transmission' provision, prohibited the knowing transmission of obscene or indecent messages to any recipient under 18 years of age (section 223(a) of the CDA). The second, known as the 'patently offensive display' provision, prohibited the sending or displaying of patently offensive messages in a manner that is available to a person under 18 years of age (section 223(d) of the CDA). A number of plaintiffs filed suit challenging the constitutionality of these provisions. The government appealed to the Supreme Court under the CDA's special review provisions.

On 11 June 1996 the United States District Court for the Eastern District of Pennsylvania granted a preliminary injunction preventing the Attorney-General from enforcing the challenged provisions, where such enforcement was based upon allegations other than obscenity or child pornography.[19]

The court found that the plaintiffs had established a reasonable probability of eventual success in the litigation by demonstrating that the challenged provisions were unconstitutional on their face to the extent that they reach 'indecency'. The court noted that, whilst the First Amendment to the Constitution enshrined the principle of freedom of speech, this did not apply to child pornography and 'obscenity' which have 'no constitutional protection'.[20]

However, the court also found, *inter alia*, that the CDA went further than was necessary to deal with child pornography and obscenity on the Internet, and would have the effect of limiting forms of speech and expression which were constitutionally protected.

The three-judge district court concluded that the terms 'indecent' and 'patently offensive' were too vague. They found that 'the special attributes of Internet communication', with regard to the application of the First Amendment, denies Congress the power to regulate the content of protected speech on the Internet. The court unanimously entered a preliminary injunction against both challenged provisions but nevertheless preserved the government's right to investigate and prosecute for breaches of certain criminal provisions dealing with obscenity and child pornography.

Judge Stewart Dalzell in the district court stated in his decision: 'Any content-based regulation of the Internet, no matter how benign the purpose, could burn the global village to roast the pig.'[21]

The Supreme Court Decision in the CDA Case and President Clinton's Response

The US government appealed the district court's decision to the US Supreme Court which affirmed, accepting the district court's conclusion that 'the CDA places an unacceptably heavy burden on protected speech, and that the defences do not constitute the sort of "narrow tailoring" that will save an otherwise patently invalid unconstitutional provision'.[22]

On 26 June 1997 the Supreme Court ruled, for the first time, that the Internet is fully protected by the First Amendment to the United States Constitution. In upholding the earlier decision of the District Court for the Eastern District of Pennsylvania, it declared unconstitutional two statutory provisions enacted to protect minors from 'indecent' and 'patently offensive' communications on the Internet in the CDA as a violation of both freedom of speech and personal privacy.

The Supreme Court agreed with the district court's first point, that the CDA lacks the precision the First Amendment requires when a statute regulates the content of speech. The Court held that, although the government has an interest in protecting children from potentially harmful materials, the CDA pursues that interest by suppressing a large amount of speech that adults have a constitutional right to send or receive: the government may not 'reduce the adult population ... to ... only what is fit for children'. Further, the Court objected to the fact that the CDA 'does not allow parents to consent to their children's use of restricted materials' and the fact that it 'omits any requirement that patently offensive materials lack socially redeeming value'.[23] In fact, the Court stated that the general, undefined terms 'indecent' and 'patently offensive' cover large amounts of non-pornographic material with serious educational or other value. It was argued that possible alternatives, such as requiring that indecent material be 'tagged' in a way that facilitates parental control of material coming into the home, were appropriate ways to approach this issue.[24]

In a dissenting opinion, Justice O'Connor stated:

> The Communications Decency Act of 1996 is little more than an attempt by Congress to create 'adult zones' on the Internet. The Court has previously sustained such zoning laws, but only if they respect the First Amendment rights of adults and minors. That is to say, a zoning law is valid if
> (i)   it does not unduly restrict adult access to the material; and
> (ii) minors have no First Amendment right to read or view the banned material.
> As applied to the Internet as it exists in 1997, the 'display' provision and some applications of the 'indecent transmission' ... fail to adhere

to the first of these limiting principles by restricting adults' access to the protected materials in certain circumstances.[25]

The district court's second point was that the Internet is a unique medium, different from television or radio, and represents an enormous opportunity as a global marketplace of ideas and a powerful new engine of commerce. As the court said, 'Neither before nor after the enactment of the CDA have the vast democratic fora of the Internet been subject to the type of government supervision and regulation that has attended the broadcast industry'.[26]

The district court presumed that government regulation will undermine the substantive, speech-enhancing benefits that have flowed from the Internet and will 'threaten to torch a large segment of the Internet community'.[27] As Judge Dalzell wrote:

[I]f the goal of our First Amendment jurisprudence is the 'individual dignity and choice' that arises from 'putting the decision as to what views shall be voiced largely into the hands of each of us,' then we should be especially vigilant in preventing content-based regulation of a medium that every minute allows individual citizens actually to make those decisions.[28]

The Supreme Court accepted this approach and rejected the government's argument that availability of 'indecent' and 'patently offensive' material on the Internet is driving countless citizens away from the medium because of the risk of exposing themselves or their children to harmful material.

On 16 July 1997 President Clinton and Vice-President Gore announced a strategy for making the Internet 'family-friendly' saying:

In the wake of the Supreme Court's decision on the Communications Decency Act, America needs a strategy for protecting children and creating a safe, educational environment on the Internet that is consistent with our First Amendment values.[29]

President Clinton said that consensus had been reached in discussions that day in Washington 'about how to pave the way to a family-friendly Internet without paving over the constitutional guarantees of free speech and free expression. The plan has three components ... new technologies, enforcement of existing laws, more active participation of parents.'

The key to this development was a so-called E-chip developed by Netscape as part of a 'whole toolbox full of technologies that can do for the Internet what the V-chip will do for television ... they give parents the power to unlock ... or to lock the digital doors to objectionable content'. The president concluded this announcement by saying that 'the Internet community must work to make these labels as common as food safety labels are today, to continue to expand access to family-friendly tools, including software to protect children's privacy from unscrupulous vendors'.[30]

The 'Focus on Children' Summit, Washington, December 1997

One of the consequences of the US Supreme Court's rejection of the CDA in July 1997 was the calling of an Internet online summit, entitled 'Focus on Children', to examine alternative strategies to promote children's interests online. This included the use of the Internet to distribute child pornography and to prey on children and means of limiting children's access to harmful material. The summit met in Washington DC from 1 to 3 December 1997.[31]

The significance of the summit to the US administration as it searches for a way forward on this issue was underscored by the very active participation of US Vice-President Al Gore, the Attorney-General Janet Reno, and the Secretary-General of Interpol, the Hon. Raymond Kendall. The summit set out to find non-legislative means of making the Internet safe, educational and entertaining for children, and the main issues on which it focused were those of appropriate content for children and personal safety. The Summit explored the development by industry of a user-friendly 'digital toolbox' of filter software, an idea endorsed by a White House meeting with industry in July 1997. The toolbox concept picks up on the idea of choice, with a range of software products and services becoming available in line with consumer demand. These allow those responsible for children's use of the Internet to restrict access to material deemed unsuitable.

The summit highlighted the strong divergence of views between civil libertarians opposed to any development that threatens the First Amendment free-speech right and conservative groups that sought more forceful action. However, it is difficult to avoid the view that the voluntary use of labelling and filtering schemes represents a realistic middle ground for progressing this issue in the United States, with all of the attendant consequences for the rest of the world which must deal with the dominance of the US industry in this field.

The summit also emphasized the need to enforce existing obscenity laws and laws against child pornography. Computer images of child pornography are now covered by amendments to the United States Child Pornography Act.[32] Janet Reno and Raymond Kendall stressed the need for police, the online industry and children's advocates to work collaboratively. At the summit, the US Internet service provider (ISP) industry announced its new 'zero tolerance' policy against child pornography, involving full cooperation with law enforcement agencies, and the use of the Cybertip line (that is, the US Government Child Pornography Internet Complaints Hotline) was also announced at the summit. Strategies for specialist training for police officers in the investigation of computer crime were put forward.

Recent US Developments in Internet Content Regulation and Policy

US Vice-President Al Gore, in an address to New York University in May 1998, called for an electronic bill of rights to protect individual privacy. On 31 July 1998 he elaborated his views on this issue, saying:

> We need an electronic bill of rights for this electronic age. You should have the right to choose whether your personal information is disclosed; you should have the right to know how, when, and how much of that information is being used; and you should have the right to see it yourself, to know if it's accurate.[33]

The vice-president announced proposed action in four key areas:

1. protecting sensitive personal information – taking new executive action, calling for tough new legislation to protect personal information such as medical and financial records and ensuring that existing privacy laws are strong enough to protect privacy as technology grows and changes
2. stopping identity theft
3. protecting children's privacy online – calling for strong new measures to protect children's privacy online by ensuring that data is not collected from children without parental consent
4. urging voluntary private sector action to protect privacy – continuing US administrative efforts towards industry self-regulation with enforcement mechanisms and acknowledging the recent establishment of a private sector 'On-line Privacy Alliance'.[34]

In relation to the broader area of US government policy for the Internet, Mr Ira Magaziner, senior adviser to President Clinton, stated in a speech in Brussels on 27 May 1998:

> Over the past three years, over one-third of the real growth of the US economy has been driven by the information technology industry … . What we are seeing is a revolution that is driving our economic growth, and this revolution is just beginning.

He added, 'We think that the same potential is available to economies all over the world, not just the United States.' According to Magaziner, the United States believes in certain principles for the new digital age:

- The private sector must lead in the movement to this new electronic age.
- The role of government 'is not to regulate but rather to set conditions for the formation of contracts ... . We need to undergo a complete deregulation of telephone and broadcast television, and we need to keep the Internet unregulated'.
- When governments act in areas such as taxation and intellectual property protection, government action 'should be minimal, precise, and transparent'.
- Whatever actions are taken must respect the nature of this new medium – 'All of our policies have to be technology neutral'.
- International agreements are needed on how to make the Internet global marketplace work: 'We believe these agreements should be reached among governments to help set a predictable legal environment for industry and assure industry that government is not going to act in certain areas.'[35]

Yet, despite the US Executive's views, US legislators have not given up the fight for more onerous legislative restrictions on cyberspace content. On 23 July 1998 the US Senate approved the first legislation restricting content on the Internet since portions of the CDA were ruled unconstitutional by the Supreme Court on 26 June 1997. Senators unanimously passed a major spending bill with controversial amendments – one of which is known as the CDAII – that would make it a crime for web sites to distribute 'harmful' material to children. Another provision would require most schools and libraries to filter federally funded Internet access, and the last would ban most forms of Internet gambling. However, the US House of Representatives has yet to vote on its own version of the spending legislation. The two chambers of Congress would have to resolve any differences before sending the bill to President Clinton.

On the same day the US Senate voted overwhelmingly to restrict Internet gaming by tacking on Senator John Kyl's 'Internet Gambling Prohibition Act' to the spending bill. Despite a report by the Justice Department that called Kyl's bill over-broad and subject to constitutional challenges, the Senate voted 90 to 10 to add the proposal as an amendment to the appropriations bill.

The July 1998 Senate vote is reminiscent of the passage in the CDA that made it a criminal offence to send indecent material to minors over the Internet and was buried in the massive Telecommunications

Act of 1996. However, it also indicates the US Congress's ongoing interest in assuring constituents that elected officials are not ignoring concerns about children's exposure to Internet pornography and other adult-oriented material.

If President Clinton eventually signs the law, a lengthy court battle is likely to ensue, with the result that children will be no more protected by Internet content restriction laws than they were in 1996 when the CDA was enacted. Civil liberties groups in the United States argue that parents, not Congress, are best suited to control their children's access to objectionable material. On the other hand US law-makers believe that they should have a role in limiting unfettered entry to 'adults-only' areas online.

Citing the US Supreme Court's ruling that the CDA is vague and broadly infringes on adults' rights to free speech, US First Amendment rights advocates have said that they will fight to overturn the Internet amendments to the spending bill if they are signed into law. 'Congress [and state law-makers] have put their stamp on many Internet censorship bills that the courts have later determined to be unconstitutional. Today will be no exception,' said Emily Whitfield, a spokeswoman for the American Civil Liberties Union (ACLU), which filed the initial lawsuit challenging the CDA.

Earlier, in July 1998, the US Senate also added Senator Dan Coats's 'son of CDA' legislation to the fiscal 1999 appropriations bill for the departments of commerce, state and justice.

The Coats amendment prohibits 'commercial' web sites from allowing under-age surfers to view adult-oriented material deemed 'harmful to minors'. It would apply to any communication, image or writing that contains nudity, actual or simulated sex, or which 'lacks serious literary, artistic, political, or scientific' value. Violators could be fined up to $50 000 and be imprisoned for up to six months. 'Children can move from Web page to Web page, viewing and downloading free images with no restrictions,' said Coats in a previous statement. 'My legislation requires the commercial distributor to remove the free images or require a credit card or PIN number in order to view them.'

Also a part of the spending bill is a measure by Senator John McCain requiring public schools and libraries that receive federal discounts on Internet access to install software on their computers to filter out material that is 'inappropriate for minors'.

Mirroring their arguments against the CDA, civil liberties groups oppose the Coats and McCain bills on the grounds that they violate free speech. The law could have applied to web sites, chat rooms, or e-mail and involved anything from safe sex information to works of art and literature. 'Coats tried to make his legislation more narrow, and I don't have any doubt that it will be litigated as the CDA was,' said Marc Rotenberg, Executive Director of the Electronic Privacy Information Centre. 'Any effort to restrict publication of content is on its face a First Amendment problem.' The ACLU's Emily Whitfield added, 'There is a lot of socially valuable information online for younger people, and the Coats and McCain bills don't take that into account.'[36]

LEGAL AND POLICY DEVELOPMENTS IN AUSTRALIA REGARDING REGULATION OF CYBERSPACE CONTENT

Australia has traditionally been a country with a rapid rate of uptake of new technologies. Take-up of use of the Internet in Australia has matched this trend. As in the United States, the growth in use of the Internet in the 1990s led to growing community concerns about the problematic content it contained. Political and media concern led to demands for heavy-handed legislative and regulatory solutions. In 1995 the Australian government sought the assistance of the Australian Broadcasting Authority (ABA) in investigating issues concerning the content of online services.

The 1996 ABA Report on its Investigation into the Content of Online Services

The Australian Broadcasting Authority (ABA) was established pursuant to the Broadcasting Services Act 1992 by the Commonwealth of Australia with responsibility for regulation of the broadcasting media in Australia. In 1995 the then Australian minister for communications and the arts directed the ABA to report to him on issues arising nationally and internationally in relation to online content. This report was finalized on 30 June 1996 when two of the key developments which have influenced so much of the subsequent direction and pace of international cooperation on this issue had just occurred. The first of these was the striking down, on 11 June 1996 by the United States District Court for the Eastern Division of Pennsylvania of the United States Communications Decency Act on the grounds of unconstitutionality.[37] The second was the development of the Platform for Internet Content Selection (PICS). This resulted from the August 1995 consortium of US-based organizations including Netscape, Microsoft and public interest groups such as the Information Highway Parental Improvement Group (IHPIG), which set up its headquarters at the Massachusetts Institute of Technology in the United States and later also at the Institut National de Recherche en Informatique et en Automatique in France.

As discussed earlier, PICS sets out both to separate the content labels from the selection software and to provide the infrastructure for content labelling on the Internet. This type of labelling can be direct, enabling content providers to voluntarily label the content that they create and distribute online or alternatively, a third party labelling agency could label the material directly in accordance with an established system. In the United States, in fact, a number of online labelling systems were already being developed using PICS by mid-1996, the most significant of these being by the Recreational Software Advisory Council (RSAC), based loosely on the system then being used for labelling computer and video games. The PICS concept offered Internet users the possibility of programming their systems so that unlabelled material could not be received, or so that only material bearing certain PICS classification labels could be accessed by particular individuals – for example, minors in a domestic environment.

The ABA *On-line Report* identified the advantages of the PICS protocol in Australia as:

- the ability to incorporate Australian standards into a labelling system for Australian material;
- speed and inexpensiveness of service;
- international application and the ability to label overseas material according to Australian standards;
- the ability to accommodate different labelling dimensions and criteria for assigning labels;
- the ability to distinguish between different applications in that PICS recognizes labels, not only on the World Wide Web sites, but also on material accessed through FFP and Gopher systems, and labels on newsgroups and IRCs;
- the ability to apply filtering at the user level or at a proxy server run by an on-line provider;
- the ability to label an entire site, a directory within a site or a page of a document;
- the ability to use labels created by first or third parties, for example a commercial content provider and a ratings organization may apply separate labels to the same resource;
- sites and documents can carry more than one label simultaneously;
- labels can carry classification information, including rating level and content advice; and
- message integrity checks ('MIC') that verify the label source through a digital signature, enabling the user to check whether changes have been made after the creation of the label.[38]

Thus, at the very time when the US Congress, in the name of protection of minors, was attempting to impose draconian restrictions on the Internet through the CDA and was failing on the grounds of infringement of the freedom of speech provisions of the US Constitution, a US consortium was identifying a serious potential solution based on voluntary conduct by service providers and accessors of the online services that could provide a key ingredient in the framework for self-regulation of content on online services. The ABA's 1996 *On-line Report* recommended in favour of a scheme of substantial industry self-regulation for online services with voluntary codes of practice supported by the labelling of online content using PICS. Its proposals have received widespread acceptance in Australia and overseas and, to a considerable extent, are reflected in the various efforts to establish international cooperative measures in a range of key international and national fora.

Recent Developments and Draft Legislative Principles in Australia

Following on from the ABA report, the Australian minister for communications and the arts and the Australian attorney-general announced, on 15 July 1997, 47 principles for a national approach to regulate the content of online services such as the Internet. At the heart of these principles was the view that 'material accessed through on-line services should not be subject to a more onerous regulatory framework than "off-line" material such as books, videos, films and computer games'.[39]

Under the proposed principles, Australia's Broadcasting Services Act 1992 would be amended to establish a national framework of effective industry self-regulation for online service providers, supervised by the ABA in relation to content transmitted through online networks.[40] This regulatory regime would aim to:

1. encourage online service providers to respect community standards in relation to material published by means of their service
2. encourage the provision of means for addressing complaints about content published by means of an online service
3. ensure that online service providers place a high priority on the protection of minors from exposure to material which may be harmful to them.[41]

The proposed legislation would encourage the development of self-regulatory mechanisms and, in particular, avoid inhibiting the growth and development of the online services industry by placing unreasonable regulatory constraints on the online service providers industry regarding the publication and transmission of material.[42]

The proposed legislation would also codify the responsibilities of an online service provider in relation to objectionable content and other content that is of concern to the community, accessed by means of the online service provider's network.[43]

The principles set out to define an online service as 'a service by means of a telecommunications network, whether or not the service is available for a fee'.[44] It was made clear that this definition was 'intended to encompass only those on-line services with interaction capability; *that is*, where the service allows the multidirectional transfer of content upon demand between an end-user and other end-users connected to the network'.[45] Legislation resulting from community consultations over these principles became law in the Broadcasting Services Amendment (Online Services) Act 1999. The Australian Broadcasting Authority now has regulatory responsibility for the co-regulatory rules for Internet content in Australia from 1 January 2000. Self-regulatory Industry Codes have been registered by the ABA and the ABA administers an Internet content complaints hotline. Details of the new Australian online content regulation regime may be obtained from the ABA website: www.aba.gov.au.

The Children and Content On-line Task Force Report, June 1998

On 28 August 1997 the Australian Minister for Communications, the Information Economy and the Arts, Senator Richard Alston, issued the second directive to the ABA to continue its investigation into matters relating to future regulatory arrangements in Australia for the content of online services. To assist in its work pursuant to this directive, the ABA formed a Children and Content On-line Task Force which reported to the ABA in June 1998 and identified the following principles:

(1) Children should be encouraged to use the Internet, as it offers them access to a range of services that can be educational, entertaining and exciting, as well as allowing them to be socially interactive.

(2) Adults should be free to access material in the on-line environment that they are legally entitled to view in other media, including material not suitable for children.

(3) It is desirable to minimise children's exposure to unsuitable material in the on-line environment.

(4) Parents and other adults with responsibility for children are usually in the best position to determine the appropriateness of content for children in their care, having regard to age, values and the special needs of the child(ren).

(5) Direct supervision of children and the setting of house rules or

guidelines are the best ways to ensure that Internet use in the home is a rewarding and safe experience.

(6)   Filtering, rating and labelling systems should be encouraged to support and supplement the management of children's use of the Internet when direct adult supervision is not possible.

(7)   The use of filtering software, rating and labelling should not create a significant barrier to the expression of diverse opinion and content on the Internet.

(8)   The use of filtering software, content labelling and rating must be voluntary for users and content providers.

(9)   The primary responsibility for content on the Internet must reside with the content provider.[46]

In reflecting on the broader issue of the protection of children in the online environment, the Task Force identified three key areas that affect children:

- contact and safety issues
- illegal content
- unsuitable content.

The Task Force also considered the community needs associated with these three key issues and developed a set of ten practical recommendations which aim to address these key areas under the following headings:

1.   Develop key messages for children and parents.
2.   Industry's role in relation to on-line advertising and targeting of children.
3.   Establishing a hotline for reporting child pornography.
4.   Role of Internet service providers.
5.   Content rating, filtering and labelling issues.
6.   Implementation of the findings of the report.
7.   Community education campaign.
8.   Some specific tools and strategies.
9.   Review of existing community education and information campaigns.
10. Delivery of the campaign.[47]

Recent Australian Policy Developments relating to Online Content

On 22 June 1998 the Minister for Communications, the Information Economy and the Arts extended the currency of his direction to the ABA to continue its work on online regulation to 31 December 1998, pending consideration by the Commonwealth of Australia Parliament of legislation flowing from community consultation on the 47 principles.[48] A further Ministerial Direction continued this role through to 31 December 1999. On 1 January 2000 the new Australian Online Services legislation came into effect.

In July 1998 the Ministerial Council for the Information Economy in Australia issued, for public consultation, a preliminary statement of the Australian government's policy approach on the information economy.[49] That statement identified four guiding principles that the Australian government believes are necessary 'to ensure the lives and work of Australians are enriched, jobs are created, and the national wealth is enhanced, through the participation of all Australians in the growing information economy':

(1) All Australians – wherever they live and work, and whatever their economic circumstances – need to be able to access the information economy at sufficient bandwidth and affordable cost; and need to be equipped with the skills and knowledge to harness the information economy's benefits for employment and living standards.

(2) The role of government is to show the way – as a user, supplier and purchaser of electronic services; to provide direction, education and encouragement to business and consumers; and to provide a legal and regulatory framework that ensures the information economy is safe, secure, certain and open.

(3) For electronic commerce to flourish, the private sector must continue to take the lead. The government encourages industry self-regulation, and supports the efforts of private sector organisations to guide the successful expansion of electronic commerce and to build confidence in its use.

(4) Because electronic commerce crosses national boundaries, the government favours national approaches to strategic issues that are consistent with those evolving in a wide range of international fora. Australia is committed – and already working – to help develop a set of norms and conventions for international governance of electronic commerce across national boundaries, that accords with Australia's national interests and ensures the openness, safety, security, and fairness of all transactions.[50]

These principles are consistent with the broad direction in which much of the international debate has been heading on the best means of dealing with access and content issues for cyberspace.

THE CompuServe CASE AND EUROPEAN INDUSTRY RESPONSES

A recent German experience provides an important example of the futility of a heavy-handed legal response in relation to cyberspace content.

The German CompuServe Case

The case against Felix Somm in Bavaria highlights the dilemmas facing governments, law enforcement agencies and the judiciary if they attempt to impose and enforce draconian laws on online content against Internet service providers.

The defendant was, at the time of the alleged offences, managing director of CompuServe Deutschland, a 100 per cent subsidiary of CompuServe USA. CompuServe Deutschland provided local dial-up access to CompuServe USA's facilities (proprietary content and access to Internet services) for the latter's German subscribers.

At the end of 1995 the German police served on the defendant a list of 282 Usenet newsgroups that, in its view, contained images of violence, child pornography and bestiality. The incriminating content was stored on CompuServe USA's newsgroup servers. CompuServe USA blocked access to the vast majority of these newsgroups for all its subscribers worldwide. It then made available parental control software to its subscribers and unblocked the newsgroups. On subsequent access by police to newsgroups through CompuServe, messages allegedly containing images of violence, child pornography and bestiality were found. The charges against Felix Somm related to 12 of these images.

The judge held:

(a)   The defendant, together with CompuServe USA, made access to material containing violence, child pornography and bestiality publicly available, contrary to Article 184 Abs 3 StGB of the Criminal Code.

(b)   CompuServe USA was technically able to block at any time access to the newsgroups containing the images.

(c)   In restoring or failing to block access to the newsgroups in question, CompuServe USA acted deliberately, in full knowledge of the fact that they contained images of violence, child pornography and bestiality, and with a motive of commercial gain. (The judge found that the defendant shared the knowledge and the motive.)

(d)   It was no defence that parental control software was made available to subscribers, since giving access to adults to the incriminated content was illegal.

(e)   The defendant was an accessory, because CompuServe Deutschland provided access to CompuServe USA's services for the latter's German subscribers as a business activity, sharing the revenue with CompuServe USA.

(f)   The defendant could not rely on the provisions of Article 5 of the *Teledienstegesetz* (TeleServices Act) restricting liability of Internet service providers since CompuServe Deutschland was not an access provider within the meaning of paragraph 3. Access to third-party services was provided by CompuServe USA. CompuServe USA had the technical means of blocking access and so had no defence under paragraph 2; therefore nor did CompuServe Deutschland.[51]

On 28 May 1998, the Munich judge imposed a two-year suspended sentence on Felix Somm, despite the intervening passing of a German multimedia law which provides that Internet service providers should not be liable for material which they carry on their services unless they knew about it and had the technical capacity to block it.[52] This decision attracted widespread international criticism and has led to no discernible reduction in the volume of obscene material available on the Internet.[53] On 17 November 1999, a German higher court in the state capital Munich reversed the decision against Felix Somm and overturned the conviction on charges of aiding the distribution of pornography. Judge Ember lamented the lack of an effective legal and technical means to eliminate child pornography and other illegal content from the web, saying he expected the issue to continue to plague the industry in years to come.[54]

The European Internet Service Providers' Response to the CompuServe Case

Partly in response to the German CompuServe judgment, Europe's leading Internet service providers met in Brussels on 22 July 1998 to launch an industry coalition intended to promote industry codes of conduct. The companies, hoping to fend off what they perceived to be stifling government intervention, aimed to draft pan-European principles on issues such as how to keep illegal material off the Internet and protect children from harmful online content. The primary focus was on implementing a working process for the industry to discuss how to regulate itself. The 22 July meeting also responded to an EU initiative asking the Internet services industry to implement measures such as codes of conduct and telephone hotlines to deter misuse of the Internet. AOL Bertelsmann – a joint venture between the US online services giant America On-line and the German media company, Bertelsmann – has spearheaded the coalition drive.

The group hoped to draw up Europe-wide principles to govern national codes of conduct before a major global conference on electronic commerce held in Ottawa in October 1998. The principles were also intended to cover issues such as consumer and privacy protection. The group hoped to educate users on how to protect children from harmful Internet material and also look at some initiatives with a broad base of support from governments, educators and consumer groups to try to promote practical tips on using the Internet for parents and teachers. This would include the use of filtering technologies and rating systems to screen out violent or obscene sites.[55]

On 27 February 1999 the Bertelsmann Foundation convened an International Network of Experts on Internet Self-Regulation to work on the development of concepts for self-regulation of Internet content.[56] This fed into the Internet Content Summit held in Munich from 9 to 11 September 1999, which received a statement of principles for self-regulation of internet content resulting from the work of the Network of Experts. Amongst the key principles are:

1. Mechanisms have to be developed to deal with illegal content, to protect children online as well as to guarantee free speech.
2. The need for a systematic, integrated and international approach to self-regulation of Internet content.
3. The need for codes of conduct to be adopted to ensure that internet content and service providers act in accordance with principles of social responsibility.
4. To be effective, codes of conduct must be the product of and be enforced by self-regulatory agencies.
5. Self-regulation must be supported by public authorities through a range of mechanisms.
6. Complaints hotlines are required to ensure users can respond to content in the Internet that they find of substantial concern.[57]

INTERNATIONAL FORA AND PROCESSES FOR DISCUSSION OF CYBERSPACE CONTENT REGULATION

These various national debates about the best means of dealing with cyberspace content have been reflected in a number of major international fora, a number of the most important of which are dealt with below.

The European Community and the Global Business Dialogue

At the international level, the primary policy interaction in this field occurred during 1998 and 1999 between the United States and the European Union.

Within the United States, the policy struggle is between a Congress that has overreacted legislatively and an industry that has been resistant to any form of content rules on the Internet, with the Executive attempting to find some middle ground between those two positions. In the European Community, by contrast, there has been a ready and rapid convergence between industry, some national governments and the European Commission about the need for strategies that will allay public concerns about online content. Some of the key events that have encouraged this convergence include: criminal prosecution by one German state government (Bavaria) against officials of an ISP for content carried on that service; industry concerns in the UK that if industry did not act on its own then some form of heavy-handed government intervention might result; and the tragic events in Belgium involving the kidnapping and deaths of several young Belgian girls that fuelled an EU-wide alarm about international networks of paedophiles using the Internet to convey and store child pornographic material and also to contact young people. The development of a cohesive EU position on harmful content on the Internet is beginning to constitute a powerful countervailing force against an American view that no action is necessary. The reality is that, in respect of transborder commerce on the Internet, the European market is crucial for US service providers and they cannot ignore or avoid the policy developments there.

One of the starting points for European developments in this area was the realization in 1995 by a number of the ISPs, including British Telecom (BT), that, if they were to nurture the development of new Internet services as a revenue-generating business, they would have to address the way in which complaints from the public might be serviced. As a consequence, they initiated a small complaints-handling function within BT. However, it rapidly became clear that this complaints-handling service needed to be made more widely available to service providers. In conjunction with the UK Department of Trade and Industry (responsible UK government policy on online services) and with some initial-funding provided by one of the service providers, a body called Internet Watch Foundation was established in 1996 to provide a hotline for public complaints about harmful content on the Internet.[58] By 1996 a basic form of industry self-regulation was in place for Internet services in the UK.

Generally speaking, complaints to the Internet Watch Foundation are investigated and, if material is found to be problematic, it is removed from the site by the ISP. This does not derogate from the proper role of criminal law in prosecuting those who place such material on the Internet.

In late 1998 the Department of Trade and Industry conducted a review of the Internet Watch Foundation and found that it was making an important contribution to protecting potentially vulnerable sections of society who may come into contact with illegal and offensive material on the Internet.[59] This review found that the Internet Watch Foundation had played a critical role in providing a service to UK Internet users:

- Through its work in receiving complaints about potentially illegal material, and where appropriate, by advising ISPs to remove the clearly illegal material from their servers; and
- Through its work in the development of rating systems, noting research that indicates people are reassured by the presence of such protection tools in using the Internet.[60]

As these UK developments took shape, the pressure was growing on the European Commission to take strong action in respect of harmful content on the Internet, largely as a result of the public concerns about paedophile rings fuelled by the Belgian scandals of 1996. As in the UK, so within the European Commission, the policy has largely been driven not from the traditional areas of broadcasting content regulation but rather from DGXIII, the generally deregulationist area responsible for telecommunications under Commissioner Martin Bangemann.[61]

In speeches given in Geneva on 8 September 1997 and in Venice on 18 September 1997, Dr Bangemann made the following indicative points:

- It is no longer possible to keep the network industries (telecoms, cable, Internet) separate from the content providers (broadcasters, publishers), which means that current regulatory frameworks governing telecommunications and the media (broadcasting, publishing) must be transformed in order to allow new business to take off.
- There is a need for an international framework of principles, guidelines and rules for global communications for the twenty-first century, which could be embodied in an International Charter.
- Such a charter would not set out detailed regulations for the Internet, but would refer to agreed principles, standards or rules that would be utilized in different countries of the world.
- Within the European Community it may be necessary to design a 'European Communications Act' to bring together legislation

on the provision of infrastructure, services and content and on conditions for access to that content, and one day a single European regulatory authority may be necessary to achieve these objectives.

An international charter for global communications, governing activities carried out over the Internet in particular, could provide a suitable framework covering such issues as the legal recognition of digital signatures, encryption, privacy, protection against illegal and harmful content, customs and data protection. The tools for achieving these objectives would include mutual recognition, self-regulation and, if needed, regulation.[62] The task of advancing the international discussion of the matters raised by Dr Bangemann has now been taken up by the Global Business Dialogue (GBD) established by business leaders in the United States, Japan and elsewhere in response to the 29 June 1998 initiatives by Commissioner Bangemann to participate in a round-table discussion on global communication issues. This GBD focuses on clearly identifying solutions and providing input on regulation or business self-regulatory codes of conduct in consultation with governments and international organizations.[63]

At this stage, the European Commission itself at this stage opted for the implementation of a set of guidelines, which it announced on 26 November 1997 in its 'Action Plan on Promoting the Safe Use of the Internet', and which build on the self-regulatory approach developed in the UK and some other EU member states. Amongst the key principles set out in this Action Plan are:

- promotion of self-regulation and creation of content-monitoring schemes including a European network of hotlines to achieve a high level of protection (especially dealing with content such as child pornography and racism);
- demonstration and application of effective filtering services and compatible rating systems, which take account of cultural and linguistic diversity; and
- promotion of awareness actions directed at users – in particular children, parents and teachers – to allow them to use Internet resources provided by industry safely and with confidence.[64]

The Action Plan identified that illegal content must be distinguished from harmful content, each of which require different measures to deal with them. The European Commission noted that illegal content must be dealt with at source by law enforcement agencies, and that their activities are covered by the rules of national law and agreements of judicial cooperation. The industry can, however, give important help in reducing the circulation of illegal content (especially

child pornography, racism and anti-Semitism) through properly functioning systems of self-regulation (such as codes of conduct and the
establishment of hotlines) in compliance with, and supported by, the
legal system and with the support of customers.

In tackling harmful content, the priority actions should include
enabling users to deal with harmful content through the development of technological solutions (filtering and content rating systems),
to increase parental awareness, and to develop self-regulation that
can provide an adequate framework, particularly for the protection
of minors.[65]

The Action Plan covers a four-year period from 1 January 1998 to
31 December 2001 and has an expenditure programme of 30 million
ECU over that period to help self-regulatory organizations to develop
guidelines for codes of conduct at the European level, to build the
consensus for their application and assist with their implementation,
and to ensure that filtering and rating will be applied and will offer
workable solutions for users, parents and teachers. And, since the
practical application of filtering and rating by European content providers has not yet achieved critical mass, it includes a call for proposals
to select projects validating the rating systems in liaison with European content providers and to demonstrate and validate third-party
rating systems. Provision is also made for funding for an international
conference to ensure coherence between European activities and those
undertaken in other parts of the world, and also to share experience.[66]

The critical aspects of the European Commission approach to note
are the determination to pursue the path of self-regulation by industry associations using PICS-type content labelling schemes and
hotlines–complaints networks as the key ingredients at member state
levels.

The Bonn Ministerial Declaration on Global Information Networks, 8 July 1997

From 6 to 8 July 1997, the German government hosted an international conference in Bonn on the topic 'Global Information Networks'.
The Conference was attended by Ministers from the Member States
of the European Union (EU), Members of European Commission
(EC), Ministers of the European Free Trade Association (EFTA) and
of countries of Central and Eastern Europe (CCEE). Guests at ministerial level from the United States of America, Canada, Japan and
Russia and representatives from industry, users and European and
international organizations also participated.[67] It resulted in the adoption of the 'Bonn Declaration', as well as declarations by industry
and user participants. For the purposes of this chapter, the key

aspects of the Bonn Declaration relating to international cooperative measures on online services are:

- recognition of global information networks as a highly positive development presenting opportunities for business, citizen and public administration alike
- recognition that the Internet is already starting to create new businesses, new high-value services and new employment opportunities
- recognition of the special characteristics and fundamentally transnational nature of the Internet
- recognition of the need to avoid divisions between the information 'haves' and 'have nots' in Europe and globally
- recognition of the key role the private sector is playing in the emergence of global information networks, in particular through investments in infrastructure services
- recognition of the role that the private sector can play in protecting the interests of consumers and in promoting and respecting ethical standards, through properly functioning systems of self-regulation in compliance with and supported by the legal system
- encouragement for industry to implement open, platform-independent content rating systems, and to propose rating services which meet the needs of different users
- recognition that the general legal frameworks should be applied online as they are offline, with regulations being technology-neutral and kept to a minimum
- recognition that it is crucial to build trust and confidence in global information networks by ensuring that basic human rights are respected and by safeguarding the interests of society in general, including producers and consumers
- encouragement of the reinforcement of police and judicial cooperation, particularly in the area of technology training and mutual assistance, to prevent and combat illegal content and high-technology crime
- support for the establishment of international networks of hotlines.[68]

The Bonn Declaration thus pointed in the direction of:

- using current national legal frameworks for the enforcement of criminal law provisions where appropriate in respect of online crime
- development by industry of common principles for schemes of self-regulation regarding the content of online services

- establishment of national hotlines for complaints regarding online content and for some appropriate interconnection and interaction between national hotlines.

The Organization for Economic Cooperation and Development (OECD)

One of the key fora in which there has been pressure for some form of international agreement on online content regulations or control has been the Organization For Economic Cooperation and Development (OECD). The initial pressure for this resulted from the unfolding of events in Belgium in 1996, referred to earlier. In January 1997 the Belgian delegation to the OECD submitted a proposal for the deposit of a Convention to outlaw the sexual exploitation and abuse of children on the Internet.[69] France strongly supported this Belgian proposal. The OECD at the 31st session of the ICCP on 27–28 February 1997 established an ad hoc process of meetings on approaches to content and conduct on the Internet; it held its first meeting on 1–2 July 1997 and the second on 22 October 1997. As a result of this process a study was undertaken of the different approaches being taken in major industrial countries to the regulation of content on the Internet. The resulting paper, 'Approaches to Content on the Internet', is an invaluable source document for directions being pursued in a wide range of industrial countries regarding online content regulation. For the purposes of this chapter, the key findings were:

- that the Platform for Internet Content Selection (PICS) represents a very significant industry-wide response to attempts to regulate content on the Internet
- that industry self-regulation is considered to be the most appropriate approach for harmful content, as opposed to illegal content
- that voluntary industry codes of conduct are being developed in at least seven OECD member states
- that complaint hotlines are being implemented in some countries as part of a self-regulatory approach.

The ad hoc meeting of 22 October 1997 concluded by acknowledging the primary role of the private sector in regulating the Internet. It also agreed that a joint OECD/Business and Industry Advisory Committee forum be held on 25 March 1998 in Paris to provide a forum for discussions among key stakeholders on the development, implementation and objectives of self-regulatory policies, mechanisms and technologies and the empowerment of users of Internet content. This forum focused on those aspects of legal issues relating to Internet content that offer the greatest opportunity for self-regulatory solutions, as well as the identification of the fields that could not be covered by them.[70]

Within these OECD ad hoc fora there was a major divergence of view between the United States, which basically favoured no international action and particularly no international regulatory framework for the Internet, and nations such as Belgium, which favoured substantial international agreement and activity. With the completion of the 25 March 1998 forum, the OECD resolved to do no further work in this area. It therefore appears that the OECD may not be the organization to progress the development of any international framework on cyberspace. The OECD Ministers for Information met in Ottawa in October 1998 and no further work on Internet self-regulation content emerged from those discussions.

UNESCO

At the 29th session of the UNESCO General Conference in Paris from 21 October to 12 November 1997 the director-general of UNESCO made a preliminary report on the feasibility of an international instrument on the establishment of a legal framework relating to cyberspace. An interesting aspect of this was a recommendation on the preservation of a balanced use of language on cyberspace, which represented the concerns of non-Anglophone countries about the domination of English as the language of the Internet.

A number of countries including Australia, Germany and UK were concerned that UNESCO should not overreach itself in terms of what might be realistically attainable in the realm of cyberspace regulations.

The UNESCO General Conference did resolve that UNESCO should be the organization of the United Nations systems to take the intellectual lead in this area and that the UNESCO director-general should continue the work on legal, ethical and societal aspects of cyberspace, and in particular:

(a) pursue further consultation and collaboration with member states, interested bodies and competent international organizations inside and outside the UN system including the private sector;

(b) prepare and organize regional and international meetings of experts to clarify policy priorities in line with the needs of member states;

(c) report to the thirtieth session of the General Conference in 1999; and

(d)   prepare a draft recommendation on the promotion and use of multilingualism and universal access to cyberspace to be submitted to the thirtieth session of the General Conference in 1999.[71]

As a result of this decision, UNESCO hosted or supported the following main meetings devoted to the issue of international cooperation in relation to the Internet: the Asia-Pacific Regional Expert Meeting on the Legal Framework of Cyberspace, Seoul, 8–10 September 1998; the International Experts Meeting on Cyberspace Law, Monte Carlo, Principality of Monaco, 29–30 September 1998; and the Asia-Pacific Internet Forum, Bali, Indonesia, March 1999.

All these processes have identified the need for international cooperative principles for the Internet and this work is expected to be considered by UNESCO in the next biennium 'to promote consensus-building on ethical and legal principles applicable in cyberspace'.[72]

The International Working Group on Content Rating/Internet Content Rating Association and Alliance

An international consensus appears to be developing on a way forward in cyberspace, which is structured around a number of principles:

- the need for coordinated national, if not international, criminal laws to deal with *illegal* content on online services
- the need for national schemes of industry self-regulation to deal with harmful content on on-line services, codes of practice, content labelling schemes such as PICS, and complaint hotlines
- the need for national schemes of industry self-regulation to be broadly consistent with each other, requiring ongoing international dialogue
- the need to protect children online and the consequent need to consider the role which content labelling and filtering can play in this area
- the need for widespread public education in the use of such services.

One of the key ingredients in the concept of industry self-regulation relates to content labelling or rating. In association with the mid-1997 Bonn Council of Ministers Meeting, Steven Balkam of the Recreational Software Advisory Council (RSAC), Kaaren Koomen of the ABA, David Kerr of the Internet Watch Foundation, Nigel Williams of Childnet International and Michael Schneider of ECO, an industry association in Germany, formed a discussion group called the International Working Group on Content Rating (IWGCR). The prime objective of the group is to consider the viability of developing an internationally acceptable content labelling scheme for the Internet in order to 'to promote self-regulation by Netizans and to stave off government censorship'.[73] The first working meeting of IWGCR took place in the UK in September 1997 when the group began work on a set of principles and an action plan for funding and progressing the issue.[74]

The group aimed to consider and, if possible, develop an internationally acceptable labelling system that is appropriate for cross-cultural use. The group agreed on some fundamental principles, including the proposition that the labelling system be voluntary and based on self-labelling. It also agreed that an international labelling scheme should describe, rather than evaluate, Internet content. By providing information to users about the content on a particular site, a descriptive scheme would allow users to apply their own standards and values to the labels based on that information.

One of the issues for the group is whether the US-based RSACi system should be the basis for the international approach to content rating on the Internet. European participants have indicated a preference for the development of a new non-US-derived system. The very nature of the dispute highlights the extent to which the key axis in this whole arena of international cooperation and agreement lies in the North Atlantic between the United States and the European Union.

At its December 1997 meeting in Washington, the IWGCR considered the November announcement of the European Commission Action Plan on promoting safe use of the Internet – particularly its endorsement of PICS-compatible rating systems.[75] In late 1998 this group was absorbed into the Internet Content Rating Alliance which in turn in early 1999 became the Internet Content Rating Association with commercial memberships from the United States, Europe and Japan.[76]

All these international discussions have pointed clearly towards the need for some form of national and international approach to cyberspace content, based on concepts of industry self-regulation and using content labelling technologies. However, the search for the way forward raises significant legal and moral issues which require resolution, not least those relating to access and to the balancing of demands for freedom of expression in cyberspace against demands for responsibility and restraint in relation to illegal and harmful material.

Global Business Dialogue

On 29 June 1998 EC Commissioner Martin Bangemann invited business leaders from around the world to participate in a round-table discussion on global communication issues. The objective of the meeting was to explore the need for strengthened international coordination.[77] The Global Business Dialogue (GBD) was formed as a result and resolved that further progress on this initiative should be based on the following principles:

- It should avoid legislation, where possible, and concentrate on market-led industry-driven self-regulatory models. Any regulation should ensure competition.
- It should focus on a well defined list of issues on which quick progress can be made with the close cooperation of business, consumer groups and government.
- Participation should be open to players from all countries.
- Work on these issues should be industry-led and coordinated with relevant international bodies.

Two organizations were particularly closely involved in this process, the Transatlantic Business Dialogue and the US–Japan Business Council. The first meeting of the GBD's Business Steering Committee took place in New York on 14 January 1999 and consisted largely of representations from major corporations from Europe, Japan and the United States.[78] However, because the GBD did not consider the issue of Internet content to be amenable to relatively swift solutions, it is not receiving immediate attention from this group.[79]

The International Network of Experts on Internet Content

In early 1999 35 participants were invited to join the International Network of Experts on Self-Regulation for Responsibility and Control on the Internet. This Network was brought together by the Bertelsmann Foundation, a charitable foundation which owns the controlling interest in Bertelsmann Corporation, the German media and publications enterprise, and is part of its advocacy of self-regulatory solutions to the problems of Internet content. The Network held its first meeting in New York on 27 February 1999 and brought together a diverse group of well known academics and participants in the implementation of Internet self-regulatory policy including:

- Professor Nadine Strossen, President, American Civil Liberties Union

- Professor Stephen Balkam, President, Recreational Software Advisory Council
- Mr David Kerr, Chief Executive, Internet Watch Ltd
- Mr Nigel Williams, Director, ChildNet International
- Mr Richard Swetenham, European Commission Directorate General XIII (Telecommunications, Information Markets)
- Mr Akio Kokubu, Executive Director, Electronic Network Consortium, Japan
- Mr Michael Schneider, President, European Internet Service Providers Association
- Madame Agnes Fournier de Saint Maur, Head, Trafficking in Human Beings Branch, ICPO-INTERPOL, France
- Ms Yvonne Gartner, Microsoft Europe
- Professor Eli Noam, Director, Columbia Institute for Tele-Information, Columbia University, New York
- Mr Gareth Grainger, Deputy Chairman, Australian Broadcasting Authority.

The three regulatory agencies represented at the meeting were the Australian Broadcasting Authority, the Canadian Radio Telecommunications Commission (Mr Ted Woodhead) and the Singapore Broadcasting Authority (Ms Ling Pek Ling), all of which are actively dealing with the issues of self-regulation of harmful content on the Internet.

The background paper to the establishment of the Network of Experts highlighted five developments that need to be addressed in dealing with Internet content:

- National regulatory frameworks do not meet the requirements of the global nature of the Internet.
- Prosecutors are under pressure to pursue child pornography and other illegal content on the Internet but lack knowledge and competence in filter technology and, in some countries, lack awareness of who to contact to tackle cases of realized Internet misuse.
- Content providers rarely use available self-rating mechanisms.
- Internet service providers are not able to control the carried information but are concerned about securing acceptance of the new medium of the Internet.
- Users lack knowledge and competence in filter technology and, in some countries, lack awareness of who to contact to tackle cases of realized Internet misuse.

In setting up the Network, the Bertelsmann Foundation accordingly aimed to facilitate acceptance of an essentially self-regulatory system for content on the Internet with four key areas of responsibility:

1. industry codes of conduct
2. self-rating and filtering mechanisms
3. hotlines
4. prosecution/law enforcement.

The identified operational goals for this Network were to:

- identify best practices within each area of responsibility
- initiate and support the process of cooperation and coordination between the areas
- support each initiative within the areas of responsibility in implementing the developed concepts in workshops.

Fundamental to the whole approach to the work on the Network is the common understanding that it is ultimately the responsibility of individual nations, industry participants and users to facilitate the development, acceptance and use of appropriate schemes of self-regulation in relation to Internet content.

At the 27 February 1999 meeting, the following four papers were given:

1. 'Self-regulation on the Internet', by Professor Stefan Verhulst and Professor Monroe Price of the Comparative Media Law and Policy Programme, Oxford, United Kingdom
2. 'Self-rating and Filtering Systems', by Professor Jack Balkin, Director, Project on the Information Society, Yale, United States
3. 'Hotlines', by Professor Herbert Kurkert, Department of Media and Information, University of St Gallen, Switzerland
4. 'Responsibility on the Internet: Law Enforcement', by Professor Ulrich Sieber, University of Wurzburg, Germany.

Amongst the key points to emerge from the presentation and surrounding discussion were:

- Progress should be made on commercial establishment of the Internet Content Rating Association taking over the work on RSACi.
- Bridges need to be built between hotlines in different countries.
- Much greater emphasis needs to be placed on community awareness programmes about use of the Internet.
- It should be understood that co-regulatory schemes, such as those proposed for Australia, are acceptable as appropriate variants of self-regulatory arrangements.
- The strong US constitutional obligations in respect of freedom of expression and the likelihood that the US Congress's

legislatively-imposed restrictions on Internet content are most likely to be struck down in the United States pose a difficulty

- Recent research shows that many US citizen want the US government to intervene in the field of Internet content, despite the US constitutional constraints.
- It is difficult to achieve genuine harmonization of national laws in respect of Internet content.
- It is desirable to identify and promote concepts for minimum requirements in respect of industry codes, hotlines and labelling and rating schemes as part of a process of advancing international cooperation on Internet content.
- Public disquiet and heavy political pressure results from negative and sensationalist media coverage of Internet content issues.
- The work of the Network needs to be focused on practical and attainable outcomes that are genuinely useful in advancing the international and national discourses on these issues.

Four working parties were established to concentrate on the four key themes of industry codes, self-rating/filtering, hotlines and law enforcement. The work of this Network resulted in the Internet Content Summit (Munich, 9–11 September 1999) reported on earlier (see p.92). It has been organized and funded by the Bertelsmann Foundation in cooperation with INCORE (Internet Content Rating for Europe) and supported by the Bavarian State Chancellery and Ministry of Interior. The Bertelsmann Foundation presented the 'Memorandum on Self-Regulation of Internet Content'.[80]

LEGAL AND MORAL ISSUES RAISED BY CYBERSPACE

In a 1996 article entitled 'Thinking Globally, Acting Locally', John Perry Barlow described cyberspace as offering:

> … the promise of a new social space, global and antisovereign, within which anybody, anywhere can express to the rest of humanity whatever he or she believes without fear. There is in these new media a foreshadowing of the intellectual and economic liberty that might undo all the authoritarian powers on earth.[81]

Barlow's words capture the image of a move into new frontiers, the opening-up of uncharted or hitherto unoccupied territories, in which the individual can be free to explore and roam without hindrance from others. It is an ostensibly noble vision and recalls the excitement of all frontier and expansionist movements – not least the westward movement of European civilization in North America. Yet, as Ziauddin Sardar has noted in *Cyberfutures*:

> Western civilisation has always been obsessed with new territories to conquer [and now] cyberspace is a conscious reflection of the deepest desires, aspirations, experiential yearning and spiritual angst of Western man. It is resolutely being designed as a new market and it is an emphatic product of the culture, world-view and technology of western civilisation ... . Cyberspace frontier, then, is set to follow the patterns of the old West. And like the old West, it is a terrain where marshals and lawmen roam freely bringing order and justice whenever and wherever they can. The lawmen of cyberspace and the new heroes of the West are hackers, whiz kids who break into computers, punish those who break the code of Netiquette and terrorise other users.[82]

We have here two sharply contrasted views, and yet they both draw on the same images – of open land being claimed and tamed. The Barlow view is that the morality and law of cyberspace is to be that of the freedom-loving individualist. The Sardar view is that the individual explorer and conqueror of cyberspace territory is ultimately an agent of longstanding forces of Western expansionism which act to sweep aside the morality, culture and legal foundations of other civilizations.

For those who seek nationally or internationally to develop principles for the governance of cyberspace, it is the reconciliation of these two views that must be sought. Cyberspace is a reality, just as the Roman Empire, the British Empire, and the Soviet Union have been historic realities in the past two millennia. As we enter the twenty-first century we are simply facing a new reality that, in addition to the nations of the world and the planet's individual geographical territories, there is a new domain that seems to coexist with geography and transcends national boundaries – namely, the domain of cyberspace. Like every other territory that has existed in the experience of human history, it will succumb to human occupation, and it will acquire customary mores, concepts of morality and principles of law. The challenge for us is resolutely to accept the responsibility to influence its mores, to shape its concepts of morality and to enact, to the extent necessary, those laws that are appropriate to such a transnational domain. In so doing we must acknowledge that the domain of cyberspace has emerged from a particular Western civilization and that it has the potential to reach into every home, school, university, office and workplace on the planet. We may not find a better place to begin to consider how this should be dealt with nationally or internationally than to go to the point of origin of the Western view of international law, and to its father Hugo de Groot,

Grotius, who, in his two most famous works *De Jure Belli ac Pacis* and *Mare Liberum*, propounded the view that the sea is *'res communis'* and is thus common to all mankind and cannot be appropriated by individual nation states.[83] However, the developers of concepts of international law later conceded that even the ocean within three nautical miles of land is the territorial possession of the neighbouring state and comes within the jurisdiction of that state and its laws.[84]

By analogy it may be argued that, to the extent that cyberspace is outside of the territory of an individual nation, it should be subject to its own laws. The flaw in this proposition is that content is almost always physically located on systems, and systems are actually almost invariably accessed within national jurisdictions. Therefore, it seems appropriate to accept that, to the extent that the location of content and its access comes within the territory of individual nations, it should be subject to the laws of those states. If this approach is accepted then there is a clear need for a two-tiered set of principles for cyberspace: one at the international level and the other at the national level. Therefore, one of the challenges for those who seek to identify moral and legal issues in this field will be to identify what morality and what law is appropriate at each of those two levels, but fundamental to the process ought to be a recognition that there is a proper role for both international cooperation and also for national law-making bodies in dealing with the issue of cyberspace. Cyberspace law and cyberspace morality will only go out of control if we fail to exercise our collective will, nationally and internationally, to give it a framework of morality and governance that is the mark of civilization in every other space which humans occupy.

I would like to suggest in this chapter that matters of morality very much relate to individual citizens and their cultures and personal views of what is appropriate for them so far as belief and behaviour are concerned. As individuals are usually citizens of a nation-state it may be more appropriate for the concerns of individual morality to be aired and reflected within the framework of individual nations and their laws. If this view is to be preferred, then moral issues relating to cyberspace ought to be dealt with – to the extent that the domain of cyberspace comes within the territorial scope of a national state – as national issues. In terms of international cooperative measures for cyberspace, these might preferably be value-neutral on moral issues unless those moral issues are considered to be so universally accepted as to demand and require the force of legal principles recognized by international law. I suggest that there are three potential moral issues that may fit within this category of demanding recognition as principles of the international law of cyberspace. These are as follows:

1. The production and dissemination of paedophiliac material (across national frontiers) constitutes an offence against the rights of the child.
2. The production and dissemination of information (across national frontiers) for the purposes of assisting terrorism constitutes an offence against humanity.
3. The production and dissemination of information for the purposes of assisting in the fomenting of racial, ethnic or religious hatred (across national frontiers) constitutes an offence against humanity.

In the domain of cyberspace beyond the reach of national territories, matters that are appropriately the subject of legal, as opposed to moral, regulation ought to be identified as being those appropriate for the safe carriage and conduct of cyberspace such as:

*   transborder or international carriage (including technical–technological standards)
*   transborder access
*   privacy
*   encryption (potentially all access issues)
*   domain names
*   content labelling/rating
*   international network of hotlines
*   copyright.

At the national level, it would seem appropriate for national administrations to have responsibility for:

1. ensuring compliance with agreed international principles
2. criminal law in respect of illegal content – for example, paedophiliac material, terrorist material and racial/ethnic/religious hatred material consistent with established principles of international law
3. working on schemes to regulate harmful content, including industry self-regulatory codes, content rating schemes tailored to national cultural mores and hotlines
4. encouraging local language content on cyberspace
5. community education on the use of cyberspace
6. facilitation of local access to cyberspace.

ACCESS TO CYBERSPACE

Towards a Goal of Universal Access to Cyberspace

One of the most pernicious myths about the Internet is that it provides free access to all the information about everything to everybody everywhere at any time. To begin with, access to the Internet is not free. Individuals working in organizations, universities and research institutions have 'free' access because their institutions pay. For individuals without institutional support, Internet access is an expensive luxury: there is the cost of the computer and necessary peripherals (£2000 or approximately US$3200, recurring every two years as both the hardware and software become useless within that period); payment to the Internet provider (£180 or approximately US$300 per year) and the telephone bills (around £500 or approximately US$800 per year). One can feed a family of four in Bangladesh for a whole year for that sort of money. Thus the Internet is only available to those who can afford a computer and the connection and the telephone charges that go with it. In the West, this means educated households with incomes in the upper brackets. In the United States, for example, households with incomes above $75 000 are three times more likely to own a computer than households with incomes between $25 000 and $30 000. That leaves most minority households out in the cold. (However, Asian and Pacific Islanders are more likely than whites to own a home computer and therefore have access to the Internet.) In the Third World – that is, those countries with telecommunication infrastructures – only the reasonably well-off can afford access to the Internet. That leaves most of humanity at the mercy of real reality.[85]

The grim comment by Ziauddin Sardar, reproduced below, should cause all who work on legal and policy issues about cyberspace to take a deep breath and reassess the reality of what we are dealing with. The view of cyberspace from Australia, the UK or the United States is not the same as it is from, say, Chad, China, India, Peru, Tonga or Uzbekistan. In Sardar's words:

> The cyberspace is inhabited not just by the white, middle-class male, but a particular type of white, middle-class male – or more appropriately two main types of white, middle-class males. The first and the most predominant type of male on cyberspace is the college student. Seven out of ten institutes of higher learning in the United States provide free Internet access to their students. Apart from spending most of their time 'netsurfing,' game playing, chatting on-line, these students also create 'home pages' as advertisements for themselves.

There are countless such home pages on the World Wide Web containing 'information' on what they eat and excrete, what they would look like if they were Martians, and their musings on God, Hegel, Chicago Bears and the Grateful Dead. This group of Internet users has the same demographic profile as Playboy readers: that is, both groups are aged 18 to 35, 80 to 90 per cent are male, they are well-educated and have a higher than average income.[86]

David Carter raises the concept of universal access to telematic services:

[I]f there are to be benefits to be gained from the development of the information economy, in terms of new training and employment opportunities, improved information, cultural and entertainment services and the ability to use such services in fully interactive ways, then everyone – regardless of whether they personally have a phone, a TV or a computer (or the money to buy one) – must have the right to access these facilities as a public service.[87]

In March 1999 Rafael Arias Salgado, Spain's Minister of Public Works and the Economy, called on the European Union to accept that the Internet must form part of what we consider universal services.[88]

If developed countries, such as Australia and the United States, are some distance from the implementation of such a principle of universal access to cyberspace, its application to the larger part of the world's population may appear fanciful, remote and unattainable. Yet, if that is not the direction in which we are committed to heading, then another gulf will be opening and widening between the world's 'haves' and 'have nots'. This would seem incompatible with every other effort which is being made by national and international aid programmes to bridge and reduce such gaps. Any discussion of an international legal framework for cyberspace must therefore confront and deal with the concept of universal access.

Encouragement of Languages in addition to English in Cyberspace

In discussing universal access, one of the first issues to tackle is the language of cyberspace. Clearly, the predominant language is English, since this has been the dominant language of late twentieth-century communications. Perhaps second only to English may be the peculiar forms of English-based cyberargot that have developed in cyberspace over the last 20 years. Each of these, of course, rule out the capacity of those who cannot use these *lingua francas* to participate in the exchange of information and ideas. As the significance of cyberspace in global trade, banking finance and economy grows, it will result in the exclusion of non-English speakers from free and equal access to, and participation in, the domain of cyberspace.

Yet this constitutes no reason to argue that there should be some rule about the use of language on cyberspace. The very phrase *lingua franca* reminds us of a previous dominant language in international trade and diplomacy – namely Latin. It would be foolish and futile for anyone to seek to restrain the current ascendancy of English in cyberspace, as it reflects the origins and current users of that domain. The more appropriate strategy would be for individual non-English speaking nations to encourage far greater participation by their citizens and institutions in cyberspace, to interconnect their own cyber-domains, such as France's Minitel, with the wider world of cyberspace, to facilitate the development of content in languages other than English and to improve the quality of automatic translation capacity on the Internet. Only by so doing will cyberspace become of greater interest and usefulness to the non-English-speaking world.

Rules to restrain the use of English, or to compel the use of some other language on cyberspace, are unlikely to be more fruitful or successful than were attempts to preserve the use of Norman French in medieval England or the use of Latin in the modern Roman rite of the Catholic Church. There are considerable challenges here, but they are not ones that should be taken up by those who seek to develop any form of international legal framework for cyberspace. They belong with individual nations and their citizens.

FREEDOM OF EXPRESSION AND REGULATION OF INFORMATION IN CYBERSPACE CONTENT

Democracy both presupposes and supports the freedom of expression and communication amongst citizens, and between them and the state. Official secrecy and censorship contradict such liberties. Yet free speech may be limited in a democratic society – for example in wartime – just as libel, defamation and obscenity do not enjoy legal protection. Many see censorship in cyberspace as being less justifiable, and claim that the exclusion of certain participants from Internet discussion groups throws into question the open-discourse quality of the 'Information Superhighway'. Kapor,[89] however, points out that the ambiguity of the public or private status of these groups makes controversy likely over the permissible extent of free speech. Beyond informal regulation of this kind lies legislation promoting, for example, 'communications decency', as in the United States. These matters of law and etiquette inhabit a grey area concerning the applicability of rules and norms, and the permissibility of surveillance.[90]

The above statement highlights the key elements of the dilemma encompassed in the exploration of whether freedom of expression in online services ought to be constrained by any form of regulation in respect of any cyberspace content. It also presupposes universal understanding of the concept of liberty of expression as enshrined in the First Amendment to the United States Constitution:

> Congress shall make no law respecting an establishment of religion, or prohibiting the free exercise thereof; or abridging the *freedom of speech, or of the press; or the right of the people peaceably to assemble*, and to petition the Government for a redress of grievances.

Since the Internet and the great bulk of its present content originate from the United States, it is impossible to avoid dealing with this issue without accepting the American context of so much of the discussion. As US District Court Judge Dalzell said in the first instance in the *CDA* case:

> If the goal of our First Amendment jurisprudence is the 'individual dignity and choice' that arises from 'putting the decisions as to what views shall be voiced largely in the hands of each of us,' then we should be especially vigilant in preventing content-based regulation of a medium that every minute allows individual citizens actually to make those decisions.[91]

Yet as US Supreme Court Justice O'Connor noted in her dissenting opinion in the same case:

> The Communications Decency Act of 1996 [is] little more than an attempt by Congress to create 'adult zones' on the Internet … . The Court has previously sustained such zoning laws, but only if they respect the First Amendment rights of adults and minors. That is to say a zoning law is valid if :
>   (i)   it does not unduly restrict adult access to the material; and
>   (ii) minors have no First Amendment right to read or view the banned material.[92]

Whether one agrees or disagrees with the US district and Supreme Court majorities in the *CDA* case, the reality is that, in the country of origin of much of the present content of the Internet, the governing national law favours a wide view on freedom of expression and will be likely to strike down other legislative or industry self-regulatory schemes that unlawfully restrict the First Amendment rights of the US citizen. Yet in Germany, which also has a Constitution that respects individual rights and freedoms, both federal and state legislatures have had no difficulty in justifying a restrictive view of what is appropriate in cyberspace conduct.[93]

The Bavarian state case against Felix Somm from 1995 to 1998, which resulted in a conviction against the managing director of a highly respected Internet service provider who was held responsible for the paedophiliac material on his company's server, indicates a willingness by at least some German judges to take a very restrictive view of the protection to be afforded to freedom of expression in online content.

Even in the United States, the Supreme Court in *Snepp* v. *US*[94] found no difficulty in restricting First Amendment freedom of expression rights where there were issues of national security.[95] Similarly, it made clear in *Ginsberg* v. *New York* that prohibitions on selling obscene material to a minor, even when that material is able to be sold to an adult, will not offend the US First Amendment right to freedom of expression.[96] As has been discussed elsewhere in this chapter, cyberspace raises serious issues about privacy. Announcements by US Vice-President Al Gore on the need for an electronic bill of rights highlighted a growing concern to protect individual privacy. Clearly, even within the United States, there is a recognition that the right to privacy demands some counterbalance against the right to freedom of expression.

Despite the fact that the Internet and so much of its present content originates from within the United States, it ought not be accepted that the US Constitution and the debates that rage around it ought to provide the fundamental underpinnings for the whole of cyberspace, either today or in the future. It simply has the status of being the law of one amongst many nations with which cyberspace co-exists. There appears to be no appropriate reason why other nations ought not take a different view in terms of entry of cyberspace content into their jurisdictions.

I would suggest that it is better to view the issue of freedom of expression in relation to cyberspace content as having no more elevated or separate status in the international discourse than many other matters that are perceived as significant, such as the protection of children from illegal or harmful material or, indeed, the protection of national cultures and mores from inappropriate intrusion by an aggressive and dominant national culture.

If this approach is taken, then it allows international discussion to proceed on the basis of a two-tiered international–national approach to the regulation of cyberspace content as set out earlier in this chapter. At the international level, the focus should be on principles for the safe carriage and conduct of cyberspace. At the national level – subject to adherence to agreed international principles – the focus should be on nationally appropriate schemes of criminal law for illegal content and self-regulatory schemes for harmful content. Key issues about morality, cultural specificity, language, community education and awareness, as well as the facilitation of universal access to cyberspace, ought to be left to national governments to negotiate with their own citizens.

When pursuing consideration of these issues at the national level, those who work on regulation of cyberspace content need to take the following factors into account.

First, attempts to impose restrictions on online content in one jurisdiction that are markedly more stringent or onerous than standards adopted in other countries are likely to be unsuccessful without the introduction of burdensome and restrictive gateways which are likely to be so resource-intensive that they would be very difficult to maintain.[97] Placing greater restrictions on local Internet service providers and other participants in one national jurisdiction than exist in other national jurisdictions is likely to cause those service providers to be disadvantaged in the emerging global market and may cause them to re-establish those businesses in other, less onerous and burdensome, national markets.[98] There are serious difficulties in imposing heavy liabilities on Internet service providers for content which they have not generated and about which they are not aware until it is brought to their attention or where they actually supply or endorse content.[99] The primary responsibility for content on online services should centred on content providers themselves.[100] Self-regulatory industry codes and systems of complaint hotlines should recognize this primary responsibility and the secondary role of Internet service providers. If adults are permitted to read, hear and see material in forms other than on online services, then they should be permitted to have access to such material on online services as well. Children should be protected from material that may harm or disturb them. Everyone should be protected from exposure to unsolicited material that they find offensive.

Second, parental and teacher supervision and involvement is the most effective means of guiding children's use of online information. If there is a genuine desire to develop the opportunities for communication, education and business offered by online services, then any regulatory policy, whether national or international, should concentrate on encouraging further development of online technology rather than stifling it with burdensome and unnecessary restrictions.

The future of cyberspace content demands reconciliation between freedom of expression and concern for community standards – particularly the protection of children from illegal or harmful content. The solution lies not in the victory of one of these positions over the other. Responsible cyberspace content regulation will facilitate an appropriate environment in which its positive opportunities and advantages can be nurtured, developed and accessed by a growing number of citizens while permitting the proper concerns of potential and actual users to be addressed. For cyberspace to be a safe place does not mean that it has to be insipid. Nevertheless, it should be a responsible place, and responsibility requires the establishment and implementation of tools that allow parents, teachers and other users of online services to feel confident that they are empowered to determine the basis on which they access those services in their homes and workplaces. The international discourse on this issue has already provided a fertile and successful array of methods for ensuring that this occurs, through the development and implementation of content-rating and labelling systems, the establishment of industry codes of self-regulation and the implementation of complaint-hotline services to allow concerns about content to be voiced and addressed. All this requires industry, governments and parents to accept their own share of the responsibility demanded by this exciting new domain. Freedom of expression is worthless if there is no one willing to listen to the speaker.

SUGGESTED INTERNATIONAL PRINCIPLES FOR CYBERSPACE

Clearly there is a broad level of international consensus emerging about some basic principles for the governance of cyberspace. These have been articulated in Europe, North America and the Asia-Pacific region, including Australia. These principles are well suited for inclusion in a UNESCO declaratory statement which, even without the full force of international law, would at least and very usefully serve to reinforce the direction in which these issues are moving and would provide worthwhile guidance to those countries yet to have an active discourse on the issue. The use of the term 'Legal Framework for Cyberspace' might best be avoided, carrying, as it does, unnecessary and inappropriate overtones of heavyhanded interference, when what is really being proposed is simply a body of broad principles largely based on the notion of international cooperation, national responsibility and industry self-regulation.

The key principles should include:

1. Acknowledgement of the enormous and positive benefits to humanity that the rapid growth of online services offers in the fields of information, communication and understanding.
2. Recognition that any rules for the governance of cyberspace should be about nurturing it as a place in which citizens, academics, and industry and public administrators can have confidence as online users and participants in their homes or workplaces.

3. Acknowledgement of the need for a principle or long-term goal of universal access to cyberspace, recognizing that the present development of online services favours the economically privileged and users of English. If the gap between the world's information rich and information poor is to be bridged, then very serious measures will be required to assist the people of developing countries to have reasonable and useful access to these services and to the tools and training that cyberspace requires.

4. Acknowledgement that, in both developed and developing countries, there is a significant and growing need for community and parental education on the use of online services and that this needs to be built into a wide range of education programmes and processes.

5. Acknowledgement that there is a difference between content in cyberspace that is appropriately identified by national authorities as unlawful and that which is appropriately identified as not unlawful but harmful to segments of national communities, such as young people, while recognizing the likely impact of cultural differences on approaches that different nations will take when considering what may be 'unlawful' or 'harmful'.

6. Acknowledgement that it is the right of national authorities to declare material on online services to be unlawful – for example, because it relates to the commission of an illegal offence such as paedophilia or terrorism, and to take appropriate national measures against suppliers or possessors of such material.

7. Acknowledgement that, in relation to harmful content on online services, the emphasis should more appropriately be on self-regulatory schemes of industry governance, whether or not underpinned by national schemes of supporting legislation.

8. Acceptance of a body of principles for self-regulation of online services in relation to harmful content that should include:

   – development of national schemes of self-regulatory codes of conduct by Internet service providers;
   – development of linked schemes of national hotlines to enable immediate complaints to be made about the illegal or harmful content on online services and to enable ISPs to take swift remedial action once informed of a problem;
   – development and implementation of technological solutions such as filtering and content rating systems, which empower parents and those responsible for young people to take appropriate action to protect those people from harmful material;
   – broad-based filtering and content rating systems which are adaptable to different countries and cultures, enabling

issues of community standards to be addressed within countries;

- a high priority placed by online service providers on the protection of children and young people from exposure to material that may be harmful to them;
- the encouragement of children and young people to learn how to use online services and the opportunity for access to, and education in, the use of such services;
- the right of adults to access material in the online environment which they are legally entitled to view in other media, including material deemed not suitable for children but which is not illegal;
- community and parental education on the best ways to use online services in the home.

9. Acknowledgement that issues of individual morality are more appropriately the domain of national authorities and national discourses to the extent that they relate to the rights and conduct of citizens within the territory of a state.

10. Acknowledgement that there are some moral issues which have such universal acceptance that they must be recognized as part of the fundamental rules of both national and international governance of cyberspace and that these may include:
    - prohibiting the production and dissemination of paedophiliac material;
    - prohibiting the production and dissemination of information for the purpose of assisting terrorism;
    - prohibiting the production and dissemination of information for the purpose of assisting in the fomenting of racial, ethnic or religious hatred and accepting the responsibility of national and international agencies for the enforcement of such laws.

11. Acceptance of the principle that cyberspace is common to all mankind and that it cannot be appropriated by individual nation-states other than to the extent to which it comes within the territorial jurisdiction of an individual state.

12. Acceptance of the principle that it is appropriate for international laws and regulatory frameworks to be developed relating to the safe carriage and conduct of cyberspace where it is beyond the reach of territorial jurisdictions, in particular recognizing the following areas as being appropriate for international agreement:
    - transborder or international carriage of cyberspace (including technical/technological standards);
    - transborder or international access to cyberspace;
    - privacy;

- encryption;
- domain names;
- content labelling/rating;
- international networks of hotlines on cyberspace content;
- copyright.
13. Acknowledgement that all international and national rules for cyberspace should be consistent with multilateral trade agreements and obligations in respect of goods and services and should aim for transparency, flexibility, business and user certainty and minimal restrictions on trade between nations.

FUTURE PROCESSES

The adoption and enforcement (as far as possible) of appropriate national laws and international agreements, added to the close collaboration of all concerned national authorities, can certainly contribute to making our relations in cyberspace more orderly and civilized.[101]

These words from Henrikas Iouchkiavitchious, Assistant Director-General of UNESCO's Sector of Communication, Information and Informatics, suggest a two-tiered approach of national laws and international principles in order to ensure that this remarkable new domain of cyberspace is enabled to achieve its full potential. The need for collaboration and understanding is clear, but the steps by which these are to be advanced and achieved have yet to be identified. Many of the world's current 'netizens' fear the development of any schemes which seem to restrict or structure the Internet's current anarchic free-for-all. Many of those seeking to establish commercial services in cyberspace fear restrictions or obligations that hamper business opportunities and impose legal responsibilities for content which has its origins in lands other than their own.

There is an equal desire for the online environment to grow so that messages can reach far more widely than they do now. There is a wish to see increased interconnectivity between different online systems, such as the Internet and Minitel. There are also concerns about the privacy of individual information, confidentiality of commercial information, national security and harm caused by terrorists and fomenters of intercommunal hatred. Not least, there is the concern of individual parents and teachers charged with nurturing humanity's future – its children – about the potential harm that lurks in a domain with which so many are unfamiliar. As has been remarked elsewhere in this chapter, cyberspace is simply another domain discovered by humans, and no domain coming within the reach of humans has yet resisted the human urge to explore, occupy, civilize or govern. This is happening with cyberspace and it will continue to happen so long as it remains a useful, interesting and engaging place for humans to be. The question is not one of knowing whether to govern it, but rather how, and in a manner that permits it to continue to flourish, grow, reach out and build bridges between people, business, institutions and nations.

UNESCO's adoption of a statement of principles for the governance of cyberspace is one step that can usefully be made, although the fact that the United States is not a member of UNESCO will restrict its significance and impact. EC Commissioner Martin Bangemann's call for an international convention to discuss principles for an international charter also has considerable merit. The resulting Global Business Dialogue will help advance these issues, as will the Internet Network of Experts on Internet Content. These processes can complement one another, and the principles pursued should endeavour to be consistent.

It seems inevitable that some form of international consensus will emerge about the appropriate governance of cyberspace; indeed, it is already emerging. Such a consensus seems the best means of ensuring the removal of fears and barriers to the future growth of online services within the realm of cyberspace.

SUMMARY AND CONCLUSIONS

While the rapid take-up of online services is continuing exponentially, a vigorous and healthy dialogue is taking place at national and international levels between industry, users and governments about the best means of ensuring that appropriate safeguards are developed and put in place in respect of harmful content on these services. Whilst those who fear the unknown remain vocal, their voices are becoming increasingly muted as an increasing number of people worldwide realize that cyberspace is a magnificent and important opportunity for humankind. Obviously, of course, schemes of national legislation must deal with criminal or illegal content and these legislative schemes have to link with those of other countries. It is also becoming increasingly clear that the principal area of concern centres around the need to protect children from harmful content for which in other arenas, such as videos, movies and television, many countries already have well developed safeguard schemes.

There is a form of international consensus being reached between Europe, the United States and other parts of the world, including Australia, Japan, Korea and Singapore, that national schemes of industry self-regulation, utilizing codes of conduct, hotlines and labelling schemes, provide the logical way forward. The European Commission's November 1997 Action Plan, and the funds allocated to it over the next few years, are a certain promise of serious progress.

Commissioner Bangemann's call for an international agreement, combined with the UNESCO and OECD processes, is capable of producing some useful outcomes: *ex post facto* endorsement of the direction that a number of key international actors, such as the United States and the European Union, will have already taken; and effective schemes of self-regulation supported by appropriate government policies. This is the approach which the ABA identified in 1996, and we still believe that it represents the best way forward. However, there is no room for complacency. Public concern has been allayed for the time being, but it will be awakened and with renewed vigour whenever the next major Internet-related scandal erupts. There is an urgent need for international cooperative measures regarding illegal and harmful content on the Internet, but the responsibility for pursuing those measures lies as much with industry and users as it does with governments and international agencies.

NOTES

1   This paper was presented at the UNESCO International INFOEthics 98 Congress, 'Ethical, Legal and Societal Challenges of Cyberspace, and the Expert Meeting on Cyberspace Law', Monte-Carlo (Monaco), 29 September–3 October 1998, and was updated to the beginning of 1999 to take account of more recent developments.

2   W3C homepage: http://www.w3.org/ and PICS homepage www.w3.org/pics.

3   RSAC homepage: http://www.rsac.org/.

4   Safesurf homepage: http://www.safesurf.com.

5   Cyber Patrol homepage: www.cyberpatrol.com.

6   Safesurf homepage: http://www.safesurf.com.

7   Nortel homepage (manufacturers of Cyber Patrol): http://www.nortel.net/index.html and www.cyberpatrol.com.

8   SurfWatch homepage: www.surfwatch.com.

9   Results reported at http://www.epic.org/reports/filter_report.html.

10   For details see http://family.netshepherd.com/frameset_about.him.

11   Press release: http://www.w3.org/Press/RDF.

12   Named after Dublin, Ohio, where the system was conceived.

13   For a description of the categories, see http://purl.oclc.org/metadata/dublin_core_elements.

14   http://www.w3.org/Metadata/RDF/.

15   For a description of the categories, see http://purl.oclc.org/metadata/dublin_core_elements.

16   M. Hudson and M. Armstrong, *Internet Content*, Melbourne, RMIT, 1998, pp.29–31.

17   See www.epic.org/free-speech(cda/cda.html. The relevant sections were cited more fully in the CDA Case, discussed at III.B., *infra*. Section 223(a), the

'indecency' provision, subjects to criminal penalties of imprisonment of no more than two years, or a fine or both, anyone who:

(1) in interstate or foreign communications ...
    (B) by means of a telecommunications device knowingly
        (i) makes, creates, or solicits, and
        (ii) initiates the transmission of, any comment, request, sugges-
        tion, proposal, image, or other communication which is obscene or indecent, knowing that the recipient of the communication is under 18 years of age, regardless of whether the maker of such communication placed the call or initiated the communication;
(2) knowingly permits any telecommunications facility under his control to be used for any activity prohibited by paragraph (1) with the intent that it be used for such activity.

Section 223(d), the 'patently offensive' provision, subjects to criminal penalties anyone who:

(1) in interstate or foreign communications knowingly
    (A) uses an interactive computer service to send to a specific person or persons under 18 years of age, or
    (B) uses any interactive computer service to display in a manner available to a person under 18 years of age, any comment, request, suggestion, proposal, image, or other communication that, in context, depicts or describes, in terms patently offensive as measured by contemporary community standards, sexual or excretory activities or organs, regardless of whether the user of such a service placed the call or initiated the communication.
(2) knowingly permits any telecommunications facility under such person's control to be used for an activity prohibited by paragraph (1) with the intent that it be used for such activity.

18 See http://www.access.digex.net/Çepic/cda/cda_opinion.html.
19 *ACLU* v. *Reno*, 929 F. Supp. 824 (EDPa. 1996).
20 *Alliance for Community Media* v. *FCC*, 56 F.3d 105, 112 (DCCir. 1995).
21 *ACLU*, 929 F. Supp. at 882.
22 *Reno* v. *ACLU*, 117 S. Ct. 2329, 2349 (1997).
23 Ibid. at 2332.
24 Ibid. at 2333.
25 Ibid. at 2353 (O'Connor, J. dissenting).
26 Ibid. at 2343.
27 Ibid at 2350.
28 *ACLU*, op. cit., 929 F. Supp. at 881 (citations omitted).
29 Remarks by President Clinton at event on the E-chip for the Internet (1997) at http://www.whitehouse.gov/WH/New/Ratings/19970716-6738.html.
30 Ibid.
31 www.kidsonline.org.
32 Remarks at Internet summit. Janet Reno, US Attorney-General Washington DC (1997) at http://www.kidsonline.org/archives/reno/shtml. Child Pornography Prevention Act of 1996, codified at 18 USC § 2251.
33 www.usia.gov/products/washfile.htm, White House Briefing Room, *Media Release*, 31 July 1998, *Vice-President Gore Announces New Steps Toward an Electronic Bill of Rights*, at p.1.
34 Ibid. pp.1, 3.

35   For the full text of Mr Magaziner's speech at the Telecommunications Conference, Brussels, see http://pdq2.usia.gov/scripts/cqcgi.

36   News Release, *Senate Oks CDA II, Gambling Bill*, www.news.com/News/Item/0,4,24533,00.

37   *ACLU* v. *Reno*, 929 F. Supp. 824 (ED Pa. 1996).

38   Australian Broadcasting Authority, *On-Line Report*, Sydney: Australian Broadcasting Authority, 1996, at pp.156–7. ABA web site: www.aba.gov.au.

39   Senator Richard Alston, Minister for Communications and the Arts, *Joint Media Release*, 15 July 1997, www.dca.gov.au.

40   Principle 1, Principles for a regulatory framework for online services in the Broadcasting Services Act 1992, *Joint Media Release*, 15 July 1997. www.dca.gov.au.

41   Ibid., Principle 2.

42   Ibid., Principle 3.

43   Ibid., Principle 4.

44   Ibid., Principle 11.

45   Ibid., Principle 12.

46   *Report of the Children and On-line Task Force*, June 1998, www.aba.gov.au/what/online.

47   Ibid.

48   Australian Broadcasting Authority (Investigation) Direction No. 1 of 1997 (Amendment No. 1 of 1998). See www.aba.gov.au/navigation/newsrel/1997/86nr97.htm.

49   Ministerial Council for the Information Economy, *Towards an Australian Strategy for the Information Economy*, Canberra July 1998, www.noie.gov.au/national strategy.

50   Ibid., p.8.

51   http://www.qlinks.net/comdocs/somm.htm. See also Professor Dr Ulrich Sieber's comments on the CompuServe Case at http://www.beck.de/mmr/Materillen/Compuserve-urtoch.htm.

52   C. Macavinta, CNETNEWS.COM, *CompuServe Manager Convicted*, 28 May 1998, http://www.news.com/News/Item/0,4,22525,000.html.

53   E. Andrews, *CompuServe Executive Indicted in Germany on Pornography Charges*, http://www.healey.com.au/antony/News/CompuServe1.html.

54   Reuters Financial Report, 17 November 1999.

55   *European ISPs to Talk Net Rules*, Reuters, 14 July 1998, CNET News.com, http://www.news.com/News/Item/0,4,24177,00.html.

56   Self-regulation of Internet Content, Bertelsmann Foundation, Gutersloh, 1999.

57   Australian Broadcasting Authority, *Update* (75), April 1999 and Australian Broadcasting Authority, *Update* (81), October 1999, pp.12–14

58   Australian Broadcasting Authority, *The Internet and Some International Regulatory Issues Relating to Content. A Pilot Comparative Study Commissioned by the United Nations Educational, Scientific and Cultural Organization (UNESCO)*, Sydney, ABA, October 1997, www.aba.gov.au/what/online/unesco/htm.

59   Department of Trade and Industry, *Review of the Internet Watch Foundation*, 25 January 1999, http://www.dti.gov.uk/iwfreview/iwfreview0.html.

60   Ibid., Executive Summary.

61   In the UK, broadcasting policy has been handled by the Department of National Heritage (now Department of the Media, Sport and the Arts) as successor of the Home Office, the responsible regulator being the Independent Television Commission (ITC). In the European Commission, DGX is responsible for broadcasting and audiovisual content policy.

62   For this point, refer to page 9 of Martin Bangemann's speech of 8 September 1997 to the International Telecommunications Union in Geneva, *New World*

Order for Global Communications: The Need for an International Charter, Geneva: ITU.
63   Global Business Dialogue at http://www.gbd.org/structure/orgin.htm.
64   Commission of the European Communities, *Final Action Plan on Promoting the Safe Use of the Internet*, 26 November 1997, Com (97), p.582.
65   Ibid., p.2.
66   Ibid., p.582.
67   Press release of 8 July 1997 from the Global Information Networks Conference, www2.echo.lv/bonn/pressrel.htm.
68   *Ministerial Declaration*, Bonn Ministerial Conference, 8 July 1997, www2.echo.lv/bonn/final.html.
69   OECD-DSTI/ICCP/REG(97) 8, p.2.
70   OECD, *Directorate for Science, Technology and Industry Forum on Internet Content Self-Regulation*, 25 March 1997, Agenda.
71   UNESCO, *Report of the 29th General Conference*, 29C/COMIV/2 29C/83, pp.20–21, www.techweb.com/sc/directlink.cgi.
72   For easy reference, see draft 30 C/5, p.153, para. 04126, (a)(i).
73   *Internet Group Plans Global Rating System*, Tech Wire Press Release, 30 June 1997.
74   www.iwf.org.uk/p011097.html.
75   Australian Broadcasting Authority, *Update*, (62), February 1998, p.20.
76   Ibid., (75), April 1999.
77   Global Business Dialogue: http://www.gbd.org/structure/.
78   http://www.gbd.org/structure/steering/htm.origins.htm.
79   http://www.gbd.org/structure/steering.htm.origins.htm.
80   Australian Broadcasting Authority, *Update*, (75), April 1999. Bertelsmann Foundation web site, update December 1999
81   J.P. Barlow, 'Thinking Globally, Acting Locally', *Cyber-Rights Electronic List*, 8 February 1996.
82   Z. Sardar, 'Cyberspace as the Darker Side of the West', in Z Sardar and J.R. Ravetz, *Cyberfutures*, London, Pluto Press, 1996, ch.1, pp.15, 16 and 22.
83   S. Dreyfus, *Droit des relations internationales*, Paris, Cyas, 1978, p.39.
84   Ibid., p.40.
85   Sardar and Ravetz, *Cyberfutures*, op. cit., pp.23–4.
86   Ibid., p.25.
87   D. Carter, 'Digital Democracy' or 'Information Aristocracy', in B.D. Loader (ed.), *The Governance of Cyberspace: Politics, Technology and Global Restructuring*, London: Routledge, 1997, p.138.
88   IRIS, *Spain Sees Net as Universal Right*, Update, 3 March 1999.
89   Mitch Kapor, Chief Executive Officer of Lotus Development Corporation, Chief Executive Officer of On Technology Corporation, Adjunct/Visiting Professor at MIT, President/Board Member of Electronic Frontier Foundation, and President of Kapor Enterprises Incorporated.
90   C.D. Raab, 'Privacy, Democracy, Information', in B.D. Loader (ed.), *The Governance of Cyberspace*, op. cit., p.156.
91   *ACLU v. Reno*, 929 F. Supp. 824 (ED Pa. 1996) (emphasis added).
92   *Reno v. ACLU*, 117 S. Ct. 2329 (1997).
93   German CompuServe judgment, Quick Links homepage at http://www.qlinks.net/comdocs/somm.htm.
94   444 US 507 (1980).
95   J.B. Ferguson, 'Information Warfare and National Security', in S.J.V. Schwarzstein (ed.), *The Information Revolution and National Security*, Washington DC, Centre for Strategic and International Studies, 1996, p.42 (citing *Snepp v. US*).

96   *Ginsberg* v. *New York*, 390 US 629 (1968).
97   Note the experience of Singapore as reported in *National Internet Advisory Committee Releases Interim Report Singapore*, 25 September 1997, www.sba.gov.sg/newsrel.htm.
98   See submission of Electronic Frontiers Australia to the Department of Communications and the Arts, EFA Website: http://www.efa.org.au/Publish/doca.html.
99   Ibid.
100 Ibid.
101 H. Iouchkiavitchious, 'Law, Civil Society and National Security: International Dimensions', in Schwarzstein, *The Information Revolution and National Security*, op. cit., p.51.

BIBLIOGRAPHY

Australian Broadcasting Authority (1997), *Investigation into the Content of On-Line Services*, Sydney: ABA.
Australian Broadcasting Authority (1997), *Response to the European Commission's Green Paper on the Protection of Minors and Human Dignity in Audio Visual and Information Services*, Sydney: ABA.
Australian Broadcasting Authority (1997), *The Internet and Some International Regulatory Issues Relating to Content. A Pilot Comparative Study Commissioned by the United Nations Educational, Scientific and Cultural Organization (UNESCO)*, Sydney: ABA, October.
Australian Broadcasting Authority (1998), *Report of the Children and Content On-Line Task Force*, Sydney: ABA.
Australian Broadcasting Authority (1998), 'European Commission DGXIII: Interim Report on Initiatives in EU Member States with Respect to Combating Illegal and Harmful Content on the Internet', *ABA Update*, (62), February.
Bangemann, M. (1997), *New World Order for Global Communications: The Need for an International Charter*, Geneva: ITU, September.
Bangemann, M. (1997), 'Europe and the Information Society', speech, Venice, September 1997.
Commission of the European Communities (1997), *Final Action Plan on Promoting Safe Use of the Internet*, Com (97) 582 Final.
Commission of the European Communities (n.d.), *Green Paper on the Protection of Minors and Human Dignity in Audiovisual and Information Services*, Com (96) 471 Final.
Commission of the European Communities (1997), *Internet Content Guidelines*, November.
Corker, J. and Sala, P. (1998), 'The Supreme Court's Ruling on the Communications Decency Act: A Victory for Free Speech', *Communications Law Bulletin*, **16**(2), pp.1–3.
Department of Trade and Industry (UK) (1999), *Report on Review of the Internet Watch Foundation*, January, http:/www.dti.gov.uk/iwfreview.
Dreyfus, S. (1978), *Droit des relations internationales*, Paris: Cyas.
European Parliament (1997), *Feasibility of Censoring and Jamming Pornography and Racism on Informatics*, PE 166 658, May.
European Parliament (1997), *Report on the Commission's Communication on Illegal and Harmful Content on the Internet*, PE 219.568/final, March.
Fidler, R. (1997), *Mediamorphosis*, Thousand Oaks, CA: Pine Forge Press.
Gibson, W. (1984), *Neuromancer*, New York: Ace.

Global Business Dialogue, http://www.gbd.org.structure/origins.htm.

Goldstein, D. (1998), 'What's Hot on the Internet', *Communications Update*, pp.18–19.

Hudson, M. and Armstrong, M. (1998), *Internet Content – Balancing Community Values*, Melbourne: RMIT.

International Institute of Communications (1997), *Intermedin Special Report*, **25**(6), December.

Internet Law and Policy Forum (1997), *Self-Regulation of the Internet*, http://www.ilpf.org/selfreg/selfreg2.htm.

Loader, B.D. (ed.) (1997), *The Governance of Cyberspace: Politics, Technology and Global Restructuring*, London: Routledge.

McCrea, P., Smart, B. and Andrews, M. (1998), *Blocking Content on the Internet*, Canberra: CSIRO.

Nordicom International Clearing House on Children and Violence on the Screen (1998), **2**(1).

OECD Directorate for Science, Technology and Industry, DSTI/ICCP/REG (97)8 (work carried out by a number of international organizations for the protection of children against sexual exploitation).

OECD Directorate for Science, Technology and Industry, DSTI/ICCP/REG (97) 28 (Summary Record of the Second Ad Hoc Meeting on Approaches to Content of the Internet).

OECD Directorate for Science, Technology and Industry, DSTI/ICCP/REG (97)14 (approaches to content on the Internet).

Sardar, Z. and Ravetz, J.R. (eds) (1996), *Cyberfutures*, London: Pluto Press.

Schwartzstein, S.J.D. (ed.) (1996), *The Information Revolution and National Security*, Washington DC: Centre for Strategic and International Studies.

Sieber, U. (1998), *The 'CompuServe' Judgment of 28 May, 1998*, http://www.beck/de/mmr/Materillen/Compuserve-urtoch.htm.

UNESCO (1998), *Report of the 29th General Conference* (29C/83).

United States Supreme Court (1999), *Janet Reno, Attorney-General of the United States v. ACLU*, 26 June, available online at http://www.access.digiex.net/Çepic/cda_opinion.html or at http://www.epic.org/cda.

3 An International Legal Instrument for Cyberspace? A Comparative Analysis with the Law of Outer Space[1]

ANNA MARIA BALSANO

INTRODUCTION

This new millennium is already destined to be 'the digital age'. The ongoing development of digital technologies for the production, treatment, dissemination (transmission) and utilization of information is leading to a new type of society with radical changes in relationships between both citizens and institutions and in working and educational environments.

One of the main questions is whether our society is prepared for this new way of thinking, communication and interaction and whether its citizens are ready to become part of the new information society. This includes the question of their participation in a new culture founded on the accelerated circulation of information, ideas and knowledge.

Many governments have expressed concern at the emerging cyberspace reality, as they consider it a potential threat to their sovereignty. This has led to, a large number of legal studies and analyses aimed at reducing the risks inherent in cyberspace activities and taming the activists on this allegedly lawless frontier so that behaviour there conforms to the standards of geophysical jurisdictions.[2] Limiting access to information or monitoring its content can lead rather quickly to limiting freedom of expression but can also act as a brake on a nation's development. It is from this angle that it is of interest to reflect on experience derived from the existing treaties that govern outer space activities and its possible bearing on emerging cyberspace law.

The justification for such a comparative analysis of space law and cyberspace law can be found in analysing correlations between the 'freedoms' of outer space and the 'freedoms' of cyberspace. It may well be that cyberspace and outer space have so much in common that some other principles of outer space law could be applied – by analogy – to cyberspace. Of course, the conclusion reached might also be that the two environments differ so much in their nature and utilization that space law should be considered irrelevant to the development of cyberspace law.

As mentioned above, because outer space and cyberspace share certain characteristics, a comparative analysis and the exploration of outer space regulations in order to identify possible norms that could be useful for regulating cyberspace is justified. The most obvious similarity is the freedom of use and, as we shall see later, the absence of (direct) sovereign rights. Both outer space and cyberspace activities are carried out regardless of geographical boundaries, in a medium that is used to achieve certain goals. Moreover, space law developed gradually as space activities became established, and much the same is happening with cyberspace law. Therefore, despite the fact that the two activities operate on totally different planes (space utilization in the physical reality, cyberspace activities in a non-physical reality), there seems to be some common ground for further study.

THE DEFINITION OF CYBERSPACE

Cyberspace activities are undertaken irrespective of territorial boundaries or other traditional limitations which normally play an important role in establishing the link between entities involved in electronic communications and the rules governing their responsibilities. The legal significance of the universality of this electronic environment needs to be assessed against the background of the traditional frame of reference used to deduce the rules of the game and the responsibilities of the players.

Cyberspace is the term coined by novelist William Gibson[3] to describe a place without physical walls or even physical dimensions where the world's data are organized into a visual, traversable medium – a fluid economy of information centred on transnational commerce electrodes providing a direct neurological interface. This kind of cyberspace does not, and cannot, exist at present; it is a kind of fantasy world of electronic space.

In the real world, cyberspace is the place where ordinary telephone conversations happen, where voice e-mail and e-mail messages are stored and sent back and forth, and where computer-generated graphics are transmitted and transformed, all in the form of interactions – some real-time and some delayed – among countless users and between users and the computer itself.[4]

The simplest definition of cyberspace is 'the space where electronic entities interact'. In other words, digital actors need an electronic space to operate in. These various electronic spaces range from the literary to the architectural – that is, from spaces created entirely with words to spaces that are intentionally modelled on architectural ideals.

> Literary spaces are spaces created entirely with words. Public discussions on the Internet form a kind of space because conversations involving a group of people could otherwise only take place in a physical room. This kind of literary space is the most developed space on the Internet.
>
> At the other extreme from literary space is architectural space, electronic space that is perceived as true 4D space. Although virtual reality is too complex for use in any generally available network and Gibson's cyberspace will not appear until later in the twenty-first century, if at all, the ideas of these fully realized electronic spaces can illuminate our understanding of the networked spaces we have today.
>
> Less complicated electronic interfaces often allow for better communications between participants. The amount of time and effort it can take to master the more complex forms of electronic space can actually detract from the experience of human contact. However, these more complex spaces are clearly the wave of the future, even if only because they provide the most interesting networking problems to solve.[5]

Consequently, cyberspace is not one distinct place but many cyberspaces with any number of models from the real world that are replicated in computer-mediated communication. In addition, the new Networld offers new cyber-communities in which netizens are endeavouring to establish cyber-ethics, cyber-rules, and, indeed, cyber-laws. The Networld, where everybody can potentially be in more or less constant communication with everyone else, stimulates new behaviour and new ways of thinking.[6]

Issues that arise from this new way of interacting will have an impact on the fundamental principles applied in dividing up the social, legal and political universe along lines corresponding to physical places. What will happen to these principles, particularly when the lines along which they were drawn change or vanish? Moreover, what values do we want to preserve? And are those values in danger?

However, new technologies also provide useful tools that assist human progress,[7] so it seems beyond question that the universal principles that form the basic values and ideals of the whole of humanity, irrespective of culture or technological development, should be preserved and reinforced in the emerging new cyberspace. Nevertheless, we can already see some clear threats to the fabric of society, such as new types of crime. It is not only governments that are concerned by 'computer crime'; owners and users of private information services, computer bulletin boards, gateways and networks feel vulnerable to the new breed of invisible trespasser.

SPECIFIC LEGAL ASPECTS OF CYBERSPACE

The rise of global computer networks is weakening the link between geographical locations, as well as the power of local governments to assert control over online behaviour and its effects on individuals or entities. It also highlights questions as to the legitimacy of the efforts of a local sovereign authority of state to enforce rules applicable to a global phenomena, and the ability of a regulatory entity (limited by territorial constraints) to give notice of which sets of rules should apply.[8]

Of particular significance is the impact of cyberspace on the sovereign authority of states. Governments are recognized as having the authority to exercise prescriptive and enforcement jurisdiction over activities taking place within their territories. The exercise of sovereign authority is dependent on some level of physical engagement within the recognized borders of the state. Cyberspace not only defies the concept of borders but also challenges the legitimacy of the adoption of regulations expressed in 'physical atomic' relationships and enforced on the basis of geographically defined jurisdictions. This phenomenon (the defiance of geographical defined jurisdictions) and the legal questions that it raises of course also bears a similarity to the actual problems perceived in the 1970s when there was international concern on how to regulate the activities of the multinational corporations that equally seemed to 'ignore' nationally-based jurisdictions.[9]

The areas of intellectual property (IP) that have most bearing on cyberspace activities (for example, on the Internet) are copyright and trade mark law.[10]

Copyright is probably the first IP right that comes to mind as it deals with so many issues relating to the handling of the content of the electronic data exchanged through the Internet. Copyright infringement is certainly the first cause of concern to right-holders, as it is difficult to detect and combat in the 'cyberspace world'.

Furthermore, other legal questions arise, such as the identification of the author, the applicability of the traditional concept of originality as a condition for protection, the concept of the first publication (when in cyberspace a work can be simultaneously disseminated worldwide), and the concept of fair use.[11]

Trade mark law is based on geographical separation. Trade mark rights[12] arise within a given country, usually on the basis of use of a mark on physical goods or in connection with the provision of services within that country. Different countries have different trade mark laws, with important differences on matters as critical as whether the same name can be used in different lines of business. There is no global registration scheme. A trade mark owner must therefore also be constantly alert to territorially-based claims and to dilution arising from uses of confusingly similar marks, and must master the different procedural and jurisdictional laws of various countries that apply.[13]

Apart from IP there is also 'security' in its broadest sense, which, in cyberspace (as e-mail and the like), is quite often endangered by various criminal activities. Criminal activity can take many forms, from previously existing activities such as fraud, theft and counterfeiting, to the new computer-specific crimes of hacking or cracking, virus dissemination and so forth.[14]

The transmission of confidential information through cyberspace could endanger the secrecy needed for legal protection. Ideally, such information should be sent encrypted (this practice is allowed by law in France only to certify the authenticity of the document) and/or should be accompanied by clear notices that the information is confidential and should not be disclosed or copied.

The electronic signature of contracts through cyberspace can be legally valid only under specific circumstances and when special measures for validating the signature and the protocol have been taken. The requirements for a legally valid signature will differ from country to country according to national legislation.

Certainly the legal regime applicable to cyberspace is still far from clear, with a plethora of competing national legislation. An analysis has to be made of the applicable laws and any special requirements to be met by an entity wishing to operate a service through the Internet.

As cyberspace is expanding daily, with new services and technical possibilities, new national legislation can be expected that will regulate its use.[15]

The above issues will not be discussed in further detail, since their complexity and importance justifies a completely separate investigation. In the following sections the principal issues concerning outer space will be addressed in order to try to draw a comparative assessment between outer space and cyberspace.

THE DEFINITION AND USE OF OUTER SPACE

Before giving an overview of the most important uses of space today, the question of what is to be understood by the term 'outer space' should be briefly addressed. Outer space has to be distinguished from airspace, which falls under the sovereignty of a state, unlike outer space. There is, as yet, no legally accepted boundary between airspace and outer space. In practice it is, however, generally accepted that outer space begins at the lowest possible orbit of a satellite, which is currently at an altitude of between 80 and 120 kilometres. The delimitation of outer space is thus not well defined. Although this issue is still on the agenda of the United Nations Committee on the Peaceful Uses of Outer Space (UNCOPUOS), there have been no tangible results from attempts to formulate an internationally accepted delimitation between airspace and outer space during the 1990s.[16]

Outer space – historically dominated by the two superpowers, the United States and the former USSR – was at first used mainly for military purposes. Even today, two-thirds of the satellites operating in outer space are for such purposes. It was, typically, an activity conducted directly by states. During the 1990s, however, space activities became increasingly commercialized and satellite communications, launch services and earth observation are now important private-sector commercial activities. In addition, a number of new spacefaring nations have developed their specialized industries, accelerating the spread of space technologies and the emergence of a world space market.

LEGAL CONCERNS ARISING FROM THE EXPLORATION OF OUTER SPACE

When the first satellites were successfully launched into outer space at the end of the 1950s, a number of political and legal questions demanded to be resolved, especially since space activities had to be seen in the context of the Cold War and it was necessary to ensure that the arms race would not be extended to outer space.

The international community was unable to define where outer space started and airspace ended. At the same time, the responsibilities and liabilities of the launching state in the event of accident had to be discussed. In addition, since space exploration was the monopoly of a few states, legal concepts had to be agreed to ensure that outer space would be preserved as an area of peaceful exploration and exploitation for all mankind.

The extraterritoriality of space exploration and the global nature of the legal concerns led to the conclusion that the issues which these activities raised concerned all states equally and that the United Nations provided the best forum for a global approach to these global issues. Consequently, UNCOPUOS was set up to address the technical, political and legal aspects of space exploration.[17]

OVERVIEW OF THE LEGAL REGIME GOVERNING OUTER SPACE

Sources of International Law regulating Outer Space

Five space treaties concluded in the framework of the United Nations constitute the basis of international space law:

- The Treaty on Principles Governing the Activities of States in the Exploration and Use of Outer Space, including the Moon and other Celestial Bodies, of 27 January 1967 (Outer Space Treaty)[18]
- The Agreement on the Rescue of Astronauts, the Return of Astronauts and the Return of Objects Launched into Outer Space, of 22 April 1968 (Rescue Agreement)[19]
- The Convention on International Liability for Damage Caused by Space Objects, of 29 March 1972 (Liability Convention)[20]
- The Convention on Registration of Objects Launched into Outer Space, of 14 January 1975 (Registration Convention)[21]
- The Agreement Governing the Activities of States on the Moon and Other Celestial Bodies, of 18 December 1979 (Moon Agreement).[22]

The Outer Space Treaty provides the basic principles for the use of outer space. It serves, therefore, as a 'Magna Carta' for all activities in outer space. A number of its principles were elaborated upon in more specific provisions of the four subsequent treaties.

In addition to these five international treaties, the United Nations General Assembly (UNGA) has adopted resolutions on principles concerning direct broadcasting by satellite,[23] remote sensing by satellite,[24] the use of nuclear power sources in outer space[25] and international cooperation in the exploration and use of outer space for the benefit and in the interest of all states.[26] The principles spelled out in these texts give an indication of the current state of the law.

A second source of international space law, of a more particular character, consists of (cooperation) agreements concluded by states, international organizations and national space organizations – for example, with respect to the International Space Station Programme, and bilateral or multilateral treaties that provide for the implementation of certain space activities.

Also part of the international legal framework for outer space activities are the conventions and agreements establishing mainly intergovernmental organizations such as the International Telecommunication Union (ITU), INTELSAT, INMARSAT, ESA, EUTELSAT, EUMETSAT, INTERSPUTNIK and ARABSAT. All these organizations, by adopting their own specific rules and regulations, contribute to the body of international space law.

Finally, space law also includes national laws applicable to space activities, such as those existing in Russia, South Africa, Sweden, the UK or the United States.

The Status of Outer Space

The following main principles, relevant to this discussion, are applicable to space activities.

The Right to use but not to appropriate Outer Space

The principle of the right to use but not to appropriate outer space is embodied in Article I of the Outer Space Treaty ('Outer space ... shall be free for exploration and use by all States') and Article II of the same Treaty (prohibition of 'national appropriation by claims of sovereignty, by means of use or occupation, or by any other means'). Outer space is considered a *res communis* where every state is free to undertake activities but may not obstruct the same free use by another state.

The Obligation to use Outer Space for Peaceful Purposes

The principle restricting the use of outer space to peaceful purposes is laid down in Article IV of the Outer Space Treaty. This Article is divided into two parts:

- a prohibition against placing nuclear weapons, or other weapons of mass destruction, in orbit around the earth
- the obligation to use the moon and other celestial bodies for exclusively peaceful purposes.

The Treaty specifies that the moon and other celestial bodies are to be used for exclusively peaceful purposes and thus cannot be militarized. In the rest of outer space, on the other hand, only nuclear and other weapons of mass destruction are prohibited.

Combining Article IV with the preamble to the Treaty (the use of outer space for peaceful purposes) and Article III (outer space activities shall be carried out in accordance with international law and the Charter of the United Nations), the doctrine emerges that outer space can be used for military purposes but only in a non-aggressive way.

State Responsibility for, and Supervision of, Private Activities

Under Article VI of the Outer Space Treaty, a state is responsible for the activities in outer space of its private-sector entities. In order to ensure compliance with the Treaty, the state must authorize and continually supervise non-governmental activities in outer space. Some states (Russia, South Africa, Sweden, the UK and the United States) have therefore enacted domestic space legislation defining the conditions for obtaining permission for private entities to carry out space activities.

The Registration of Space Objects

The obligation to register space objects is set out in the Registration Convention. Registration is recorded in national registers and the international register kept by the Secretary-General of the United Nations, which only gives a general indication of the designation, functions and orbital parameters of each object, the frequency used, and the date and location of launch.

Retention of Jurisdiction and Control

Article VIII of the Outer Space Treaty provides that the state of registry retains jurisdiction and control over an object while it is in outer space.

Liability for Damage

The Outer Space Treaty (Article VII) provides for state liability for damages to a third party. The 'launching State' is absolutely liable for damage occurring to the surface of the earth or to aircraft in flight. The only exception is gross negligence on the part of the victim (in which case partial or total exoneration is possible). With regard to damage to other objects in outer space, the launching state is liable if it is at fault. No description of 'fault' is given by the Outer Space Treaty. Fault normally refers to negligence or *culpa*; however, the degree of negligence or *culpa* for attaching liability is unclear. The 'launching State' is defined as the state that launches or procures a launch or from whose territory or facility the space object in question is launched.

The Application of International Law

Space law is a *lex specialis* of international law. Article III of the Outer Space Treaty stipulates that activities in outer space shall be carried out 'in accordance with international law, including the Charter of the United Nations'.

Jurisdiction and Space Activities

As stated above, outer space, like the high seas and Antarctica, is an area outside any state sovereignty and cannot be appropriated. According to general international law it can be considered a *res communis*. This raises a problem with respect to the legal regime applicable to activities carried out in this area, as jurisdiction (applicability of national laws) has to be constructed without relying on territorial sovereignty.

According to the Outer Space Treaty, a state is internationally responsible for 'national activities in outer space', including those undertaken by 'non-governmental entities', in order to monitor their compliance with the rules of space law. Under the same provision, this responsibility leads to the requirement of 'authorisation and continuing supervision' by the 'appropriate State'. However, the terms 'national activities' and 'appropriate State' have not been defined by the Outer Space Treaty, or any other legal document.

Two basic approaches can be distinguished in the literature. The first approach focuses on the interpretation of the word 'national', as meaning that the private actor undertaking the activity should possess the nationality of the state concerned. This would fit well with the concept of jurisdiction of states over their nationals, to be used for exercising legal control over the activities of their nationals as defined above. The other approach proposes an extension of the jurisdiction of states over their territory, which would mean that a state would also be considered internationally responsible for activities undertaken from its territory. In either case, the 'appropriate State' could then be seen as the state whose responsibility is at stake.

The second way to construe jurisdiction basically borrows the notion of the 'launching State' from the other principle of accountability, that of liability. Thus, the 'appropriate State' should be interpreted as being the 'launching State' of the space object involved in the violation of space law, and 'national activities', as a consequence, are (re)defined as 'activities of the launching State'.

National Space Laws

States are recognized as bearing international responsibility for the exploration and use of outer space. As noted above, such responsibility includes authorization of outer space activities conducted by the growing number of private enterprises, continuing supervision of these activities, retention of jurisdiction over space objects and, where necessary, making liability and insurance arrangements. As well as being bound to comply with international obligations assumed under the Space Treaties, every state has the sovereign right to anticipate developments in outer space, particularly as they affect its citizens, and arrange for the continued enjoyment of benefits arising from outer space exploration.

From this perspective, a number of states have adopted national legislation governing the exploration and use of outer space. The United States (1962 and 1984), Sweden (1982), the UK (1986), South Africa (1993) and the Russian Federation (1993) have all passed national legislation on space activities variously regulating issues such as licensing, insurance and administrative procedures.

In addition to general national legislation on space, specific domestic regulations exist in some countries regarding the launching of space objects, satellite communications and the export of space-related materials.[27]

The space laws of Sweden and the UK are summarized below.

Swedish Space Law

Sweden established its Act on Space Activities together with a Decree on Space Activities in 1982. The Act encompasses all space activities defined as 'activities carried on entirely in outer space' and, in addition, 'the launching of objects into outer space and all measures to manoeuvre or in any other way affect objects launched into outer space'.

Anyone carrying on space activities (as defined by the Swedish Act) and any Swedish natural or legal person carrying on space activities anywhere else requires a licence from the Swedish government. With this comprehensive scope, Sweden asserts jurisdiction over its territory and over nationals with respect to space activities.

Both the potential international responsibility of Sweden and its potential international liability with respect to privately conducted space activities are thus dealt with. The Decree accompanying the Space Activities Act establishes a National Board for Space Activities as the government authority for granting licences and maintaining the national register of launched space objects.

UK Space Law

The UK adopted its Outer Space Act of 1986 with the express intent to 'confer licensing and other powers on the Secretary of State to secure compliance with the international obligations of the United Kingdom with respect to the launching and operation of space objects and the carrying on of other activities in outer space by persons connected with this country'.

The licensing obligation established as a consequence (in section 3 of the UK Outer Space Act) pertains to a comprehensive list of space activities: the launch or procurement of the launch of a space object, the operation of a space object, or any (other) activity in outer space.

Parties falling within the scope of the Act are 'United Kingdom nationals, Scottish firms, and bodies incorporated under the law of any part of the United Kingdom' – in other words, any natural or legal person with UK nationality. The place where the activity in question is undertaken is not of relevance in this respect.

The UK's international responsibility has been addressed – at least to the extent that 'national activities' should be interpreted as 'activities undertaken by nationals'. Finally, the Act has also established a national register of licensed space objects, maintained by the Secretary of State.

In general, these national space laws contain provisions on obligations potentially incurred by the state concerned on the international level in cases of private involvement in space activities. This is achieved by explicitly or implicitly defining a category, or a number of categories, of private entities – both natural and legal persons – to whom the law applies. Also, the legislation of both Sweden and the UK creates a licensing system with respect to space activities conducted partially or completely by the categories of private entities thus defined.

INTELLECTUAL PROPERTY RIGHTS AND SPACE ACTIVITIES

As discussed above, the technical and economic developments currently driving the spectacular growth in the use of the Internet pose problems regarding the legal regime to be applied to this new area of activity. In this respect, the questions which will be discussed later for cyberspace law can be compared with discussions concerning intellectual property and space activities, where rapid technological developments and expanding economic interests are posing problems for the current legal structure. The new services and products resulting from space activities are difficult to integrate into the existing legal doctrine. An example can be found in the international cooperation between Canada, Europe, Japan and the United States on constructing and operating the International Space Station.

Following the decisions taken concerning the actual implementation of the International Space Station Programme, intellectual property rights and space activities have been the subject of discussions in several international fora, especially within the European space community. In general, it has been concluded that, due to the special character of outer space and the territorial working of national patent laws, it is unclear whether the use in outer space of an invention covered by a patent falls under any patent regulation and thus whether patents in outer space can be protected. This applies to all countries with the exception of the United States which, in 1990, adopted the Patents in Space Act which extends its national patent law to objects in outer space.[28]

The two basic questions arising from activities in outer space in relation to inventions are the patentability of inventions made in outer space[29] and the protection of patents used in outer space. When we look at the national patent laws of European countries we see that they have largely been harmonized. However, none of them has expressly been made applicable to outer space or to space objects registered by the country concerned. In some countries patent laws could only be made applicable to registered space objects by accepting a broad concept of territoriality. This presumption is at best uncertain and, as a consequence, the protection of European patents in outer space is problematic.

It has to be pointed out that some uses in outer space – notably experimental and scientific ones, which are for the near future the main purposes of manned space stations – are in all European systems, excluded from the exclusive right of patentees. European patent laws do, however, afford partial protection of the use of a patent in outer space.

In contrast to the European legislation, US patent law clearly provides for its applicability to US-registered space objects. The United States has thus precluded debate on the subject of the patentability of inventions made in outer space and the protection of US patents in outer space.

In ratifying the intergovernmental agreement (IGA) on the Space Station, each European country must specifically declare the applicability of its patent law to the ESA-registered elements. Only Germany ratified the original IGA (signed in September 1988) in such a way that it made its patent law applicable. On 29 January 1998, the representatives of fifteen States (that is, the United States, Russia, Japan, Canada and eleven Member States of ESA) signed a new IGA in Washington concerning international cooperation on the civil International Space

Station. This agreement which, when brought into force, will replace the 1988 IGA, formalizes Russia's integration in the partnership, confirms major changes in the Partners' contribution and an evolution of the rules put in place for this cooperation, with the exception of Article 21 on Intellectual Property Rights, which remains unchanged. Even assuming that the European countries solve the specific patent issues arising in the case of the IGA, questions remain as to the applicability of patent laws to outer space activities outside its scope.

It is evident from the above that, if commercial uses in outer space are to be stimulated, a clear regulatory framework for the protection of inventions in outer space is needed. This would facilitate international cooperation on space activities, prevent legal uncertainty over the protection of private rights in outer space and thus encourage private investment.

The situation with respect to intellectual property rights in outer space is generally unclear and confused. The remarkable exception is the legal situation in the United States, where a simple amendment to national patent law declared the law applicable to space objects under the jurisdiction or control of the United States (so that it is out of line with the Outer Space Treaty and could have detrimental effects on the legal regime of a space object not under US jurisdiction). Without a similar provision the applicability of national patent laws of the other spacefaring nations in outer space can be seriously doubted. This raises a question mark over patent protection in outer space, beyond the territorial limitations of national patent laws.

As Europe becomes more integrated, European regulation would, of course, be preferable to the national option, and would create the harmonized situation needed for space activities carried out through ESA (or another European organization) and under international cooperative projects. For the creation of a specific European legal regime for inventions in outer space, additions should be made to the existing provisions; this would involve including the issues of intellectual property and space activities in the debate concerning the patent system in Europe.

THE SIGNIFICANCE TO CYBERSPACE OF THE REGULATION OF OUTER SPACE

The foregoing has shown that basic differences exist between outer space and cyberspace. The two belong in different worlds – namely, the world of atoms and the world of electrons. Nevertheless, there are many similarities which justify a comparative assessment.

Cyberspace is not limited by territorial boundaries. It operates beyond known and recognized political boundaries and negates such boundaries. In essence, it is a realm globally open to all mankind, although, as we shall see, this creates specific political and regulatory problems.

Cyberspace raises many legal and institutional issues that challenge the rationale of centralized and territorially-based governance. Its extreme sense of independence from governmental control and its potential for causing harm and defying national and international laws is of great concern to governments, and to some of its users as well.

Outer space, on the other hand, is a realm regarded by the international community as a *res communis*, open to anyone capable of exploring and using it for the benefit of mankind. National appropriation of outer space is not permitted but the exercise of jurisdiction over nationally registered space objects is allowed. States are responsible for their own space activities and for those conducted from their territories, for which authorization is required. States are consequently required to ensure continuing supervision over national space activities. More importantly, the regulation of outer space activities does not originate from national laws. A set of principles was agreed upon internationally to guide outer space activities irrespective of the state involved or of the nationality of the private entity involved. The basis for outer space regulation has been the *a priori* acceptance of a set of obligations applicable to all states.

The development of space law is thus very different in nature to cyberspace law. Cyberspace regulation is currently a patchwork of national regulations reflecting the various stages of legal appreciation of the activities that are carried out in the different countries. This is logical in comparison with outer space activities, as the development of cyberspace activities was much faster and access to cyberspace has never been restricted to a limited number of privileged states that possessed the necessary technology and means. Therefore, it can be stated that, although the object of the two sets of regulations may bear a number of similarities (as analysed above), the way in which the international community is attempting to tackle the legal issues that arise from the activities in question has been fundamentally different. This difference in approach up to the present, does not, however, prevent us from drawing lessons from the experience gained from the regulation of outer space activities. It seems clear that, since cyberspace activities have been the subject of a variety of national regulations, international coordination and harmonization are essential in order to prevent interstate conflicts as to what activities should be prohibited in cyberspace and to prevent private entities from profiting from the uncoordinated state of regulation by using 'flag states' where regulations are not yet developed. To avoid this situation a set of basic principles is needed that will provide, on the one hand, mechanisms for concerted actions permitting or prohibiting certain activities in cyberspace and, on the other, an international standard for activities in cyberspace. In both cases, the machinery for discussing and developing regulations, the basic principles for further development of regulations and the experience gained in regulating space activities can be of great use.

As to the forum in which principles could be agreed, the United Nations would be a logical choice. As with COPUOS, a committee would be needed that combined technical and legal expertise for arriving at consensus on basic legal principles that should be agreed. Contrary to the outer space experience, it is likely that the emphasis in such a committee should be laid on the legal and political aspects, as various national legal principles have already emerged with respect to the use of cyberspace. Also, since cyberspace activities have a more or less direct impact on society, more expertise would be needed from social sciences. This could be compared with the experience of space lawyers when discussing regulations for satellite television broadcasts. As cyberspace can be considered to be an international realm with the potential to bring benefits to all mankind, in common with outer space, regulation of these activities should also be coupled with programmes for (technical) assistance to less developed user groups.

From a more practical point of view, the extraterritoriality of both activities means that only internationally accepted standards can lead to a regulatory environment in which activities that will be of interest to all mankind will be further developed and potential undesirable effects of new technological developments will be limited. Moreover, only internationally accepted norms for attaching jurisdiction to entities active in cyberspace will lead to efficient regulation. A parallel could be drawn here with space telecommunications where the coordination of activities and frequencies takes place in the International Telecommunication Union (ITU) on the basis of a number of internationally agreed principles laid down in regulations. These activities are coordinated within the framework of the ITU on the basis of consensus, and the international community and private entities active in space telecommunications are well aware that efficient use of this extraterritorial area is possible on this basis alone.

Since all such regulatory efforts are bound to take considerable time, requirements for the near future could perhaps be covered by developing a code of conduct which would lay down basic 'rules of the road' for entities active in cyberspace, as has been done for certain space activities. These rules could constitute a point of departure for further more formal regulations.

CONCLUSION

Cyberspace activities are currently subject to a wide variety of national regulations that reflect the state of the activities taking place in a given country and the legal appreciation in that country of those activities. This situation is the reverse of the way in which space law developed; at first only internationally agreed principles were formulated and, in some cases, later 'transposed' into some national regulations. However, as with space activities, the basic legal problems arise from the inherently extraterritorial character of activities, which can have effects outside the control of individual states.

Also, cyberspace law, like space law, will have to address distinct branches of law such as intellectual property, criminal law, administrative law, insurance law and so forth, as it will have to be framed especially for regulating activities taking place in a specific area.

In this respect, cyberspace can certainly learn from the experience of developing legal norms for space activities and profit from the success of the general space law principles which guided states in their exploration and exploitation of outer space. One lesson that can be learned is the need to avoid the pitfalls that occurred when the international community attempted to regulate specific space applications – for example, direct satellite broadcasting – on the basis of their technical characteristics rather than their general effects on states.

It will take some time to assess the impact of cyberspace on society. This new phenomenon will need to be constantly monitored and assessed. That process will determine when to adopt an international agreement or to adopt an international code of conduct applicable to service providers and controllers of access to gateways. It is in the interest of all states to facilitate cyberspace activities in such a way that there can be an equitable distribution of benefits arising out of them and an orderly development that reflects the interests of citizens.

NOTES

1   The views and opinions expressed in this article are those of the author and do not commit the European Space Agency (ESA).
2   A.W. Branscomb, (ed.), *Emerging Law of the Electronic Frontier*, The Hampton Press Communication Series, Communication and Law, 2000.
3   Cyberspace was popularized by Gibson in his classic science fiction novel, *Neuromancer*, in 1984.
4   L.H. Tribe, *The Constitution in Cyberspace: Law and Liberty Beyond the Electronic Frontier*, http://www.io.com./ss/tribe.html.
5   Clay Shirky's attempt to grasp some of the difficulties we encounter when we attempt to describe the Internet in terms of 'space'. By using the language

which comes most naturally to this strange environment, we end up oversimplifying, because metaphor always explains the strange in a familiar way.

6   See Branscomb, *Emerging Law*, op. cit.: the author defines five different categories of legal activity in the Networld that are challenging legislators' and lawyers' capabilities to be innovative, responsible and creative.

7   It is certainly true that closed-circuit television and one-way mirrors, for example, changed the basis of the criminal procedure and led to a reinforcement of the protection of the witness while at the same time weakening the impact produced by the physical confrontation of the parties.

8   D.R. Johnson and D.G. Post, *Law and Borders: The Rise of Law in Cyberspace*, http://www.cli.org/.

9   The presence and activities of multinational corporations in the developing world have been the subject of controversy in discussions on development policy. The theoretical background for the negative verdict is largely from the ideological Left (for example, the theory of peripheral capitalism and Latin American dependency theories). The scepticism shown is often partly based on negative experiences in the late 1960s and early 1970s, with blatant examples of incorrect behaviour – for example, inappropriate influence of political decisions, exploitative wages and poor social conditions. In recent years the impact on developing countries of multinational corporations has been judged more favourably. Comparative surveys by the International Labour Organization (ILO) of social conditions, effects on employment, choice of technology and training by multinationals and local companies paint a positive picture for multinationals – certainly in comparison with local companies. This view is confirmed by studies from the United Nations Centre for Transnational Corporations (UNCTC) since the early 1980s.

10   Protection by copyright laws covers: literary works (including compilations, tables and computer programmes); dramatic, musical or artistic works; sound recordings, films (including video recording and any moving image); broadcasts or cable programmes (including some publicly accessible online databases), and the typographical arrangement of a published edition.

11   The Digital Era Copyright Bill addresses the Internet and WIPO Treaties in *Patent, Trademark and Copyright Journal*, **55**(1352), 20 November 1997. Report Rick Bauker (R-Va) on 13 November 1997 introduced legislation (HR3048) to amend the Copyright Act to better accommodate the Internet environment and implement recently negotiated copyright treaties.

12   Trade mark law protects any material signs that are verbal (name, geographic name, fantasy denomination, numbers, initials,and so on), figurative (a design, a model or colours, the form of the product, the combination of colours and so on), or complex (that is, a sign that is composed by a combination of verbal and figurative signs).

13   A legislative fix on domain name issues would be premature: *Patent, Trademark and Copyright Journal*, **55**(1351), 13 November 1997.

14   Bills on copyright technical corrections, Internet theft and publication are published in *Patent, Trademark and Copyright Journal*, **55**(1350), 6 November 1997. Representatives on 4 November 1997 passed a Bill (HR2265) that would create stiff criminal penalties for wilful copyright infringements by electronic or other means.

15   For instance, 'La Charte de L'Internet: proposition pour une autodiscipline dans la communication électronique', *Droit de l'Informatique et des Télécoms*, **1**, 1997.

16   See note 17 below.

17   In UNGA Res. 1472 (XIV), 'International Co-operation in the Peaceful Uses of Outer Space' (12 December 1959), an ad hoc COPUOS was set up:

(a)   To review the area of international co-operation and to study practical and feasible means for giving effect to programmes in the peaceful uses of outer space which could appropriately be undertaken under United Nations auspices, including, inter alia:

   (i)   Assistance for the continuation on a permanent basis of research on outer space;
   (ii)   Organisation of mutual research programmes for the study of outer space, and the rendering of all possible assistance and help towards their realisation;
   (iii) Encouragement of national research programmes for the study of outer space, and the rendering of all possible assistance and help towards their realisation;

(b)   To study the nature of legal problems which may arise from the exploration of outer space.

The ad hoc committee was given permanent status in 1961 with the adoption on 20 December 1961 of UNGA Res. 1721 (XVI).

18   Entered into force on 10 October 1963. 480 UNTS, 43.
19   Entered into force on 3 December 1968. 610 UNTS, 205.
20   Entered into force on 1 September 1972. 961 UNTS, 187.
21   Entered into force on 15 September 1976. ILM, vol. XIV, 43.
22   Entered into force on 11 July 1984. ILM, vol. XVIII, 1434.
23   Adopted on 10 December 1982. UNGA Res. 27/92.
24   Adopted on 3 December 1986. UNGA Res. 41/65.
25   Adopted on 14 December 1992 UNGA Res. 47/68.
26   UNGA Res. 51/122. Declaration on International Cooperation in the Exploration and Use of Outer Space for the Benefit and in the Interest of all States, Taking into Account the Needs of Developing Countries, adopted on 13 December 1996.
27   See P.L. Meredith and G.S. Robinson, *Space Law: A Case Study for the Practitioner: Implementing a Telecommunications Satellite Business Concept*, The Netherlands: Martinus Nijhoff, 1992, pp.10–13.
28   A European Space Agency study (ESA SP-1209), a follow-up to earlier research by ESA and the European Centre for Space Law (ECSL), analysed international and national patent regulations and space regulations in order to come to an overall assessment of legal problems encountered when using patents in outer space or when inventing in outer space. The study concentrated on the regulatory situation in Europe and examined the extent to which national intellectual property laws and regulations, in so far as patents are concerned, can be applicable to space activities. Also discussed are the national legislations of Canada, Japan, Russia and the United States.
29   Space-related inventions can theoretically be made either on earth or in outer space. The use of inventions can also be either on earth or in outer space. As a basic concept, inventions in relation to outer space activities can be divided into: (a) inventions made on earth for space applications; (b) inventions made on earth for terrestrial applications as a result of space activities (including telecommunications); (c) inventions made in outer space for terrestrial applications; (d) inventions made in outer space for space applications; (e) inventions patented on earth for space applications and used in outer space.

4 Some Considerations on Cyberspace Law[1]

YVES POULLET

... We should like to stress the State's vital obligation to intervene at a time when, in our opinion, deserting the Internet and withdrawing from the field of regulation to such a point that it no longer even decides the general framework, would notably put at risk public order, fundamental liberties and other basic values.[2]

INTRODUCTION

The Characteristics of Cyberspace

'As cyberspace develops increasingly into a zone of human exchange, the need for balanced and well-adapted rules of the game gains in importance.'[3] Are these rules new? Opinion has long held that the Internet revolution has to be matched by a revolution in law. As noted by the Working Document of the Expert Meeting on Cyberspace Law which took place in Monte Carlo in September 1998:

> In this respect, the most authoritative legal writers admit that today's Internet revolution, which will be confirmed by tomorrow's information society, must in any case be matched by a revolution in the law in the broad sense of the term.[4]

Two characteristics of cyberspace have been amply highlighted in this context. First, cyberspace ignores frontiers: yet law, which is based essentially on the notion of territorial states, is intended for the control of situations that are localized. 'Cyberspace calls into question frontiers, which it bypasses, and the state laws, which it challenges.'[5]

Second, cyberspace is never confined, but is continually being redefined to favour the hyperlinks of its users. The distinctions with which law seeks to regulate communication begin to melt when faced with such infinite possibilities:[6] distinctions separating the parties themselves, at a time when anyone may be producer, intermediary and consumer of information simultaneously; distinctions of media, at a time when written text, printed text and sound are becoming mixed; and classical opposition between the products' regulations and the services' regulations at a time when digitalization of the so-called 'informational products' make this distinction inoperative and dangerous. Moreover, the concept of a 'work' need no longer be linked to a person and a particular medium but simply to an object and a process in which any number of persons may be involved. Finally, the distinctions between communication in the public and private domains are becoming increasingly blurred.

Thus the 'natural' place for the intervention of law and the structures and concepts that govern its operation are vanishing into our 'global village'.[7]

The Aims of this Chapter

This chapter is intended to explore a number of ideas on the basis of the position outlined above.

The first section is intended to make jurists aware that the latest developments in technology and communications not only call for an expansion of traditional concepts but, beyond this, frequently modify the system of checks and balances enshrined at their heart, thereby giving rise to new demands for legislation.

Following on from this, questions are raised on the means by which law is created in a modern context. There is a great temptation to hand over the task of legislating social behaviour in cyberspace to self-regulation and regulatory technology. This gives rise to questions on the role of the state and the potential dialogue between different norms, state regulations and self-regulations.

Finally, the values with which the law should be concerned with promoting so that our society may be both informational and democratic are discussed.

A LAW ON THE BRINK: FROM GROWING CONCEPT TO WIDENING DEBATE

Digitalized, flashed across vast distances via world-embracing networks, processed in a variety of ways and transferred from one medium to another, information is becoming uncontrollable. From the legal viewpoint it is breaking the confines of tradition in every way. The restraining duty of the jurist – in other words, his or her obligation to confront novelty with ancient concepts and their associated values, is in natural opposition to such an explosion; he or she abides by an established concept until analysis reveals, clearly and evidently, either the impossibility of its satisfaction or the necessity, induced by a new disequilibrium, of protecting new values.[8]

Two debates illustrate this: the first concerns the electronic signature, while the second considers the consequences of so-called Electronic Copyright Management Systems (ECMS). The conclusions drawn from these two examples will serve to highlight certain reflections on the meeting of law and technology.

Signatures in all their Forms

Expanding the Law: A Functional Approach

The problem of an electronic signature's validity seems, since the works of UNCITRAL[9] and European Draft Directive 98/297/EC on a common framework for electronic signatures, to have been resolved by way of a functional approach. The answer to the question 'Should we profoundly alter our legislation to admit the reality of computers and communications technology?' was in the negative. The 'providential' openness of the legal concept of the signature permits the inclusion of this new reality by demanding the technical means for the creation and appending of an electronic signature, the same practical demands as are placed upon its handwritten equivalent – the signatory's identification and the authentification of a document to which his or her signature must remain attached. Thus, as we are frequently made aware, the development of information technologies is an opportunity for the revitalization of traditional concepts. The danger of ad hoc solutions must be emphasized: despite the advantage of apparent simplicity, they can create long-term turbulence in jurisprudence.

Previous attempts to legitimize electronic proof by means of exceptions to the signed document principle have proved ill-fated. Such solutions showed their limitations whenever particular laws called for a hand-signed document and, more seriously, encouraged an over generous acceptance of electronic proof, without demanding sufficient security requirements in its creation. That said, the idea of an equivalence in principle between manuscript and electronic signatures certainly does not close the debate. Many other questions may be asked beyond the narrow regulatory bracket in which, until now, the legal dispositions covering the legal issue of the signature alone have been inscribed. The points developed below illustrate the necessity of extending this debate.

Technical Normalization: Society's Risks

The first question takes us back to the statute and the setting up of norms. The actual requirements to be met by an electronic signature before it can pretend to the quality of its handwritten counterpart develop as technological evolution advances. Thus the robustness of a signature, if it is to serve as proof of identification, presupposes the use of ever more perfect and secure methods of cryptography.

> The content of such requirements must develop in accordance with technological evolution and the functions drawn from each concept. There can be no question of defining, once and for all, on the basis of a given state of technological development, the precise implications of each of these functions. Thus the robustness of a signature may suppose the use of ever more perfect and secure methods of cryptography.[10]

The difficulty that a company or administrative authority, wishing to take advantage of electronic proof, faces in demonstrating the quality of its security measures can readily be imagined. This leads inevitably to movements towards standardization in the context of ad hoc public or, more frequently, private institutions. This normalization, without being obligatory, nonetheless represents a standard acceptable to the courts, with the reservation of such expert evaluation as these may consider appropriate. The advantage of such normalization is its relative flexibility. Openness to the possibility of participation in such a normalization process, also by consumer representatives, would be advantageous (compare, on this matter, the statutes of the ETSI).

Questions of system interoperability and the laws of competitive trading are closely linked to the issue of technical norms. The normalization of a particular cryptographic system may enable a company to corner a market. We must bear in mind the requirements of 'transparency' in normalization and the need for legislation permitting every operator to enjoy this 'essential facility'.

Finally, the development of the cryptographic procedures that underlie electronic signatures gives rise to other concerns: legitimate public security issues permit wire- and phone-tapping under certain strict procedural conditions. What will happen to this legitimate state security concern if undecipherable messages are circulating on the information superhighways of tomorrow? This sensitive discussion provided the backdrop to the OECD guidelines on cryptography which were adopted on 27 March 1997.

The Question of Fundamental Rights

The growing demand for a move to electronic signatures for access to all kinds of services, including government online services, raises other questions – namely, the right of every citizen to an electronic signature and to sign anonymously, the corollary right to request that government authorities maintain paper procedures for 'cyber have-nots' and, finally, the right to use several signatures in order to avoid the signature becoming a unique identification liable to be subjected to numerous processes.[11] The Meeting of Experts on Cyberspace Law convened by the UNESCO Director-General in 1998 underlines, in Principle No. 8, the importance of the fundamental right of every person to privacy, including the right to communicate confidentially using certain techniques such as cryptographic systems and pseudonyms.

A New Role for the Signature

There are two aspects to this: first, recognition that the electronic signature will cause the emergence of new agents whose services may require regulation and, second, the fact that the electronic signature functions in a different manner to its manuscript cousin.

Regarding the first point, electronic signature technology, which is based on asymmetric cryptography, requires the intervention of new parties, particularly certification authorities responsible for publishing signatories' public codes in open registers and guaranteeing their authenticity of content. Their work will be the object of new regulations establishing their responsibilities and fixing the conditions for the official recognition of their activities.

As to the second point, the disappearance of exchanges based on the physical proximity of parties whose identities are previously known to one another, in favour of transactions concluded across non-territorial virtual space, fundamentally changes the very nature of contractual relations. This has repercussions, notably on the function of the signature which can no longer be perceived simply as the *a posteriori* confirmation of a transaction for the purposes of proof. The signature itself becomes a condition for the recognition of the contractual parties and therefore a prior condition for the drawing up of a transaction.

Must this recognition necessarily be that of an individual, or can it be that of a legal entity? What the manuscript signature did not permit yesterday can now be authorized by the electronic signature. A legal entity may, in future, dispose of a signature in the fullest sense of the term and be able to initiate operations without recourse to an individual signatory; this will be especially true of automatic systems dealing with ordering and invoicing.

Preliminary Conclusions: The Fracturing of Disciplinary Boundaries

To conclude, electronic signature law certainly invites us to revisit the law in this new light, expanding traditional concepts and, beyond this, exploding the disciplinary divisions of law. The signature, classically a question of civil contract law, veers into the field of human rights with such issues as the right to a signature, the right to eavesdrop electronically, and the protection of privacy, as well as into the field of fair trade law with the right to free competition and the issue of establishing norms. The second example highlights the dual concern confronting the jurist involved in information and communications technology: the need to reread the law and to be aware of the fracturing of disciplinary boundaries that the legal recognition of information and communications technologies provokes.

ECMS or the Death of Copyright?

Electronic Copyright Management Systems (ECMS)

The Internet is clearly no longer the grand university forum of ideas celebrated at the time of its creation, but is becoming daily more and more like a trade fair. Cryptographic systems and signatures and, more generally, such technological methods as 'tattooing' permit control of, and limited access to, information that is better protected by these means than it would be in a bank vault.[12]

Such systems, among which can be found programs for managing 'works', substitute for the protection classically assured by copyright, or more recently by other rights considered *sui generis*. They provide far more effective technical and contractual protection not only to works effectively protected by the Act, but equally well to types of information not previously afforded any legal cover.[13]

Towards the Death of Copyright

It would certainly be useful to ask what the legal limits of protection technology are.[14] Such systems render the protection by judicial regime irrelevant, assuring the holders of simple informational property protection of a degree and effectiveness beyond the measure commonly accorded by rights of intellectual property, with the exception of the sacred principle of the free circulation of ideas.

What is to become of, *inter alia*, the right of quotation, the exceptions for the benefit of scientific research, and copying for personal use and education if technology is capable of blocking all non-contractual use? Would it not be more appropriate, rather than bemoaning the demise of the laws of intellectual copyright, to insist instead that technology should conform to them?[15] The rights of quotation, the rights of scientific researchers and the right of copying for private use must be specifically recognized, however advanced technical protection may become. More fundamentally, the above-mentioned Expert Group brought together by UNESCO at the second Monte Carlo Info-Ethics Conference (September 1998) stressed that:

> Public bodies should have an affirmative responsibility to make public information widely available on the Internet and to ensure the accuracy and timeliness of the information. This information could include government information, information concerning cultural heritage, and archival and historical information .... States should preserve and expand the public domain in cyberspace.[16]

The development of vast ECMS systems invites further reflection. Who runs these systems? What role should be granted to copyright protection agencies? Once again, questions of fair trade and normalization, particularly with respect to the encryption of works, are sure to be raised.

Finally, the use of such systems will generate nominative data, and it will become important to determine what rights to the exploitation of this data will be granted to the various parties, from the system operators to the authors themselves.

From a Service to an Information Product

I will approach the issues relative to this second example via certain remarks on the subject of the responsibilities involved in online data banking.

Traditionally speaking, the supplying of information was regarded as a service, the service provider being obliged to deliver the required dispatch to his client. The introduction, between the producer of information and the internaut, of a technical tool capable of responding in a standard way to varied demands for information pushes us towards another analysis of the process and, as recent jurisprudence demonstrates, to question – in the case of incomplete or inexact information – the very quality of the 'data product'. By 'data product' we understand the entirety, including both the technical (software and programming) and organizational means (collection method and sample quality), as well as content (integrity, contemporary nature). It becomes an issue of the conformity of the product to the internaut's expectations.[17]

Clearly, the online information service producer and distributor must now view their responsibility in terms of product quality and no longer in terms of delivery.

Site Labelling and Filter Techniques

Technology comes to rescue the law. It is in this context that we can explain the tendency to develop labelling techniques (such as Webtrust and Trust-e), just as for conventional consumer products and, building on this, to introduce filter systems such as Platform for Internet Content Selection (PICS) and even negotiating systems like Platform for Privacy Preferences (P3P). The idea is simple. Every 'data product' can be examined for its conformity to threshold standards for decency, violence, respect for privacy (compare, in this regard, Trust-e), consumer protection and so forth. Such labelling would operate *a priori* in connection with filter techniques enabling the internaut to select sites according to personal preference and even to negotiate with these sites an individual protection or, conversely, discard it.[18]

Undoubtedly, labelling laws still have to be drawn up: what criteria would decide which sites required labelling? Can we even envisage contesting criteria? What degree of transparency must be expected of the criteria? What will be the responsibilities of labelling authorities? What legal recognition should be granted to such labels? What role has the state to play as regards the recognition of the labelling authorities? And, finally, what private or public sanctions should be levied for failure to respect the conditions applied?[19]

Second Conclusions: On the Interaction Between Law and Technology

We must admit that technology can strengthen the law's effectiveness and that, without such reinforcement, it would either become a dead letter or be poorly served by classic judicial procedures that are neither rapid nor effective. A revisionist site would certainly be better countered by such mechanisms as filtering or blocking its access, as envisaged by the 'Internet Charter', than it would be by the condemnation by a tribunal of something that is essentially unseizable and currently sailing somewhere far out on the global chart of the World Wide Web. In another order of ideas, as indicated above, ECMS are more effective than legislation at protecting an author's copyright. All these remarks support the opinions of certain authors[20] that the so-called *lex informatica* – that is, regulation by technical means – is preferable to classic legal ones.

When this argument is stretched to highlight the various facets of this legal–technological axis, it is clear that it is as much the parties themselves who are calling for legal measures to legitimize technical solutions as it is the law calling on the parties to take whatever technical measures are necessary to ensure its effective respect.[21]

The former role – that of legitimizing technical solutions – is definitely the one being sought by the promoters of Internet services.

The electronic signature, as the first example analysed, demonstrates the need for security in commercial relationships on an open network such as the Internet; it also justifies service providers' requests for legal recognition of electronic certification services – those famous electronic notaries known as the 'certification authorities' or 'trusted third parties' such as Belsign or Isabel whose activities have already been legalized in some states (Germany, Italy and the United States) and will shortly be so in others. As regards ECMS, the recent reform of the Berne Convention on authors' rights criminalizes any attempt to outwit the technological protection systems offered by copyright management services.

On the other hand, the law may call for either direct or indirect technical measures to be taken. Applying the principle of responsibility could lead a judge to sanction, in either a civil or a criminal suit, access providers and servers who have not taken currently acceptable and appropriate technical measures to prevent possible harm to clients using their services. It is in response to such fears, and particularly the fear of a legislative intervention: in the form of a 'Decency Act' that American industrialists and others have developed the filter standard known as the Platform for Internet Content Selection (PICS) (see above).

It is important that lawyers should carefully examine the 'privacy', 'copyright', and 'consumer protection' enhancing technologies to ensure that they strictly conform to both the letter and the spirit of the law. This is not always the case: thus ECMS do not always operate in accordance with the equilibrium established by copyright legislation between the interested parties. Similarly, in the case of 'privacy enhancing technology', the P3P system would permit the user to negotiate his or her right to privacy, including rights that are not negotiable, being directly linked to fundamental liberties.[22] In other words, the technology should comply with the law.

THE VARIOUS REGULATORY TECHNIQUES ON THE INTERNET AND THE ROLE OF STATE LAW

Clearly, technology can serve to regulate behaviour on the information superhighway. However, there are other regulatory models with which the law may even maintain a dialogue.

Below, I first identify the different regulatory techniques applicable to the Internet or to information superhighways in general; I then analyse the various responses in state and supranational law to these different regulatory techniques and envisage some criteria for the legitimization of non-state regulatory systems.

On the Diversity of Regulatory Models

Preliminary Considerations

The goal of regulation is the prescription of behavioural norms. That said, the diversity of regulatory models and the application of norms could be divided into four categories: the object, the author, the subject and the sanction of the norm.

We may note at the outset that the international dimension of the Internet leads to a degree of competition between different national regulations. As soon as one country decides to regulate certain activities, the parties concerned by the legislation are free to move their activities to another country with a more flexible and less strict regulatory framework. This phenomenon of 'regulatory dumping' is real.[23] On the other hand, advantages can accrue to the consumer who prefers the security that is granted by a regulatory environment that takes better care of his or her interests. This second aspect should not be neglected.

An Enumeration

It is impossible to number all the many normative sources of law on the Internet. Those public sources of law – the national state and international norms – contrast with the private ones, based either on contractual liberty or on the sort that tends to be called self-regulatory; one may now distinguish aspects of certification and usage that some regard as an emerging *lex electronica*, parallel to *lex mercatoria* but developed within an electronic context. The technology itself (see 'Second conclusions', p.154 above) may also have a normative effect on behaviour.

As regards these private sources, we may observe that the actors themselves have developed means to ensure that the self-regulatory code passes from the letter into action. Thus the coordinators nominated within discussion groups are expected to vet incoming messages. The sanctions peculiar to the network, such as disconnection and 'flaming', are strangely reminiscent of vigilante justice. The hotlines created within the framework of certain codes of conduct to permit the denunciation of activities contrary to those codes are a further example of the means put in place to assure adherence to network discipline. More interesting still are the labelling and rating mechanisms developed by certain servers (see 'Site labelling and filtering techniques' p.154 above) which both guarantee and inform the user of the quality of the service being offered (such as the 'privacy-friendly' label or the one relating to web sites of journalistic information on respect for the press code). Naturally, the value of any such classification depends on the certifying body which defines, issues and controls it. It is appropriate to mention the North American initiative to create 'virtual magistrates', online arbitrators or mediators who are authorized to adjudicate conflicts arising out of network use, whether they concern matters of defamation, intrusion into the private sphere or non-respect of the rules of a news group. These alternative dispute resolution (ADR) mechanisms have recently been promoted by the European Draft Directive on Certain Legal Aspects of Electronic Commerce in the Internal Market.

Briefly, we can see that private regulatory sources set up their own mechanisms for expressing the rules, controlling their application and, finally, sanctioning non-respect; such sanctions are pronounced by their own 'magistrates'. The following reflections will develop certain summarizing remarks concerning the various private and public sources.

State Norms

It is clear that the nation-state constitutes a legitimate authority for Internet regulation. The modalities for the development of the norm are meticulously described in the texts and procedures surrounding this development, thereby guaranteeing a democratic discussion. Application of the norm is granted to 'professional' jurisdictions, surrounded by guarantees of independence and contradictory function.

With regard to 'electronic environments',[24] we may observe two distinct tendencies in state law. One is a preference for notions of variable content, called standards, and the other the entrusting of the interpretation of these standards to relay bodies, sometimes qualified as independent administrative authorities. If we take the Belgian model as a simple example, insofar as the other Western European countries have similar institutions, we would point out the creation of multiple institutions, notably as regards: questions of privacy – the Privacy Protection Commission (Commission de Protection de la Vie Privée); regulation of the audiovisual sector – the Higher Audiovisual Council (Conseil Supérieur de l'Audiovisuel) or the Media Council (Mediaraad); and the telecommunications sector – the Belgian Institute of Post and Telecommunications (Institut Belge des Postes et Télécommunications).[25]

The international dimension of information superhighways leads states to search, at the international level, for models with which to develop the law, or for cooperation between the national authorities entrusted with the application of national laws.[26] Whether through international conventions, such as those of UN, UIT, WTO, WIPO and OECD, or bodies such as the G7 or at the level of treaties for police cooperation between those engaged in the fight against cyber-crime (as illustrated by the draft of an International Internet Charter presented by France to the OECD), a number of public initiatives have been taken to maintain the state's role in the protection and safeguarding both of individual rights and of the overriding public interest. Some[27] go so far as to suggest the creation of an 'International Cyberspace Authority' as a reaction to movements for the emancipation of Internet law and in the face of the increasing power of private norms – an issue we shall now discuss. Global Business Dialogue promoted by the European Commissioner, Martin Bangemann, stresses the importance of setting up this global authority and fixing global rules for electronic commerce.

Private Norms

Contracts   The interactivity of networks gives the consent of the Internet's user unprecedented implications. Whether to say 'yes' or 'no' to a 'cookie', to agree to a particular process, to reveal his or her identity or not, to object to non-solicited correspondence – whatever the issue, technology renders the internaut responsible for his or her actions.[28] Tempted by the contractual paradigm inherent in the Internet environment, some authors consider that the state's responsibility to regulate behaviour has been usurped by the substitute responsibility of the citizen, who by his or her consent chooses to authorize or forbid this or that operation.

The principles of autonomous will and the law of covenant, unanimously recognized in every jurisprudence, gives this approach considerable weight, founded as it is on the responsibility of the individual internaut. The contractual approach evidently requires that the technology permit such choices, hence the questions: 'Does the Internaut wish to be identified?' 'For what finalities?' 'Within what time limit?' The internaut must be the object of onscreen choice pages, and the system's configuration must guarantee the respect of such choices.

Self-regulation   Trudel defines this as 'norms voluntarily developed and accepted by those who take part in an activity'.[29] We are familiar with the proliferation of such codes, sometimes drawn up locally in a university or in a newsgroup, sometimes on a larger scale for a direct marketing sector or even for the broad mass of activities on the net (such as national charters). The Internet Society, a purely private organization entrusted with ensuring international cooperation and coordination in technology and programming for the Internet, publishes directive guidelines for Internet and network use. In the words of its president:

It is no longer adequate to base guidelines for conduct purely on the basis of who pays for the underlying network or computer systems resources. Even if that was once sensible, the diversity of constituents of the Internet makes it a poor basis for formulating policy. Thus guidelines for conduct have to be constructed and motivated in part on the basis of self-interest. Many of the suggestions [herein] are based on the theory that enlightened self-interest can inform and influence choices of behavior.[30]

The justification for this galloping self-regulation is a triple one. The argument concerning the technical and evolutionary nature of the object with which this self-regulation is designed to cope is joined by the argument that only the authors themselves are capable of perceiving the risks involved in particular solutions or, more importantly still, of assessing the adequacy and effectiveness of sanctions. The immediate blockade by access providers of a site that has been denounced via a hotline mechanism constitutes a more appropriate and effective response to a pornographic site than any judicial condemnation.[31] The possibility of their development and expansion at a global level serves as a supplementary argument, at a time when the global dimension of cyber-highway problems is uncontested.

Beyond the establishment of norms, self-regulation claims to offer models for applying these norms in virtual communities, as distinct from spatial communities localized in a given territory and subject to national legislation. For some time now we have been aware of the role played by network 'moderators', of the first experiences of 'cyber-magistrates' and of virtual tribunals charged with resolving litigious issues in the virtual world. The creation of councils charged with the application of Internet charters represents another demonstration of self-regulation's aptitude not only to develop a supple system of law for cyberspace, but also to sanction it.[32] There is a considerable temptation to see self-regulation as more than just a source of law complementary to that of the state, but rather as a replacement for the latter[33] or, in any case, as a means of dispensing the state from an intrusive regulation. This means that sometimes the private norm will take the place of legislation: for example, the manner in which the delicate question of the attribution of Internet domain names is currently dealt with certainly makes a good case for the integrity and sufficiency of self-regulatory solutions.[34] In other cases – and the current debate between the US administration and the EU authorities about the 'safe harbour' privacy principles is a good example – the adoption of a code of conduct or some other self-regulatory instrument, even if it is promoted or simply requested by the public authorities, will help to avoid the setting up of an intricate administrative and regulatory system which is not considered useful. Further to the entry into effect (25 October 1998) of the European Directive on the protection of personal data (95/46/EC), the European Commission and the United States (US) Department of Commerce have been involved in a dialogue with a view to establishing a legal framework for the transfer of personal data to the US. It has led the US Department of Commerce to publish the 'Safe Harbour' privacy principles on 15 and 16 November 1999. If the European Commission found these principles acceptable, a decision (under article 25.6 of the data protection directive) could be issued recognising them, as providing adequate protection for the transfer of personal data from the EU to the US.

Certification   In a global environment where the network represents the sole means of communication, the definition of certification as a procedure by which a third party guarantees the specific quality of a person or product seems a happy solution.

The aim of certification is to assure the internaut first of the existence and address of his interlocutor and, second, of the other's professional status (see 'Signatures in all their forms', pp.149–52, concerning the electronic signature). There then arise questions of conformity of the other's products to this or that norm, of his or her processes to this or that privacy legislation, of his or her practices to required consumer protection standards and, finally, of the general security of sites. All such problems can be the object either of specific certificates (as, for example, the label delivered by the Internet Consumer Protection Agency (ICPA) or by Trust-e, which deal solely with questions of conformity to privacy standards) or of certification of a more global nature (such as the 'Webtrust' initiative developed by the Association of American Accountants).

Certification presents a solution that may complement either a state normative source or self-regulation, inasmuch as it refers either to a law or to a code of good conduct. Essentially it is based simultaneously, on the one hand, on the quality of the certifying authority and its verification procedures (namely, its independence and expertise) and, on the other, on the effective responsibility of that authority in the event of the unwarranted issue of a certificate. Finally, certification permits easy and effective sanctioning, inasmuch as the company or individual fears the loss of certification and the negative publicity that this would entail.[35]

Practice and the lex electronica   Beyond the codified and well identified sources we have so far referred to, we must also deal with principles, whether or not they are more diffuse, which are to be found in the 'Acceptable Use Policies' proposed by Internet access providers, the servers. This 'netiquette' is a sort of 'Ten Commandments' or highway code of fundamental rules for Internet surfers:[36]

1. You shall not use a computer to harm another person.
2. You shall not interfere with another's work.
3. You shall not ferret about in another's files.
4. You shall not use a computer to steal.
5. You shall not use a computer to bear false witness.
6. You shall not use or copy a program for which you have not paid.
7. You shall not use the resources of another's computer without authorization.
8. You shall not misappropriate another's intellectual creation.
9. You shall envisage the social consequences of the program you are writing.
10. You shall use the computer in a manner which shows consideration and respect.

When these rules are contravened, sanctions can take the form of an organized or individual reaction: 'flaming', the disconnection of an indelicate user, the threat of contacting the police and so forth.

The comparison between such practices, spontaneously developed by virtual communities, and the rules of conduct habitually practised by trading communities, gives the impression that *lex electronica* is close to *lex mercatoria*.[37] The similarity is all the more seductive when some authors[38] denounce the dominant economic debate as one which would 'lead to the submission of the information society in general, and the activities of the Internet in particular, solely to the laws of the international marketplace'.[39]

This parallel tends to lend authority to the reflections which now follow on the role of state law in the face of diverse regulatory techniques.

The Role of National Legislation in the Reception and Promotion of 'Private' Sources of Cyberspace Law

Trudel, paraphrasing an observation by Perritt, wrote:

> The parties engaged in international transactions, for example, have developed law-creating practices. Interesting parallels can be drawn here with regard to the regulation of electronic–commercial environments, even though we cannot currently speak of the emergence of a genuine corpus of generally applicable rules. The future of this process of normalization will be favored by the development of more general practices of international arbitration, carried through without regard to differing national legislations. Even if the customs and practices of a given field of activity are often taken into account and, to a certain degree, integrated into national legislation, the nub of such a

norm still rests in its capacity to autonomously organize behavior and transactions among the members of a community. Respect of these customs and practices is, under certain circumstances, an essential prerequisite for a participant's admission to a given community. Certainly, if the importance of the community justifies it, these customs and practices can constitute a complete regulatory technique, parallel to national legislation, regulating the relationships of members of a community and administered by their own authorities. The model of lex mercatoria from the middle ages is frequently cited as an example. Several current debates are involved with the opportunity of developing a similar legal framework for the regulation of cyberspace; this issue will be analyzed here.[40]

This doctrinal reflection on *lex mercatoria* has led a number of authors[41] to see in it the opportunity for a clear and indisputable recognition of our essential legal pluralism. Developing this idea, Rigaux writes:

> The citizen of a State may possess goods in, or reside in, another State, adhere to an organized religious confession, be a member of a transnational professional organization. The law of each of the States to which he is subject, the law of the church to which he is affiliated, the contractual engagements to which he subscribes in the exercise of his individual economic rights, these all present a variety of distinct legal authorities, each one but imperfectly suited to the others.[42]

From this perspective, self-regulatory acts and, more generally, those private sources of legislation that some choose to refer to as 'soft' law, seem in fact to be legal systems in the full sense of the term, even though their creation may seem less legitimate than a more traditional public process of enactment.

In other respects, without being naive, we must realize that such a system of regulation by the parties themselves is far from being gratuitous. Operators are concerned by such measures either to sidestep national legislations or to subject them to a 'soft' interpretation, yet notably avoid the levelling of grave accusations. The debate on Internet pornography arising from certain recent events, and the resultant proliferation of self-regulatory measures in this respect, well illustrates the argument.

The 'Reception' Given Private Sources by State Law

The three laws: contract, fair trade and responsibility   The general and universal principles of national law – particularly those of contractual autonomy, fair and equitable trade and responsibility – can be taken initially as a control model for private sources of 'cyber-law'.

In that context, the different targets pursued by the authors of a code of conduct should be emphasized. Traditionally, the sole target of self-regulation was to fix the rules of behaviour between the actors, authors or those represented in the process of setting up the code of conduct. The main aim, then, is to avoid unfair, uncontrolled competition between them. Sometimes, the code of conduct will pursue another goal and provide solutions with external effects outside the circle of the natural addressees of the code – the authors or representatives of the actors concerned by it. So, when the self-regulation defines the professional behaviour acceptable *vis-à-vis* third parties concerned by the operations regulated by the code of conduct, it is clear that the code of conduct is intended to have effects *vis-à-vis* third parties, including in particular, but not only, parties contracting with the actors submitted to the code of conduct. To take an example, if a direct marketing association forbids or, on the contrary, accepts certain advertising methods or messages, its attitude might affect the third parties independently of the fact that they will become contractual parties. From the legal point of view, this external effect of the code of conduct is more questionable than the internal effects.

As regards the external opposability of the code of conduct to persons who are not only third parties but will become contracting parties and, in that quality, will be considered as submitted to the content of the code of conduct, it would doubtless be sufficient for a judge to go 'to the limits of contractual logic', as Vivant[43] assures us, to become aware of the absence of fully free and informed consent on the part of the internaut in accepting a 'policy' or a code of conduct that barely respects his or her interests. This approach places a question mark not only over the content of the private norm, its conformity with the legal rules, its clarity and its possible unfair character, but also over the integration of the code of conduct within the scope of the contract, which might be questionable when the code of conduct is referred to only by a hyperlink that is difficult to activate.

The other 'third parties' might consider themselves prejudiced by a behaviour which, although in strict conformity with the content of the code, has recourse to standards such as 'good faith' and *in pater familias* – those 'as well as possible' forms often permit lip service to be paid to the adoption of an ethical code, respectful of its norms of prudence and diligence and its sanctioning of violations of a norm developed by a private judicial system, to the degree to which that norm represents a professional standard whose contravention automatically constitutes a fault.[44] However, recourse to standards authorizes the denunciation of self-regulation or systems of certification whose content does not seem to respect those standards.

The adoption by one faction of 'codes of conduct' or of 'technical norms' may be intended to prejudice the competition in some way. It will be sufficient to invoke the principles of free and fair trade to strip them of all value.

Rejection of private judicial systems where public order has been contravened   The body of jurisprudence dealing with the activities of associative authorities, both at the time of enactment of disciplinary rules and during their application, permits us to extrapolate certain rules which are relevant when tackling the subject of self-regulation in cyberspace. This applies equally to legal systems whose right to create norms is undisputed. While not contesting the autonomy of the norms enacted by a given profession, jurisprudence has sometimes nonetheless called them into question, particularly in situations when the professional norm is in conflict with a state norm judged to be in the public interest.[45] So, for example, if a code of conduct authorizes a server to process data obtained by means of cookies, without prior information of the Internaut concerned, it would constitute an infringement of the principle of transparency upheld by the data protection directive. Furthermore, the space available for self-regulation is reduced each time a conflict involves a superior motive or fundamental value. State law will either by decree or recognition proclaim such norms as being in the public interest. This assertion should, however, be nuanced by the following consideration: the efficacy of the state norm can be reduced insofar as state authority does not possess the means to enforce it. In such a hypothesis, the state recognized norm is granted a value more symbolic than real, and self-regulation may represent the lesser evil.

Jurisprudence has also sometimes questioned professional norms in situations when the application of the norm represents an abuse of rights inasmuch as the sanction is disproportionate to the infraction concerned, or its levying has not taken into account the minimum right to defence according with Article 6 of the European Convention of Human Rights. This question is delicate in so far as the self-regulation pretends to external effects particularly when privacy or consumer protection questions are addressed by the code of conduct or by technical norms. One would like to underline the very interesting solution foreseen by Article 17 of the draft proposal of the Directive on certain legal aspects of the electronic commerce: 'Member States shall ensure that the bodies responsible for out-of-court settlements of consumers apply the principles of independence and transparency, the adversarial principle, and the principles of effectiveness of the procedure, legality of the decisions, liberty of parties and representation.

In an Internet context there are certainly instances of sanctions which, through their unilateral application by less than transparent authorities without any external control, may be deemed abusive of a party's rights. Thus the immediate revoking of a server's certificate for alleged behavioural non-conformity to a code of conduct may seem to be an unacceptable censure to a state authority concerned with the respect of freedom of expression and the principle of unrestricted defence.

The Promotion of the Private Legal Authority: Reflections on the 95/46 Data Protection Directive

Two types of promotion   Taking as a departure two provisions of the Directive referred to, we should like to show:

- with reference to Article 27, how state law articulates both public and private norms and thereby promotes the adoption of the latter
- with reference to Article 25, how a national legal authority, while respecting the culture and system of other legal authorities, can establish certain criteria for the recognition of private norms conceived in those other legal authorities.

'Monitored codes of conduct'   Article 27, paragraph 1 of the Directive affirms that the Commission's member states 'encourage' the enunciation of codes of conduct destined to contribute – depending on the specific nature of the sectors concerned – to the correct application of national provisions. The editors of such codes can submit them to monitoring authorities that would verify their conformity with existing regulations. The text also envisages the drawing up of community codes for submission to a European data protection group which would examine their respect for national provisions.

Once the codes have been submitted for their inspection, both the national monitoring authority and the European group can, 'should they deem it appropriate', gather the opinions of the persons concerned or their representatives. Finally, depending on whether the code is national or European, each of these authorities respectively can take steps to ensure publication.[46]

The principle enacted by the Directive is a simple one: both self-regulation and certification systems represent effective tools for the enactment of the provisions laid down in the Directive. They contribute to the improvement of the brand image of those who submit to them and increase the confidence of the internaut. Their flexibility and specificity make them suitable tenders for evolutionary solutions adapted to the particularities of each sector. Finally, their European character serves to guarantee equivalence of protection with regard to electronic processes operating in any corner of the continent.

Recognition by state authorities of these codes of conduct takes two forms. The formal procedure of confirmation does not only apply to the basic criteria which constitute respect for the provisions of the directive, but also to more procedural criteria: the publishing of the content of self-regulation or criteria for certification, the transparency and openness of debates, taking into account the range of parties interested in these processes, in particular those directly concerned.

In any event, the codes of good conduct cannot exempt the server from applicable areas of national legislation derived from the directive which guarantee, admittedly in general terms, the respect of subjective rights and the possibility of appeal to justice for the persons concerned. Such submission to the law brings to codes of otherwise restricted range, if only indirectly, a certain legal weight, given the fact that the law, accompanied by the restraining force of justice, remains the ultimate guarantee of the effectiveness of the principles enunciated therein.

The European Council Recommendation of 24 September 1998 'on the development of the competitiveness of the European audiovisual and information services by promoting national frameworks aimed at achieving a comparable and effective level of protection of minors and human dignity'[47] goes further. A number of indicative guidelines, aimed at ensuring the full participation of all interested parties (public authorities, consumers, users and industries) in the drafting, implementation, evaluation and control of the respect of the codes of conduct, are annexed to it. This participation is regarded as necessary in order to legitimate the recourse to self-regulatory solutions.

The amended proposal for a European Parliament and Council Directive on certain legal aspects of electronic commerce in the Internal Market establishes, in the same way, that 'In so far as they may be concerned, consumer associations shall be involved in the drafting and implementation of codes of conduct. Moreover, the actors must ensure their complete transparency and accessibility including as regards their evaluation.'[48]

'Adequate' protection, or how a state authority can impose its values in a flexible manner on a third country in the global information society   By virtue of Article 25.1 of the Directive:

> … the Member States stipulate that, in the event of a transfer to a third country of personal data as the object of a process, or intended to be subjected to a process after transmission, such a transfer may not take place unless, subject to national provisions taken in application of other provisions of the present directive, the third country in question can assure an adequate degree of protection.

The principle is therefore to prohibit transmission unless the third country can prove an adequate level of protection.

The Directive, rendering this yet more precise in Article 25.2, goes on to say that an evaluation of the adequate nature of data protection in a third country must take into account 'all circumstances relating to a transfer or type of transfer' and in particular the different factors, of which some are integral to the type of transfer being considered, such as the nature of the data itself, the finality and the duration of the process, the country of origin and the country of destination, and others concerning the level of protection in the third country such as 'current legal provisions both general and sectorial, as well as professional rules and the security measures which are respected there'.

In particular, the text of Article 25 presumes a functional approach – that is, that protection should be evaluated as much according to the risk of attack on the data's protection and risk arising from the type of flow in question, as according to the specific or general measures undertaken by the party responsible for the data in the third country to reduce such risks.

The evaluation of these measures should be made without *a priori* judgement. There is no question here of imposing European mechanisms developed in response to the Directive on a third country (that is, there is no European imperialism), but rather of appreciating to what degree the goals of protection pursued by the Directive are encountered there, whether in an original way or not. In this sense, the idea of adequate protection does not in any sense represent a weakening of that data protection envisaged by the Directive. In effect, the idea of adequate protection induces a confrontation between the protective demands of the Directive and the responses given to these by the third country. The aim is to ascertain whether there is a 'functional similarity'. Such a 'functional similarity' implies that we are concerned to find not a pure and simple transposition of European principles and systems of protection in the third country, but rather the presence of those elements fulfilling the required functions, even if the said elements are of a different character to those with which we are familiar in Europe. This certainly encourages a better respect for local structures and legal characteristics than would the requirement of equivalent protection, which calls for complete legislative similarity.

In particular, with regard to the protective instruments installed in the third country, Article 25 not only refers to norms established by public authority, whether general or sectorial in character, but equally to codes of conduct or technical measures, provided that these are 'respected'. Thus the person entrusted with evaluating foreign protection would be more attentive to the 'effectiveness' of an instrument than to its nature: what matters is that knowledge of the instrument in question – even if it is just a simple company privacy policy – be

widespread among the persons concerned and among those responsible for files; similarly the trustee would be mindful of the option of
claims or appeal by individuals calling those responsible to account
in the event of any act of non-respect for these instruments. Finally,
he or she would meticulously evaluate the quality of the authority in
charge of claims and appeals, its accessibility and its functional trans-
parence.[49]

Conditions of self-regulation   What conclusions can we draw from
these two provisions of the Data Protection Directive to serve as
lessons both as to the value of private norms and to the synergy
between these and the norms established by the state?

First, the private norm is the better accepted for being defined
within the framework of principles or standards established by the
state norm. Such standards not only enable an evaluation of the
private norm's conformity of content to society's expectations, but
also assure it greater effectiveness.

Second, the private norm may be deemed 'adequate' as compared
to the state norm if the procedure under which it was drawn up
conforms to certain demands of legitimacy: first, the degree to which
that procedure has permitted the expression of the opinions of, and
taken into consideration the interests of, the different parties concerned by the operations to be regulated; second, the transparency of
the norm in question; and, finally and most importantly, whether it is
genuinely effective – that is, that binding sanctions can be handed
down by an authority equipped with powers of investigation, acting
independently of the parties concerned, easily accessible to all and
whose dealings are transparent (for example, via a public report of
its activities or the publication of its decisions).

Some Conclusions

The state norm: a necessary intervention   With regard to state sources,
what is the use of a national legislature legislating when, as we have
shown, first, the international character of the network and, second,
the impossibility of mastering the space–time coordinates of exchanges, lead us to admit the impotence of nation-states in the effective
application of the norms which they have drawn up? The emotion's
aroused in 1996 by the intervention of a German court, charging
access servers with having allowed pornographic material to filter
through, shows, however, that even if state law does not have completely effective instruments at its disposal, it is nonetheless capable
of motivating private parties to put self-regulatory solutions in place
which are at least partially, if not totally, satisfactory. The state, therefore, cannot simply resign; instead, without pretending to efficiently

police the network, it should duly call attention to the social values that enshrine the norms, even if this is only to provoke appropriate self-regulatory reflexes and to serve as their basis. It is quite noticeable that even in the United States – the country which is deemed to be the leader in the defence of the self-regulatory solutions – public bodies are playing an ever greater role in promoting, or even requesting, these solutions. Thus, Mr Pitofsky, Chairman of the Federal Trade Commission, asserted in August 1998: 'Unless Industry can demonstrate that it has developed and implemented broad-based and effective self-regulatory programs by the end of this year, additional government authority will be appropriate and necessary.' Since this statement before Congress, the US Government has taken different initiatives such as the 'Global Alliance' in order to protect privacy effectively in the context of its discussion with the European Union in the matter of Article 25 of the Data Protection Directive.

Furthermore, the search within supranational bodies, such as UNESCO, for common principles and solutions in areas such as the protection of minors, consumers, the electronic signature and so on, favour the normalizing of working channels and, indeed, of cooperation between states (even if only among police forces). In the absence of such a consensus, the position taken by a supranational organization such as the European Union can serve as a departure point for international negotiation with other countries also entrusted with the search – doubtless via means more in keeping with their own legal traditions – for adequate protection *vis-à-vis* the principles enunciated by the European Union.

Confronted with the social revolution that the Internet represents – particularly in terms of the dislocation of space–time frontiers – state law, as the expression of the social regulation of behaviour, is, and has a right to remain, present. The law cannot allow itself to be content with deploring the limitations placed on its own enforcement and affirming the essential lawlessness of cyberspace. On the contrary, it must find, in the context of a pluralist normative expression, an adequate active role. As far as possible it will refer, by application, adaptation or reform of general principles, to the normative mechanisms present in the network: the application of principles via self-regulation and technical standardization. Depending on the case, it will draw its inspiration for the defining of rules of law, if possible at the international level, from the content of internal network regulation. What we are seeing here, to use Vivant's expression,[50] is without doubt the emergence of postmodern law, or what Reidenberg refers to as a new 'network governance paradigm'.[51]

Far from sanctioning the state's resignation, this 'postmodern law' – this new 'paradigm' – calls for the creation of new forms of dialogue both between diverse ethical and regulatory normative techniques and, more problematically, between the democratic authorities capable of nurturing such a dialogue and placing it at the service of the public interest.

On the one hand, the state cannot abandon Internet regulation to the sole initiative of its users. We have seen clearly that, in the absence of specific regulations, a reaffirmation of major legal principles spurs the parties to take measures and leads to the development of appropriate techniques. On the other hand, we should like to stress the state's vital obligation to intervene at a time when, in our opinion, deserting the Internet and withdrawing from the field of regulation to such a point that it no longer even decides the general framework, would notably put at risk public order, fundamental liberties and other basic values.

The precise division of labour between the drawing up of state or supranational law and the regulatory initiatives of Internet users remains to be defined. It will doubtless be a dynamic relationship, and one that must enable the users to demonstrate a certain creativity in the enactment of the framework proposed by national legislation.

The value and limitations of self-regulation   This said, there can be no question of rejecting self-regulation as a normative source in the fullest sense of the term. As Osman concluded, 'whether we choose to see in this uniquely "a question of time and context" or the proof that the law must "progressively suffer both the attraction and the yoke of the economic facts" which dominate it and to which it has become a tributary',[52] such a phenomenon can only serve to awaken the interest of jurists who have been taught that the sanction is part of the mechanism of the rule of law. Naturally they are tempted to search everywhere, even in 'soft' law. And if the criterion of the sanction as a 'characteristic of the rule of law is a false [one], despite doctrinal attempts to revive it, this is doubtless because the effectiveness of rules of social conduct, whether they "rule or regulate", does not necessarily reside in the adherence to them by the social body for which they are destined'.[53]

This reflection, which addresses the normative sources of *lex mercatoria*, certainly ought to be equally applicable to *lex electronica* but it cannot have the same range, and this, without doubt, justifies a more resolute intervention on the part of state law. First, the Internet environment, except in the newsgroup context, or in certain contexts, such as universities or trade between merchants, does not have anything like the same homogeneity as the professional environment. Second, whereas *lex mercatoria* only regulates economic questions, *lex electronica* is concerned with culture, values and liberties.

It would seem, therefore, that self-regulation should be controlled. Although it is certainly capable of representing the spontaneous expression of a particular community, this is rarely the case. Furthermore, state law is obliged at least to fix the standards which serve as a basis for the development of self-regulation and its associated normative techniques and to ensure that the mechanisms for the setting up of these regulatory techniques and the application of the content of these private norms is transparent and takes into account the interests of the various parties concerned.

THE ROLE OF THE STATE AND THE DEFENCE OF VALUES

Traditionally the role of the state is defined as being threefold in that it consists of regulation, stimulation and production. The function of production is understood as the development of goods and services. In the information society, this function tends to be whittled down, such is the degree to which the merits of free and fair competition and the financial needs of the state have led the latter to separate itself from the entities of production, particularly in the telecommunications sector in which the state formerly enjoyed a monopoly, but also in the general exploitation of telematics administrative services (such as multimedia data banks on the subject of ratable property values) where the state increasingly relies on outsourcing.

The stimulatory or catalytic function can take place in a variety of ways. In the same way that adequate regulation, including fiscal policy, can be a useful lever for the development of computerized goods and services, the transformation of processes within the government, or between the government and the people, via the introduction of information and communication technology, can lead to the people adopting that same technology. It is for this reason that all national programmes relative to the information society speak of the need for a 're-engineering' of public functions, and it is a fact that the use of electronic forms for administrative purposes, such as value added tax (VAT), is leading companies increasingly to expect electronic invoicing from their business partners.

The first function of regulation constrains the state to espouse the cause of liberty. Indeed, the earlier discussion not only stressed the complexity of the legal debates arising from the use of information and communication technologies, it also bore witness to the recurrence and omnipresence of the issue of liberties.

The following reflections derive from the recognized fact that the increasingly significant incursions of economic operators, supported in their activities by recent developments in the safeguarding of electronic messages, are radically reshaping the landscape. As stated earlier, the Internet is rapidly leaving the 'forum of ideas' which characterized exchanges within the scientific community where the Net was originally conceived, to enter the world of the 'trade fair'. Thus two worlds currently appear to exist side by side within the Internet:

> The first being cyberspace, close to the 'forum of ideas', where technology appears, on the one hand, to be a mode of expression – some would say 'free' – of each and everyone, an expression all the more free for the fact that the author of a message can decide whether or not to identify him or herself and choose the correspondents with whom he or she wishes to communicate and, on the other hand, a means of access to the free creations of others, wherever they may be in the world;
>
> The second being the 'superhighway', not unlike a 'trade fair', where technology appears as an extraordinary tool at the service of the market, enabling it to improve information production circuits, but above all to control distribution. Electronic services for copyright management and the creation of centres for the certification of messages (see Part I above) are best understood in this light.[54]

In other words, the Internet's development oscillates between two worlds: one of uncontrolled ideas and the other founded on the laws of the marketplace and the rules of property.[55] And it is in taking this revolution into account that we confirm the essential role of law and regulatory functions in maintaining a free society.

Regulatory function can be understood, in one sense, to mean drawing up the rules of the global game – rules that are valid for a given society, either general (as for example, the laws of fair trade) or specific to a particular sector (such as audiovisual law) – or, in another sense, applying those rules by means of 'new regulatory bodies', those 'independent administrative authorities' whose existence and proliferation have already been indicated (see pp.152–5 above).

Shorn of its productive function, the state concentrates its role around the defence or, preferably, the promotion of certain values. Thus even such a privatistic issue as that of contractual law nonetheless raises challenges to questions of liberties and non-discrimination. This is the case with the appearance of 'electronic notaries' and the right of every person to an electronic signature. It is the case with the need to develop, for reasons of privacy protection, the right to the use of anonymization techniques for transactions, whether towards certain parties to the transmission or the recipient. It is the case in the laws of intellectual property, as expressed in the idea of obligatory licensing, when the desire emerges not to reserve the right of information access solely to the 'haves' of this world but to guarantee it to all, if we are to avoid a two-track society. Finally it is the omnipresence of the principle of freedom of expression which, as the jurisprudence of the European Court of Human Rights reminds us, cannot be limited by superior interests and liberties except in so far as such limitation is strictly necessary for the protection of these selfsame interests and liberties, which leads the state, not only to avoid any excessive regulation, but equally to take care that self-regulation does not become a more insidious and effective tool of censure than any police surveillance could be.

Beyond this, the state will endeavour, on the one hand, by a policy called 'universal service', to ensure that each citizen enjoys the possibility of access to the benefits of the information society and, on the other, to introduce appropriate instruments to ensure a better participation of all citizens in defining the *res publica*, by avoiding the traps of what some call 'electronic democracy'. It is these last two points that will be addressed below.

Beyond the Universal Telecommunications Service: The 'Universal Service' in the Information Society

The Universal Telecommunications Service

The proposal to create a universal telecommunications service is based on an indication that the citizens of the information society demand more than that defined by the European Union following the reform of autonomous public services. The concept is defined as a service that is universal (providing access for all at a reasonable price), equal (implying non-discriminatory access quite independent of geography), and continuous (characterized by uninterrupted service of a given quality).

The concept of a universal service has the merit, while respecting the dynamism of a competitive market and therefore refusing all state monopoly, of accentuating the manner in which new technologies should permit everyone to better participate in society and in the definition of the collective will to co-exist. In this respect, the expansion of the universal service concept is evolutionary in so far as it takes into account technological developments and their increasing distribution within society.

The universal service is initially understood as access to communications technologies: to the network or today's telephone service, to e-mail and to the information superhighway of tomorrow. Until now, only this universal telecommunications service has been considered by European texts.

A second aspect of the universal telecommunications service, already present in certain European countries and encouraged by

Belgian legislation of 17 December 1997, favours the connection of schools and public libraries so that everyone may have access to technological culture.

The Universal Service in the Information Society

President Clinton and Vice-President Gore's 'National Information Infrastructure Policy' (1993) has brought a revolutionary dimension to the concept of a universal service, without much altering its definition. The universal service concept grows daily in vitality and represents a means of fighting against social discrimination.

That political will was enshrined in the Telecommunications Act (1996), section 254 of which establishes the principles of a universal service, defines its expansion and, finally, establishes a periodic revision procedure for its contents.[56]

The consequences of such a positive approach, which founds the development of an information society upon the flowering of our liberties, highlights the importance – even necessity – of a redefinition of the universal service, no longer understood only as the access to technical means of communication (infrastructure and voice transport service), but equally as the means whereby the demands of creation and provision can be introduced openly into the concept of universal service, as that which is considered 'essential' and 'vital' for assuring the people's participation in a democratic society. The task here, according to the American policy definition given in the 'National Information Infrastructure Policy' is to take care that no discrimination occurs between those with the necessary know-how and those without – the information 'haves' and 'have nots'. As proclaimed by Principle No. 1 of the UNESCO Experts Group (1998), 'The right of communication is a fundamental human right' and, therefore, 'Every citizen should have the right to meaningful participation in the information society' (Principle No. 2). This implies that 'States should promote universal services where, to the extent possible given the different national and regional circumstances and resources, the new media shall be accessible at community level by all individuals, on a non-discriminatory basis regardless of geographic location' (Principle No. 3).

Even if multiple and various expressions of this right have to be realized according to the level of development of each country, the issue is not merely one of ensuring technical access to a network or service, at a reasonable price and in a non-discriminatory manner, but of giving access to the information content itself. We are already familiar with certain well known examples in the United States, such as access to training and health care. The important thing now is to make certain services of public interest available to everyone by means of telecommunications systems of different parameters according to the type of service, if there is not to be a two-tiered society.

To this end, several national reports (Canadian, Danish, Dutch and French, *inter alia*) stress the need for a voluntarist education policy in the use of these technologies in secondary and even primary schools. Apart from the actual linking of schools to the infrastructures, the use of interactive technologies can be a valuable teaching aid, while at the same time encouraging students to master the new technology. Such an educative process should also include lessons in the reading of onscreen images, whether in the form of advertising, of general information or other, in order that future users of these new media may know how to 'decode' the messages that the network provides. In the words of the UNESCO Experts Group (1998):

> All persons should have a right to appropriate education in order to read, write and work in cyberspace. There should be specific initiatives to educate parents, children, teachers and other Internet users on the implications of their participation in cyberspace and on how to maximize the opportunities presented by the new media. (Principle No. 6)

In addition there is an interest in the creation of 'information centres' open to everyone in locations such as public libraries. Local experiments attest to the dual benefit of such centres: first, they enable populations which, for financial reasons, have difficulty in accessing electronic information services to come online at a reasonable cost; second, they stimulate direct contact between individuals grouped around a terminal and thereby diminish the risk of an 'isolating' technology, where only virtual, individualistic communication is on offer.

On the medical front, the concept of a Universal Public Health Service is being developed – in other words, a positive commitment on behalf of the government to establish online assistance services to help with the filling out of forms, and medical information services for statistical and other purposes. This is, in its turn, the source of the state's duty to subsidize certain establishments, notably in higher education, for access to, and diffusion of, such data.

Under the heading of a Universal Public Health Service is also found the creation of information infrastructures of high capacity and output between hospitals situated in low population areas with few highly qualified staff and hospitals which, either due to their geographical position or to their university status, employ highly qualified personnel. Such networks serve to improve the standard of the health service.

This strategy can be extended to other sectors; in many fields of governance, information technology could improve citizens' access to public services, whether to the social services, or for the issuing of building permits, or access to the fiscal authority, or helpline services for the filling out or sending of administrative forms, or to the public services of the judiciary for the electronic certification of messages, the lodging of complaints or the deposition or exchange of findings.

Basically, the entire functioning of a government and its attendant services can be reviewed in the light of its potential for the development of information and communications technologies.

This transformation of government services has its legal foundation in the law of mutability – a key principle of public service – and in the laws of access to government documents. Particularly in an electronic environment, this right should be understood not only in terms of ensuring citizens' right to be informed by their government (see the following section) but, in a more voluntarist context, in terms of the government's desire to be of greater service to its citizens.

The recent national legislation regarding the electronic diffusion, particularly via the Internet, of the various public regulations and court cases are an example of this.[57] But above and beyond this, the possibility for a citizen to follow the progress of his or her application for a building permit, for instance, and be further able, thanks to a decision helpline system, to understand the logic of the regulations involved in that permission, constitute even more remarkable advances in the application of the citizen's right to administrative transparency.

The Virtues of a Large Concept

To conclude, the virtue of a universal service concept is a multiple one. First, a social goal is being pursued by those advancing the concept: a dualization of society is to be avoided. Second, the necessarily evolutionary content of such a universal service calls for forum discussions by all parties involved before the public authority makes any decision, and is thus a gauge of the participation of all in defining the information society of tomorrow. Third, the concept of a universal service, in preference to a simple public service, accentuates the possibility of private sector participation in one or other of the tasks of setting up or distribution of each service deemed to be of public interest. This collaboration between government and the private sector may be seen as a better guarantee for the effectiveness of the service, provided that a private monopoly is not substituted for a public one, and that guarantees to this effect exist in the form of laws of competition, public markets and so forth.

Electronic Democracy: From Myth to Reality[58]

Technologies of Information and Communication and Democracy: A Multifaceted Dialogue

The new information and communication technologies are equally capable of promoting freedom of expression and information and, in a wider sense, democracy. They facilitate a citizens' access to public information, offer them the possibility of being consulted or of intervening more directly in the decision-making process, and can even pose a danger when used to dubious ends by political parties or lobbies wishing to influence a political decision.

Two questions relating to these themes shall be examined here. First, reflection on the subject of information superhighways is stimulating a revitalization of the laws of access to government files (Freedom of Information Acts). Thanks to the administrative transparency that these laws assure, they emerge as an indispensable prerequisite to citizens' free and informed expression of views in a democratic society. Second, these same technologies offer citizens the possibility of being consulted or of intervening more directly in all decision-making processes, particularly at the local level. This will lead to increased use by political parties of the facilities offered by the new technologies, thereby raising not only hopes, but also such fears as to justify defining certain rules of the game.

From Access to Administrative Documents to Electronic Access

The cornerstones of legislation The freedom of expression recognized in Article 10 of the European Convention for the Protection of Human Rights and Fundamental Freedoms presumes, if it is to be effective, an obligation on the part of the state which is as much passive as it is active – an obligation to inform both of the action taken and the action intended. The public's right to be informed, understood not as a subjective right but as a democratic principle, finds its primary expression in the freedom of information.

This, bearing as it does on the relationship between the governed and the powers that be, takes on a very particular sense and signifies the ability of every citizen to gain a knowledge of government files as well as information held by public authorities. Freedom of information, the instrument of transparency for public and administrative institutions, offers, through this progress towards the installation of participatory democracy, the indispensable complement to current regimes of representative democracy. The open debate within the body politic cannot take place except on the basis of access to all information held by the public sector.

This assertion has already served as a foundation for the very principle of the Council of Europe's recommendation on access to information held by public authorities, a recommendation which was taken up by numerous national 'freedom of information' laws. The use of information and communication technologies (ICTs) gives new forms – not to say a new significance – to this right of access.

Electronic access to administrative documents   Under the impulse of the American 'National Information Infrastructure Policy', simple technologies have been set up all over the United States, particularly at the local level, permitting over-the-counter access for citizens to exercise their rights under this legislation more effectively. In this way citizens can obtain information and services (population or land register, tax service, social security) from the municipality either from a home terminal or from one of the counters at different points in the town.

This is not just a matter of ensuring access to, or distribution of, statistical, geographic, demographic, administrative or legislative government databases, but of permitting an interactive electronic dialogue between the government and its citizens. Hence we can imagine citizens, thanks to the interactivity of these networks, being able to question their governments on those procedures which concern them (say, building permits, entries in the commercial register and so on) and to accomplish this without needing to leave their homes. This means that the people can continuously monitor documents which concern them.

By pushing this reasoning still further, it might be asked whether the processing of administrative data should not be conceived in such a way as to enable the people to access the process itself directly via their own terminal. These questions are the subject of current discussions in the context of freedom of access to electronic information in the United States, but it is only in Canada, at the federal level, that the law has opened up the right to include 'computer time' – in other words, the duty of public authorities to perform the necessary data programming, as a means of responding, including via electronic means, to each interested citizen requesting direct access.

The evidence of a multiplicity of developments and suggestions indicates the desire for a profound change in the right of access. This is not simply a matter of ensuring citizens' rights to be informed by their government but, thanks to information technologies, of transforming, through a more voluntarist approach, the now transparent administration into a better service for its citizens.

However, these new ICT implementations will raise the problem of accessibility for all citizens to the network. The denial of a two-tier society of 'haves' and 'have-nots' is justified not only for reasons of ethics or social justice but also in terms of democracy by which everyone is entitled to access administrative and governmental services. The state has a duty to abolish any barriers to such access to these new services. In that context, according to Wellman and Buxton,[59] three levels of accessibility should be distinguished: technical, economic and, most importantly, cultural. The 'physical' or 'technical' aspect is within reach, due to of the spectacular evolution and dissemination of the technologies; the economic aspect will shortly be resolved thanks to the continuing fall in prices, the provision of computers in public libraries and schools, and the development of the universal service concept; the outstanding challenge is the cultural aspect because of literacy problem for certain populations. In so far as the state is unable to ensure these three levels of accessibility, it is duty-bound to maintain traditional means of access to the administration.

Improving Citizens' Participation in Political Decision-making

'Civic networking', virtual towns   The interactivity of networks means that they can be regarded as a more sophisticated tool for dialogue between the citizenry, on the one hand, and decision-makers and lobbyists on the other. The Internet already offers numerous 'bulletin board systems' where messages on public-interest matters of local, national or international importance can be exchanged individually or thematically.

Professor Rodota has described the US experiment in this respect as follows:

> In the United States, alongside the Internet experiment and the other big telematics networks, numerous local experiments can be observed, of which the majority are managed by private 'civic networking' organizations. About a hundred American towns are equipped with operational Civic Networks or FreeNets (networks accessible either free or for a nominal fee). To co-ordinate their development they are grouped together in a 'network of networks', the National Public Telecomputing Network (NPTN) which groups all these appropriately called 'Digital Cities' together. These organizations not only provide Internet access, but also link citizens to public offices, libraries, archives, schools, universities, hospitals, research centres and companies. The main aim is to offer users a series of services which deal with government and legislation, administration and politics, as well as with social issues, sanitation, education and economics.[60]

Such services for popular consultation should be organized systematically by governments at every level – local, regional, national and even international – with due observance of the laws of privacy.

What is at issue here is a modern form of organization for public hearings, capable of usefully enlightening decision-makers by informing them of both individual and collective points of view. Certain rules should be followed in order to ensure the transparency of procedure both at the initiation stages and in the results, which should be accessible to both opposition and majority.

The electronic referendum   Ross Perot, the ill-starred American presidential candidate, contributed to the popularization of the concept of the 'electronic town hall'. This involves an authority – particularly, though not exclusively, a local one – in the development of electronic modes of decision for its electorate. The aim is to install, alongside representative democracy, a form of direct democracy, enabling more rapid political consultation and offering citizens a way of reappropriating the *res publica*.

This type of electronic referendum experiment favours direct democracy. However, the institution ought to be evaluated, taking account not only of its technical potentialities but also of its implications for our contemporary political systems. While retaining complementarities with the representative version, the electronic referendum nonetheless carries with it risks of derailment accentuated by its 'push-button' aspect.[61] There is clearly a risk of public manipulation inherent in this type of procedure, whether in the choice of problems to be dealt with by referendum or in the phrasing of the questions put to the population. But it is also to be feared that the technology trivializes this type of consultation and that its very interactivity – via the threshold of a screen which creates a sort of 'living-room democracy' – deprives citizens of the necessary guarantee of distance, private reflection and public debate, necessary as much for an understanding of the significance of the question being posed as for reacting to it.[62]

Undoubtedly, ethical and normative rules will need to be enacted to this end. Thus, in any hypothesis, the aim, modalities and consequences of the consultation and the authority responsible for carrying it out will have to be clarified. A prohibition against recording any personal data accruing from polls taken in this way has to be affirmed and, in cases where the electronic consultation is organized by a public authority, the following obligations imposed:

1.   Prior to the poll, the questionnaire should be submitted for discussion within the representative democratic bodies and, depending on the case, the remarks of each faction of opinion on the questionnaire should be made publicly accessible.
2.   The questionnaire and the reflections upon it should be published both electronically and otherwise, prior to the poll.

3. Modalities other than the electronic option alone should be provided for.
4. A complete review of the results of the referendum (in particular the number of persons who voted and the modalities of the poll and so on) should be published.
5. No decision should be based solely on the results of an electronic referendum.

Use by politicians and political parties of information and communications technologies   A number of examples testify to the importance of electronic media in the diffusion of party political messages. The *Berlusconi* case is often cited but, far beyond this, we can observe how each party – indeed, each politician with electronic server access – is increasingly organizing the communication of information or provoking debate on this or that subject via electronic systems.

Some authors do not hesitate to denounce the dangers of such a mediatization of the political process, short-circuiting as it does traditional forms of political apprenticeship and engendering a simplification of issues into populist slogans and caricature. Above all, using such media leads to the formation of political opinion outside the common forums (electoral meetings and so forth) where such opinion was traditionally forged.

In the circumstances, we should ensure that school curricula include courses in the critical analysis of messages via the new electronic media. Furthermore, it is vital that access to the new media should be guaranteed for all shades of opinion and that, as in the case of party political messages in the classic press and audiovisual media, similar rules should be drawn up for their operation. These should ensure the proper identification of the nature of such messages and of their authors, access for all citizens via a single terminal to the political messages of all the different parties, and the anonymity of citizens consulting such programs should they so request.

Many electoral rules – those relative to the organization of electoral campaigns, to the laws of defamation and the right of response, to the strict control of electoral advertising, to the prohibition of the publishing of exit polls during the election, to the length of campaigns – are difficult to apply outside the context of the traditional media and 'invite a certain revision of our habitual regulatory thought patterns'. Without this, audiovisual communication law will lose all coherence and shatter into a multitude of specific laws, each relating to an individual medium, and the mechanisms of electronic democracy will be subverted by the capacity of the technology.

CONCLUSION

The role of the law in the face of developments in the information society is a multiple one. Its first mission is certainly one of critical re-evaluation. There is no question of yielding to the temptation of modernity and, by a circumscription both hasty and rough, enshrining in law the originality of technological data. On the contrary, the invitation to 'reread' the law demands a period of distance to enable us to steep ourselves both in the values and balances etched at the heart of traditional concepts and in the need for awareness of the new challenges.

To resolve these new challenges, the jurist's task – and this is his or her second mission – is to become a mediator between the diverse and often conflicting interests that are spawned by the different categories of users of these new technologies. Rather than congealing into law the results of arbitrages – results which will be disputed in the short term – the law has a duty to set up mechanisms with which to measure, quite openly, the degree to which evolution is altering a fragile equilibrium that is hardly definable.

Such a conclusion pleads for a law that is more one of procedure than of content. Open and transparent spaces in which this discussion can take place have to be created. Such spaces are legion. Apart from the public sources, the norm may emanate from private circles. The law needs to recognize such norms and multiply the dialogues between public and private authors, building that 'internormativity' which characterizes the regulation of information and communications technologies. With regard to private sources, the state will remind us, meanwhile, of the demand for legitimacy for their authors and their content – a legitimacy which can only emerge from the transparency of the discussion, or at least from taking into account the interests of each party concerned by the question under debate.

The same concern for flexibility and mediation between parties with divergent interests stimulates the law to swell the ranks of the 'independent administrative authorities', granting them the same creative autonomy while demanding functional transparency and openness from them in return.

Finally, the will to define a 'willingness-to-cohabit' should lead to the creation of a place of national reflection, a place of technological vigil, for the concentration and definition of global policies – a place where, in the course of public debates, the major options of our society will be forged. We will have then created a society not only of information but of democracy.

NOTES

1   The main ideas in this text were initially presented to the Information Society Working Group of the Belgian Royal Academy of Sciences on 20 March 1998. It has been extensively reworked until the end of 1998 in the context of research carried out under the interuniversity 'Poles of Attraction' programme sponsored by, and for, the Federal Department of Scientific, Technical and Cultural Affairs of the Belgian State.

2   See p.170.

3   P. Trudel et al., *Droit du cyberspace*, Montreal: University of Montreal/Editions Themis, 1997.

4   UNESCO, 'Experts Meeting on Cyberspace Law. Working Document', Paris, UNESCO (CII-98/Conf.-601.2), 1998, para. 12.

5   UNESCO, op. cit., para. 10.

6   See Y. Poullet, 'Le droit de l'informatique existe-il?', *Droit de l'informatique: enjeux-nouvelles responsabilités*, Brussels, Conférence du Jeune Barreau, 1993; also J. Reidenberg, 'Governing Networks and Cyberspace Rule-Making, *Emory Law Journal*, 1996, p.911.

7   See C. Lamouline and Y. Poullet, *Des autoroutes de l'information à la démocratie électronique*, Report to the Council of Europe, Brussels: Nemesis/Bruylant, 1997.

8   See S. Gutwirth, 'Waarheidsaanspraken in Recht en Wetenschap, een onderzoek naar de Verhouding tussen Recht en Wetenschap met bizondere illustraties uit het informatierecht, thesis, Maklur, Antwerp, 1993.

9   See M. Antoine and D. Gobert, 'Pistes de réflexion pour une législation relative à la signature digitale et au régime des autorités de certification', *Revue Générale de Droit Civile*, 1998, pp.285–310.

10   See Y. Poullet, op. cit., p.17.

11   See Y. Poullet, 'Libertés fondamentales et société de l'information', *Revue Générale*, no. spécial, *Communication ou a-communication*, March 1999, pp.21–8.

12   See S. Dussollier, 'Electrifying the Fence: The Legal Protection of Technological Measures for Protecting Copyright', *European Intellectual Property Review*, 1999, pp.285–97.

13   The European Parliament and Council Directive 96/9/EC of 11 March 1996 on the legal protection of databases (O.J., June 23, 1996, L. 77) does consider that the marker's investment (in terms of financial resources, time effort or energy) in obtaining, verifying or presenting the contents of a database might be protected by a new economic right.

14   See P. Samuelson, *Technological Protection for Copyright Works*, 1996, http://www.sims.berkeley.edu/~pam/courses/cyberlaw/docs/techpro.html.

15   See Dussollier, op. cit.

16   See Appendix to this book, p.228 (para. II.A.9); and UNESCO, 'Report of the Experts Meeting on Cyberspace Law', Paris, UNESCO (CII/USP.EC7/99/01), 1999, para. II.A.9.

17   See E. Montero, 'Les responsabilités liées à la diffusion des informations illicites ou inexactes sur Internet: Internet face au droit', *Centre de Recherches Informatique et Droit*, (12), 1997, pp.111–36.

18   See J-M. Dinant, 'Les traitements invisibles sur l'Internet', *Centre de Recherches Informatique et Droit*, 1997; *idem*, 'Communication ou A-Communication? L'électronisation du commerce', *Revue Générale*, (3), 1999, pp.39–47; and J. Reidenberg, 'Les Informatica: The Formulation of Information Policy Rules through Technology', *Texas Law Review*, 3, February, 1998, pp.553ff.

19   On all these points see S. Louveaux, Y. Poullet and A. Salaun, *User Protection in*

the Cyberspace: Some Recommendations, 1999, http://www.jura.uni-muenster.de/
eclip.

20   See Reidenberg, 'Governing Networks', op. cit.
21   See Y. Poullet and R. Queck, 'Le droit face à Internet, Internet face à droit',
      Cahiers du CRID, (Centre de Recherches Informatique et Droit), (12), 1997, pp.231–
      49.
22   See Dinant, 'Communication ou A-Communication?', op. cit.
23   See Poullet and Queck, 'Le droit face à Internet', op. cit.
24   See Trudel et al., *Droit du cyberspace*, op. cit.
25   See Poullet, 'Le droit de l'informatique', op. cit.
26   See B. Frydman, *Quel droit pour l'Internet, Internet sous le regard du droit*, Brus-
      sels: Editions du Jenne Barreau, 1997.
27   For example, J-J. Avenue, 'Cyberspace et droit international: pour un nouveau
      jus communicationis', *Revue de la Recherche Juridique – Droit prospectif*, 1996,
      pp.811–44.
28   See R. Dunne, 'Deterring Unauthorized Access to Computers: Controlling
      Behavior in Cyberspace through a Contract Law Paradigm', *Jurimetrics Journal*,
      (35), 1994, pp.11ff; P. Trudel 'Le cyberespace: réseaux constituants et réseau de
      réseaux', in J. Frémont and J-P. Ducasse (eds), *Les autoroutes de l'information:
      enjeux et défis*, Montreal: Les chemins de recherche, 1996, pp.137–59.
29   P. Trudel, 'Les effets juridiques de l'autoréglementation', *Revue de droit de
      l'Université de Sherbrooke*, **19**, 1988–89, pp.247–86.
30   See P. Trudel, op. cit., p.251, quoting V. Cerf, *Guidelines for Conduct on and Use of
      Internet*, 14 August 1994 at http://info.isoc.org:80/policy/conduct/cerf-Aug-
      draft/html.
31   See T.I. Hardy, 'The Proper Legal Regime for "Cyberspace"', *University of Pitts-
      burgh Law Review*, (55), 1994, pp.993–1055.
32   See H.H. Perritt, 'Dispute Resolution in Electronic Networks Communities',
      Villanova Law Review, (38), 1993, pp.349–401; Dunne, 'Deterring Unauthorized
      Access', op. cit.
33   See D. Johnson and D. Post, *Law and Borders: The Rise of Law in Cyberspace*,
      http://www.cli.org/X0025 LBFIN.html.
34   See A. Wilkinson, *An Agenda for Industry Self Regulation*, Address to Mundo
      Internet 98, Madrid, 19 February 1998 available at http://www.Ispo.eec.be/
      eif/nextgen/mundoint.html.
35   See Poullet and Royen, 'Rapport de l'atelier', op. cit.
36   See A. Rinaldi, *The Net: User Guidelines and Netiquette*, http://www.fau.edu/
      rinaldi/net/index.html.
37   See B. Wittes, 'Law in Cyberspace: Witnessing the Birth of a Legal System on
      the Net', *Legal Time*, (36), 1995, pp.27ff.
38   See Frydman, *Quel droit pour l'Internet*, op. cit.; J.N. Brouir and P. Martens,
      Liberté, droits et réseaux dans la sociéte de l'information, Paris and Brussels: Brugland,
      LGDJ, 1996.
39   B. Frydman, *Quel droit pour l'Internet*, op. cit.
40   Trudel, 'Les effets juridiques', op. cit.
41   F. Rigaux, *Droit public et droit privé dans les relations internationales*, Paris: Pedone
      1977; S. Romano, *L'ordre junidique*, Paris: Dalloz.
42   Rigaux, *Droit public*, op. cit., p.439.
43   M. Vivant, 'Cybermonde: droit et droits des réseaux', *Semaine Juridique*, (3969),
      1996.
44   See J. Osman, 'Avis, directives, codes de bonne conduite, recommandations,
      déontologie, éthique, etc.: réflexions sur la dégradation des sources privées du
      droit', *Revue Trimestrielle de Droit Civil*, 1995, pp.509–31.

45 N. Decoopman, 'Droit et déontologie: contribution à l'étude des modes de régulation', in *Les usages sociaux du droit*, Paris: PUF, 1989.
46 See M.-H. Boulanger et al., 'La protection des données à caractère personnelle en droit communitaire', *Journal des Tribunaux de droit européen*, 1997, pp.121–7, 145–55, 173–9.
47 98/560/EC, Official Journal L270, 07/10/98, pp.0048–0055.
48 Amended proposal, presented by the Commission pursuant to Article 250 (2) of the EC-Treaty, of the proposal for a European Parliament and Council Directive on certain legal aspects of electronic commerce in the internal market (1999/C 30/04), COM (1998) 586 final of 18.11.1998, OJ C 30, 5.2.1999, p.4.
49 Data Protection Working Group, Working Paper, 'Transborder Data Flows towards Third Countries', Art. 25 and 26 D.P. Direct Implementation, Document adopted 24 July 1998, XV D/5025/98 – EN W.P. 12.
50 See Vivant, 'Cybermonde' op. cit.
51 Reidenberg, 'Governing Networks' op. cit., p.911.
52 Osman, 'Avis, directives, codes de bonne conduite', op. cit., p.530.
53 Osman, op. cit., p.531.
54 C. Lamouline and Y. Poullet, op. cit., pp.112–13.
55 See E. Mackay, 'Lawyering and Litigating in Cyberspace', Address to the Eleventh Colloquium on Legal Data Processing in Europe, 4 October 1993.
56 See F. van der Mensbrugghe, 'Le service universel aux Etats-Unis', *Centre de Recherches Informatique et Droit*, (14).
57 A colloquium, 'L'information juridique: contenu, accessibilité et cirulation. Défis politiques, juridiques, économiques et techniques' (Paris, 22 and 23 October 98) organised by the French ADIJ (Association for the Development of Legal Informatics) was dedicated to the analysis of the recent national government initiatives around the diffusion of legal documents (Belgium, Canada, France, the Netherlands, USA, etc.) The texts of the different interventions are available on the ADIJ's web site: http://www.adij.assoc.fr.
58 Taken up here are certain ideas that were developed in Chapter 3 of Lamouline and Poullet, *Des autoroutes d'information*, op. cit.
59 See B. Wellman and M. Gulia (1998), 'Net Surfers don't Ride Alone: Virtual Community as Community in Networks in the Global Village', Barney Wellman (ed.), (available at http://www.acm.org/ccp/references/wellman/wellman.html).
60 S. Rodota, 'Démocratie électronique: rapport générale par la Conseil de l'Europe', *Séminaire sur la demande électronique*, Paris, Palais du Luxembourg Senate, 23–24 March 1995.
61 See P. Levy, *Cyberculture: Report to the Council of Europe*, Paris: Odile Jacob, 1997, pp.228ff.
62 See S. Rodota, 'Technopolitica: La democrazia e la nuove technologie della communicazione', *Sagitari Laterza*, Rome, 1997.

BIBLIOGRAPHY

Antoine, M. and Gobert, D. (1998), 'Pistes de réflexion pour une législation relative à la signature digitale et au régime des autorités de certification', *Revue Générale de Droit Civil*, pp.285–310.
Brouir, J.N. and Martens, P. (1996), in *Liberté, droits et réseaux dans la société de l'information*, Paris/Bruxelles: LGDJ. Brugland.
Cerf, V. (1994), *Guidelines for Conduct on and Use of Internet*, 14 August 1994, available at http://info.isoc.org:80/policy/conduct/cerf-Aug-draft/html.

Couret, A., Igalens, J. and Penan, H. (1995), *La certification*, Paris: PUF.

Davio, E. (1997), 'Questions de certification, signature et cryptographie, Internet face au droit', *Cahiers du CRID (Centre de Recherches Informatiques et Droit)*, (12), pp.65–86.

Decoopman, N. (1989), 'Droit et déontologie : contribution à l'étude des modes de régulation', in: *Les usages sociaux du droit*, Paris: PUF, pp.87–105.

Dinant, J-M. (1997), 'Les traitements invisibles sur Internet', *Centre de Recherches Informatiques et Droit*, 7pp.

Dinant, J-M. (1998), *Using PICS as an Enhancing Privacy Technology*, http://www.droit.fundp.ac.be/crid/eclip/pics.html.

Dinant, J-M. (1999), 'Communication ou A-Communication? L'électronisation du commerce', *Revue Générale*, (3), pp.39–47.

Dunne, R. (1994), 'Deterring Unauthorized Access to Computers: Controlling Behavior in Cyberspace through a Contract Law Paradigm', *Jurimetrics Journal*, (35), pp.11ff.

Dussollier, S. (1999), 'Electrifying the Fence: The Legal Protection of Technological Measures for Protecting Copyright', *European Intellectual Property Review*, pp.285–97.

Electronic Frontier Foundation (EFF) (1995), *General Information about the Electronic Frontier Foundation*, Washington DC, 20pp., http://www.eff.org/EFFdocs/about_eff.html #INTRO.

Frydman, B. (1997), *Quel droit pour l'Internet, Internet sous le regard du droit*, Colloquium of 15 November 1997, Brussels: Editions du Jeune Barreau, p.295ff.

Hardy, T.I. (1994), 'The Proper Legal Regime for "Cyberspace"', *University of Pittsburgh Law Review*, (55), pp.993–1055.

Johnston, D. and Post, D. (1996), *Laws and Borders: The Rise of Law in Cyberspace*, http://www.cli.org/X0025_LBFIN.html.

Lamouline, C. and Poullet, Y. (1997), *Des autoroutes de l'information à la démocratie électronique*, Bruylant. Report to the Council of Europe, Brussels: Nemesis.

Lavenue, J-J. (1996), 'Cyberspace et droit international : pour un nouveau jus communicationis', *Revue de la Recherche Juridique – Droit Prospectif*, pp.811–44.

Levy, P. (1997), *Cyberculture: Report to Council of Europe*, Paris: Odile Jacob, pp.228ff.

Louveaux, S., Poullet, Y. and Salaun, A. (1999), *User Protection in the Cyberspace: Some Recommendations*, http://www.jura.uni-muenster.de/eclip.

Mackay, E. (1993), 'Lawyering and Litigating in Cyberspace', Address to the Eleventh Colloquium on Legal Data Processing in Europe, 4 October.

Mensbrugghe, F. van der (1998), 'Le service universel aux Etats-Unis', *CRID* (14).

Montero, E. (1997), 'Les responsabilités liées à la diffusion d'informations illicites ou inexactes sur Internet: Internet face au droit', *CRID*, (12), pp.111–36.

Montero, E. (1998), *La responsabilité du fait des informations accessibles en ligne*, Namur: PUN.

Osman, F. (1995), 'Avis, directives, codes de bonne conduite, recommandations, déontologie, éthique, etc.: réflexions sur la dégradation des sources privées du droit', *Revue Trimestrielle de Droit Civil*, pp.509–31.

Perritt, H.H., jr (1992), 'The Electronic Agency and the Traditional Paradigms of Administrative Law', *Administrative Law Review*, **44**, pp.79–105.

Perritt, H.H., jr (1993), 'Dispute Resolution in Electronic Networks Communities', *Villanova Law Review*, (38), pp.349–401.

Perritt, H.H., jr (1996), 'Jurisdiction in Cyberspace : The Role of Intermediaries', *Symposium on Information, National Policies and International Infrastructure*, 28–30 January 1996, Harvard, http://www.law.vill.edu/harvard/article/harv96k.htm.

Post, D. (1995), 'Anarchy, State and the Internet : An Essay on Law-Making in Cyberspace', *Journal of Online Law*, art. 3, http://www.law.cornell.edu/jol/post.html.

Poullet, Y. (1993), 'Le droit de l'informatique existe-t-il?' in: *Droit de l'informatique : enjeux-nouvelles responsabilités*, Brussels: Conférence du Jeune Barreau, pp.1–43.

Poullet, Y. and Havelange, B. (1998), *Preparation of a Methodology for Evaluating the Adequacy of the Level of Protection of Individuals with Regard to the Processing of Personal Data*. Annex to Annual Report 1998, XV D/5047/98, Brussels: Office for Official Publication of the European Communities.

Poullet, Y. and Queck, R. (1997), 'Le droit face à Internet, Internet face au droit', *Cahiers du CRID (Centre de Recherches Informatique et Droit)*, (12), pp.231–49.

Poullet, Y. and Royen, J. (1998), 'Rapport de l'atelier : Commerce électronique : vers la confiance', *AGORA*, (98), 16 December, 73 pp.

Reidenberg, J. (1996), 'Governing Networks and Cyberspace Rule-Making', *Emory Law Journal*, p.911. Also available at *Symposium on Information, National Policies and International Infrastructure*, 28–30 January 1996, Harvard, http://ksgwwwharvard.edu/~itbspp/reidpap2.htm.

Reidenberg, J. (1998), 'Lex Informatica: The Formulation of Information Policy Rules through Technology', *Texas Law Review*, 3, February, pp.553ff.

Rigaux, F. (1977), *Droit public et droit privé dans les relations internationales*, Paris: Pedone.

Rigaux, F. (1997), 'Le droit au singulier et au pluriel', *Revue Interdisciplinaire d'Etudes Juridiques*, (9), pp.45ff.

Rinaldi, A. (1995), 'The Net: User Guidelines and Netiquette', http://www.fau.edu/rinaldi/net/index.html.

Rodota, S. (1995), 'Démocratie électronique: rapport général par le Conseil de l'Europe', *Séminaire sur la demande électronique*, Paris: Senate, Palais du Luxembourg, 23–24 March.

Rodota, S. (1997), 'Technopolitica: La democrazia e le nuove technologie della communicazione', *Sagitari Laterza*, Rome.

Romano, S. (1975), *L'ordre juridique*, Paris: Dalloz.

Samuelson, P. (1996), *Technological Protection for Copyright Works*, http://www.sims.berkeley.edu/~pam/courses/cyberlaw/docs/techpro.html.

Trudel, P. (1988–89), 'Les effets juridiques de l'autoréglementation', *Revue de droit de l'Universite de Sherbrooke*, **19**, pp.247–86.

Trudel, P. (1996), 'Le cyberespace : réseaux constituants et réseau de réseaux', in: J. Frémont and J-P. Ducasse (eds), *Les autoroutes de l'information : enjeux et défis*. Montréal: Les chemins de la recherche, pp.137–59. (Actes du Colloque tenu dans le cadre des Huitièmes entretiens Centre Jacques Cartier, Rhône-Alpes, 5–8 December 1995.)

Trudel, P. et al. (1997), *Droit du cyberspace*, Montreal: Université de Montréal/Editions Thémis.

Vivant, M. (1996), 'Cybermonde: droit et droits des réseaux', *Semaine Juridique*, (3969).

Wellman, B. and Gulia, M. (1998), 'Net Surfers don't Ride Alone: Virtual Community as Community in Networks in the Global Village', Barney Wellman (ed.), (available at http://www.acm.org/ccp/references/wellman/wellman.html).

Wilkinson, A. (1998), *An Agenda for Industry Self Regulation*, Address to Mundo Internet 98, Madrid, 19 February 1998, available at http://www.Ispo.eec.be/eif/nextgen/mundoint.html.

Wittes, B. (1995), 'Law in Cyberspace: Witnessing the Birth of a Legal System on the Net, *Legal Time*, (36), pp.27ff.

5 Liability in Cyberspace[1]

PIERRE TRUDEL

INTRODUCTION

The advent of cyberspace, as a place of interaction, brings the question of the apportionment of responsibility among participants in electronic communication more acutely to the fore. In most countries, there is debate on who is answerable for the information circulating on open networks such as the Internet. Now that we have outgrown the idyllic conceptions of a cyberspace[2] which evades all regulation and is exempt from any conflict, and with interaction in these virtual places on the increase, the most pressing issue is that of liability. There is no escaping the question as to 'who' is answerable for information that has caused conflict or damage. It is in the laws of the different territories and countries that firm guidance on these questions is to be found.

In order to deal with this aspect, it is important to specify the scope of the problem of liability in cyberspace – a fairly new area for law. The heuristic approaches that are used to isolate the respective responsibilities of the different participants in electronic communication must then be tackled.

CYBERSPACE

Cyberspace[3] is an undefined area. It is the continually provisional consequence of the interconnections existing among computers connected in accordance with compatible protocols. Its morphology is determined by the software tools used and the links existing between the sites and the data. Thus the hypertext that is a feature of the World Wide Web produces a continually redefined and unpredictable space, fluctuating with the links that the users decide to

189

activate. The course followed by each of the participants in electronic communication depends on the choices he or she makes and the links available.

Cyberspace has four characteristics which assume importance when the problem of its regulation is considered. It is virtual space, a place for interaction, and it is characterized by the sovereignty of the user and by competing regulations.

Virtual Space

Cyberspace is not situated at a specific point in territorial space.[4] The possibility of controlling activities that take place in it has little to do with the physical location of the protagonists. It can be defined as virtual space resulting from the manifold interconnections made possible by the interoperability of the networks. Whereas, in the physical world, the location of persons and businesses within national frontiers is a basic premise of the applicability of the principles of the law of a particular state, in cyberspace everything is simultaneously present and absent at a given geographical position. A message is present wherever a computer is connected; all the states in which one of these points of reception is to be found can claim to apply their law. Few, however, are actually in a position to enforce it.

A Place for Interaction

The Internet is not just a place for broadcasting; it is much more a place for interaction. We must set aside the approaches based on the premise that this virtual space is used for broadcasting and concentrate on determining the scope of the problem of a regulatory framework for the activities going on in places of interaction. In respect of places of interaction, rules are less concerned with governing the dissemination of information than with providing a framework within which relations on the Internet may be contained. At least three areas of conflict almost always become apparent at some time or other in the environments of open or interactive networks.[5]

The first area of conflict concerns right of access to the networks: someone who is not in a network wants to gain access to it, whereas those who are already in it or who control it want to keep that person out. This type of conflict calls for a clarification of the principles governing the right of access to the networks. It presupposes the introduction of measures that will ensure equity or equality as regards access. Under what conditions should there be rules guaranteeing universal access? By what means can we ensure that basic services are available to whole populations? How can what should be regarded as a basic service and what constitutes an optional service be differentiated? These questions concern the status of the networks, the principles of their operation and the rules governing rate fixing. Furthermore, the networks are coming increasingly under the control of private bodies. While they are gateways to cyberspace on a global scale, the networks are also gatekeepers that can, in practice, decide to exclude participants in electronic communication. The question of their responsibility thus arises in two respects: as gatekeepers and as holders of certain monitoring powers of an editorial nature.

A second area of conflict affects the flow of information. Some people want to prevent certain information from circulating, whereas others want to continue to broadcast or receive such information. Information that is defamatory or violates privacy can circulate in cyberspace. The circulation on open networks of material protected by copyright is another significant source of concern. Conflicts may stem from the desire of injured parties to obtain compensation for damage suffered as a result of the circulation on a network of harmful information. The legal system governing the determining of liability as a result of the circulation of information is therefore a major component of the infrastructure of electronic environments.

A third area of conflict involves the mechanisms designed to ensure that users of a network keep their word. The kind of conflict that arises when someone on the network believes that another person has not fulfilled his or her obligations calls for the establishment of an appropriate framework to facilitate the harmonious conduct of transactions. The question that then arises is whether bodies to stand surety for certain contractors exist.

The Sovereignty of the User

Because information highways give users greater control over their choices, they consequently, incur a larger share of liability for the interaction in which they agree to take part. The absence of any centralized control means that users have to bear the burden of ensuring their own protection: no one can relieve them of this burden and claim to offer guarantees against false or otherwise misleading information. On the Internet, individuals may be dealing with a business that adheres strictly to high standards, or they may be taking the risk of entering into a contract with an imposter.

The question of responsibility must therefore be examined against the background of this wider discretion which appears to be left to individual users. The challenge to each of the sites desirous of holding its own is to offer optimum integrity, in accordance with the demands of consumers or users. Individual users can choose to visit only those sites that present guarantees of reliability and honesty or to take risks by visiting sites operating on the basis of rules offering few guarantees, if any. All in all, the option of evading regulations works both ways. In some cases, people will avoid a site because it seems too controlled and the rules in force do not suit them, whereas in other situations, particularly when integrity and credibility are required, they will be inclined to visit sites applying regulations that offer optimum guarantees of integrity and reliability. In these respects, the sites are in competition with one another, which entails competing regulations.

Competing Regulations

Electronic communication presupposes a voluntary act on the part of the user, to whom it gives the option of connecting up elsewhere. Moreover, anyone not satisfied with the rules applying in a network or a particular electronic environment can always set up other networks. This possibility has a major implication: regulation on the Internet is an activity open to competition; no authority can claim to exercise a monopoly over the laying down or the enforcement of rules.

Competition may concern the quality of the guarantees of integrity offered by each of the sites made available to users and the social pressure these users will bring to bear. If the rules do not suit the actors, they often have the option of changing their location so as to evade the unwanted rules. This means that when the problem of regulation in such an environment is tackled, the formal or state-inspired paradigms on which legal analyses are often based must be abandoned.

DETERMINING RESPONSIBILITY IN CYBERSPACE

In this section, the conditions under which the various participants in electronic communication may incur liability are set out. In order to cover the essential aspects of the question of responsibility adequately, we must refer to the principal metaphors illustrating what the persons involved in electronic communication are doing, and then draw up a list of the main factors which create liability for the circulation of information in cyberspace.

The Principal Metaphors

In cyberspace as elsewhere, the person who physically performs the tortious harmful act is, of course, the first to incur liability for it. However, in electronic environments that person is not always identifiable, or may be out of reach. Hence the importance of determining the responsibility of the other persons participating in the chain of the information transmission.

In many situations in which the circulation of information causes damage, the criteria for appreciating responsibility are based on the roles assumed by the different participants in the chain in adding value to the information. The incurring of liability rests largely on a comparison, or an acknowledgement, of similarities and differences existing in the systems developed for situations resembling communication in open electronic networks, such as, for instance, railway transport or the circulation of printed matter.[6] It is thus asked who acted as a publisher, a common carrier, a broadcaster, a newspaper and so on because the obligations and responsibilities attaching to these respective roles are well established in the law of liability. It is therefore by extrapolating from both the characteristics of the different communication contexts to be found on the Internet and analogies apparent in the roles and functions of the various persons involved that it is possible to sum up the situation as regards the law of liability resulting from the transmission of information on the Internet.[7]

In the law of a number of countries there is a close link between the control exercised over presumably harmful information and the ensuing liability. Thus the greater discretionary power to decide what will be published (or broadcast), the greater the liability incurred by such a decision.

In order to deal with the status and responsibilities of participants in electronic communication, it is a good idea to seek parallels in familiar communication contexts in order to find an adequate metaphor. Some writers advocate setting up a hybrid legal framework specific to electronic environments and taking over various concepts already applicable to existing channels of communication.[8] What helps give the impression of a so-called loophole in the law as regards the Internet is the absence of a consensus on the metaphors that should contribute to situating the roles of the participants in electronic communication, and also the various inadequacies inherent in each of these metaphors when it comes to illustrating the roles actually played in electronic communication.

While recourse to metaphorical analysis is likely to clarify matters for anyone seeking to define the responsibilities of the various persons involved, the limitations of such an approach are soon evident, as has been demonstrated by a number of authors. Whereas, traditionally, communication contexts have been well compartmentalized,[9] the advent of electronic environments has created the impression that 'the legal system is trying to fit square pegs into round holes'.[10] Care should therefore be taken not to extend a type of regulation to electronic environments solely on the basis of their possible resemblance to pre-existing environments.[11]

When attempting to identify the components of this fundamental legal framework, it is timely to observe that a number of persons play a role in cyberspace. Each of these participants involves variations and recombinations, so that, in some situations, one and the same entity may assume more than one role. In environments such as the Internet, however, there are always network operators, information providers and one or more information carriers. According to the (often very fluctuating), circumstances, one or other of these entities may take on the role of a publisher, a librarian (or distributor), an owner of premises or a carrier of messages.

The Carrier

Some of the persons involved in cyberspace assume the role of mere carriers of information. The analogy with common carriers throws light on the conditions of liability of the administrator of an electronic mail server acting solely in that capacity.

In the same way as a carrier, an electronic communication system sometimes does no more than serve as a channel for transporting information from one site to another.[12] As a rule, common carriers are exempt from liability for the content of statements they are paid by their users to carry.[13] In contrast with publishers and distributors, carriers are under an obligation to carry any message without discrimination, be it with regard to the content of the message or the person who sends it.[14]

The Owner of Premises

Some writers have argued that electronic communication requires the use of a person's property.[15] This means that persons may find themselves in a situation in which presumably harmful information is found on premises which they own. So, what is the position in regard to the liability of owners under such circumstances?

Owners are seldom rendered liable for acts committed on their premises. For instance, when a hotel lets a room to a client, it has neither the obligation nor the right to supervise what that client does there and is therefore not liable for any illegal activities taking place there.

This argument is in keeping with a principle established in the judicial doctrine of a number of countries, according to which an owner is not necessarily liable for offences committed by tenants. Obviously, a hotel which knowingly makes itself a centre of illegal activities is liable for any damage, in the same way as the web site owner would be if he or she endorsed defamatory messages transmitted by users.[16] It is, after all, recognized that the owner of a property who, having been informed of the presence of libellous graffiti on its walls and who does nothing to have them removed is considered to be a repeater of the remarks and is liable for damages in the same way as their author.[17] Accordingly, a webmaster would always be under an obligation to withdraw information he or she knew to be harmful, failing which he or she would incur liability as a repeater of the remarks.[18] Thus, if the metaphor of the owner is applied to the webmaster, the prerequisite for liability would be knowledge of the presence of harmful information on a site.[19]

The Publisher

The publisher publishes information. Publishing means communicating information to third parties in the knowledge that the information will be read, seen or heard. As publication is effected intentionally, it presupposes knowledge of the content of the information transmitted.[20] In the context of the Internet, publication may result from the transmission of files, or of discussions in the context of electronic conferences, or again the making available of information in files that can be transferred via the network.[21] Thus an access provider to the Internet who examined all messages before retransmitting them and reserved the right to forward only those messages deemed in conformity with his or her policies would be behaving in the same way as a publisher.

In situations such as this, the decision to publish invariably rests with the publisher. For the publisher it is an option: he or she is under no obligation to publish. In the sphere of the press and publishing, it is usually held that the editor-in-chief, or the publisher, is in a position to control the information circulating as a result of his or her activity.[22] Liability for the transmission of harmful information is entailed by this power of control.

In *Stratton Oakmont Inc.* v. *Prodigy Services Co.*,[23] the New York Supreme Court found that the Prodigy network was assuming the role of a publisher. A Prodigy subscriber sent a defamatory message concerning the director of Stratton over the network through a bulletin board. The Court held Prodigy to be liable for the damages caused to the slandered person. In order to classify Prodigy as a publisher, the Court examined the behaviour of the webmaster with regard to the information carried.[24] In this respect, Prodigy exercises some control over the information it carries, because its advertising announces a 'family' service. It must therefore eliminate any information that does not meet this criterion by employing, among other methods, software for censoring obscene material and personnel to examine messages and ensure that they are in line with Prodigy's policy. In this particular case, the Court found that the fact of using the technology required for the restriction of harmful messages was sufficient ground for concluding in favour of editorial control and triggering off liability: Prodigy incurred liability for the information it transmitted, since it was supposed to be acquainted with its content.[25]

Thus, in the case of a closed and controlled discussion list, it is reasonable to hold that the controller is analogous to a publisher and should therefore assume responsibility for what he or she forwards.

The Librarian

A librarian does not control the content of the information transmitted or made available to readers. For this reason librarians are not liable if that information proves to be harmful.[26] It would indeed be unthinkable for every distributor (newspaper vendor, bookshop, library) to be under an obligation to check the contents of every publication distributed to ensure that no offending, illegal or harmful information[27] was contained therein. However, distributors exercise certain choices of an editorial nature, often based on the guiding principles of their chosen calling.

On the other hand, it is recognized that librarians are under an obligation to withdraw information once they have been informed that it violates the law. If not, they may incur liability for the resulting damages.[28]

In *Cubby Inc.* v. *Compuserve Inc.*, an electronic message distributed in Compuserve contained disparaging remarks concerning a rival service provider (Cubby). The court found that Compuserve had no control over the information circulating in its system and that it could not, and had no reason to, know the harmful nature of the messages. There was therefore no liability. The court compared Compuserve with an electronic library. In the same way as a library, Compuserve had the option of circulating or not circulating a work, but once the work was in its system it had no editorial control over it. Furthermore, even if Compuserve had wanted to examine each message, their sheer numbers rendered this an impossible task.[29]

In addition, system operators often lack a legitimate reason for intervening and deleting potentially harmful information. In the name of what, and by virtue of what authority, have they to gauge the offensive or inoffensive nature of a piece of information? By virtue of what authority should they set themselves up as judges with responsibility for determining whether or not a content is offensive and harmful?

The Principal Factors in the Incurring of Liability

A number of factors are taken into consideration when it comes to determining the existence and extent of liability incurred by one or another of the participants in electronic communication. Without claiming to be exhaustive, I note that, in a number of legal systems, the factors to which importance is attached are knowledge of the information and control – whether editorial or physical – over it. Also taken into account, in the case of certain types of information, are the expertise of the person who produces it, the foreseeability of the uses to be made of it, the role of the user, the context, and the accessibility of the information.

Control over the Information

In order to determine the liability of someone who transmits the same information to several users at the same time, it is necessary to consider that person's relationship to the content of the message transmitted.[30] This criterion of control appears even to be a prerequisite for the incurring of any liability. As Perritt explains:

> In all three categories of tort liability (defamation, copyright infringement and invasion of privacy), the requisite fault cannot be proven without showing either that the actor and potential tortfeasor exercised some actual control over content or that it was feasible for it to control content and that it could foresee the possibility of harm if it did not control content.[31]

The nature and scope of the rights and responsibilities of the different persons involved in electronic communication depend not so much on their official role as on the amount of control and supervision they exercise, or are reputed to exercise, over the information and communications circulating in the open networks, or some part of them over which they have a certain control. Rendering some entity liable presupposes the possibility of identifying the persons who have control over the information in the various locations in this virtual environment.[32]

In this connection, Schlachter says:

> There is a sliding scale of control in relation to forced access. At one end of the scale are primary publishers, who have virtually unrestrained

discretion over what they print or to whom they give access or disseminate information. Also on this end are owners of private property,
who are similarly protected from mandatory or forced access … . At
the other end of the sliding scale from primary publishers are common carriers who by definition must be available to all comers and
cannot refuse to provide service in a discriminatory fashion.[33]

This sliding scale does not concern only the rights of access to electronic environments, it also finds its full application in the field of
liability. In this regard, Schlachter notes that 'Those entities with
more editorial control generally also have greater exposure to tort
liability for the statements or actions of others'.[34] This means that it is
possible to classify the degree of liability on the basis of the degree of
control which a person actually exercises over the information in a
particular situation.

Editorial discretion: control over content   Editorial discretion, mainly
exercised by a publisher or broadcaster in the traditional environments, takes the form of discretionary editorial choices – the selection
of the information to be published. It is the term denoting freedom of
expression when applied to the media as entities.[35] Editorial discretion presupposes fundamental autonomy in decisions relating to the
selection, treatment and circulation of information. However, its counterpart is liability: the holders of editorial discretion are liable *vis-à-vis*
third parties for information circulated. Charkes explains below the
close relationship between the principle of editorial discretion and
that of liability:

> Editing – selecting of material to be communicated and deciding how
> to present it – is an activity protected by the First Amendment, al-
> though less so when the editor is a broadcaster. The guarantees of our
> system of free expression rest to a large extent on the assumption that
> autonomous editors will exercise judgement responsibility and, taken
> as a whole, will provide the public with necessary access to diverse
> views.[36]

Editorial discretion does not take into account the intention of
communicating a message of a harmful nature. What counts is the
intention of communicating a message whose harmful nature should
have been known to the publisher.[37] Thus it is generally considered
that the publisher is in a position to control all the information circulating in his or her medium of communication[38] and is liable for
damages, and it matters little whether the offensive remarks are
made by an employee, or in an open letter to the editor, or in an
advertisement.[39] Liability for the transmission of information that
may be illegal or harmful is a consequence of this power of control.[40]

Editorial discretion and its corollaries apply to any publication. However, whereas print media are free to undertake the publication of any text, the discretion of radio and television media, as broadcasters, is seen differently.[41]

Owing to the public character of the frequencies, the freedom of expression allowed to broadcasters is markedly more limited than that traditionally granted to the print media. However, the basic principle remains: the holders of a broadcasting licence enjoy editorial discretion even if it is more limited than in the other media. It has generally been held that broadcasting activities, unlike those of the print media, presuppose the use of a resource considered to be in short supply – that is, radio frequencies – which is regarded as constituting public property. Furthermore, the intrusive nature of the broadcasting media and their supposedly greater persuasive capacity have also been proposed as a justification for the special treatment of these media in regard to freedom of expression.[42] Despite these restrictions on editorial discretion, which take the form of an obligation to balance programmes and ensure that they reach a certain standard, it is posited that broadcasters incur liability as editors of the information broadcast by their organizations.

By contrast, the legal arrangements governing carriers reflect a total lack of editorial control. Carriers enjoy a special privilege which exempts them from liability for the content of messages carried by them on behalf of their users.[43] This follows from the fact that carriers are under an obligation to convey any message without discrimination, in terms of either the content of the message or the person sending it.[44] Carriers may exceptionally incur liability for the content conveyed if they are themselves the authors of the message, but they are not liable for content coming from third parties, for which they are merely a channel.[45]

Stratton Oakmont Inc. v. *Prodigy Services Co.*[46] was the first case in which a court found that a service provider exercised some editorial control, and recognized that it played an editorial role, as grounds for its liability. In this case, discussed earlier in the chapter, the New York Supreme Court, by classifying Prodigy as a publisher, held it liable for the damage caused to the defamed person. What is interesting in this judgment is that the Court, in order to classify Prodigy as a publisher, examined the latter's behaviour in regard to the information carried.

Physical control Actual physical control is exercised by a person who, knowing that he or she is contributing to the dissemination of a potentially harmful message, has the possibility of withdrawing the message and stopping its circulation, not by exercising editorial discretion over the content, but by withdrawing the material embodiment of the content or the whole of the work. That such a factor is relevant to the incurring of liability stands to reason: 'an individual cannot incur liability for an unforeseeable and unavoidable act in respect of which s/he had no power to intervene.'[47]

Several examples taken from traditional communications contexts (press, radio, publishing) show that the possibility of effectively controlling the medium used to circulate the information may be one of the factors in the incurring of liability if the person implicated does not take the precautions available to remedy the harm done after publication or initial broadcasting.

In the field of online data transmission, it is considered that control presupposes preliminary preservation of the information in a medium:

> It must be realized, however, that these torts [defamation] presuppose preliminary preservation of the message in a medium. The idea is that the publisher has to control what is disseminated, but, as a counterpart, that s/he has to be in a position to do so ... . Now this point is extremely important from the angle with which we are concerned here, since a considerable part of the messages accessible on line, and hence their content, escape the service provider. The liability examined here is therefore incurred solely in the case of storage of the message (before it is made available to the public). And this irrespective of the duration: the person in charge of the service need only have been in a position to exercise the supervision expected of him or her by the law.[48]

Perritt stresses the fact that the possibility of exercising such physical control does not result solely from technological factors:

> The victim would prefer a rule that would allow a defendant to avoid tort liability only in situations in which content control is technologically infeasible. Infeasibility, however, is a concept with an economic dimension. Determining what is feasible requires balancing of risks and benefits.[49]

There is thus a close relationship between effective control over information and the extent of liability.

In the case of the liability of persons who participate in the transmission of messages over the Internet, the question then arises as to whether, in the event of damage, they were in a position to take effective action in regard to the information in order to prevent or limit the damage. To answer this question, one has to examine the possibilities of control over the information and the extent to which it is exercised. It is also important, however, to examine how far the persons concerned had knowledge of the information transmitted.

Knowledge of the Illegal or Tortious Nature of the Information

Knowledge of the harmful nature of a piece of information is closely related to a number of the factors on which liability is based. The question does not usually arise in the context of publishing, when knowledge of the harmful nature of the information goes together with a presumption of knowledge inherent in the exercise of editorial discretion: good faith on the part of the publisher does not make any difference to the liability incurred.[50] Publishing means communicating information to third parties, in the knowledge that it will be read, seen or heard. As a product of editorial discretion, publication presupposes a first-hand knowledge of the existence of the information transmitted.[51]

While editorial discretion entails a presumption of knowledge of the harmful nature of the information transmitted, in the absence of the exercise of such discretion, evidence of knowledge will have to be brought for liability to be incurred. Knowledge may be claimed in several circumstances:

> Knowledge, or the imputation of knowledge, can be established if the intermediary exercised content control over the messages on the network (for example moderator of a bulletin board conference who screens messages before posting them) or if special circumstances were present, such as the fact that the operator knew of the user's repeated transmission of defamatory messages and had knowledge that a recent message might be defamatory. This special circumstance may arise even if an intermediary that otherwise does not exercise content control receives complaints about an originator of messages.[52]

But how can it be made obligatory to prevent damage caused by the dissemination of information whose harmful or illegal nature is not likely to be established until after the hearing of both parties by a court? It is, after all, difficult for the administrator of an electronic mail server to decide as to the tortious nature of a message transmitted. The same question arises when the harmful nature of a piece of information is pointed out. What credence is to be placed on external sources of knowledge? And how should the information be subsequently reassessed?

These questions arose in an intellectual property context: *Religious Technology Centre* v. *Netcom Online Communication Services Inc.*[53] An anonymous user made available protected material of the Church of Scientology, through a discussion group. As soon as the Church was apprised of the infringement, it asked the system operator to withdraw the material. He refused to act until he had obtained additional evidence. The judge found that Netcom had incurred liability by its inaction, which was equivalent to substantive participation in the illegal distribution of the material. However, this ruling does not provide useful guidance for a number of cases that occur in electronic communication. In the particular case on which the ruling was given, the evidence revealed that Netcom had done nothing to prevent the distribution of the *potentially* illegal material, having even refused to look at the material in question. But what weight must a notification have to place an obligation on the system operator, or any other intermediary able to prevent the damage by stopping circulation of the material, when it is the policy of the system operator not to exercise editorial discretion over the contents he or she helps to circulate?[54]

Another solution is to protect the intermediaries from all liability until a ruling is given as to the harmful, illegal or infringing nature of certain information whose circulation can be stopped. Perritt, however, points out the weaknesses in such an approach, in the case, *inter alia*, of the circulation of content infringing an intellectual property right:

> That approach would not adequately protect the interests of copyright holders. It takes a long time to get a judgement on the merits in most jurisdictions and continued availability of infringing materials while the litigation process proceeds could result in substantial irreparable harm to the copyright holders.[55]

The notion of knowledge is also dependent on the damage likely to be caused by the information. For instance, in the law of most countries, defamation has to result in the person defamed being perceived negatively by third parties – a criterion estimated in terms of the perception of an ordinary average person.[56] As soon as it is presumed that the exercise of editorial discretion entails the publisher's being in contact with the whole of the content published, it is taken for granted that the publisher, as a reasonable person, knew that the remarks with which he or she was in contact were likely to have an adverse effect on someone's reputation.

In the case of information of a factual character, it is difficult for intermediaries not involved in its production (as opposed to journalists, for instance) to know that it is inaccurate and hence likely to cause damage.[57]

Expertise

The notion of expertise is not exclusive to the field of information. It constitutes one of the chief criteria for the incurring of liability in various fields of activity. When an individual has recourse to an expert, the latter may be liable for certain specific obligations.

For instance, in the law governing building operations, some authors say that general contractors can incur liability for damages resulting from a building operation under their supervision in the absence of any specific negligence on their part, for it is considered that they guarantee that the building which they contracted to erect will be adequate and feasible, since it can be considered that the owner reasonably relied on the skill and judgement of the contractors.[58] Similarly, information brokers, although not themselves information providers, will incur liability if damage occurs as the result of information that is omitted, incorrect, out of date or incomplete:

> It is the fact that we are holding ourselves out as experts and being paid for specific expertise which creates the potential liability.[59]

Sookman goes still further, making explicit the close relationship between expertise and the dependence thereon of the recipient of the information:

> Where there is a contractual relationship between the information provider and the recipient of the information and the contract between the parties is silent as to scope of the duty of the information provider, if the former holds himself out as, or is known as, possessing some special knowledge, information or expertise in the field and furnishes information in that field to the recipient knowing that the recipient is likely to rely on the information, a legally enforceable duty to exercise reasonable skill and care in furnishing the information will be present.[60]

The concept of expertise may also apply in the field of knowledge, as noted by Elkin-Koren:

> In the context of copyright law, in order to guarantee full compliance a BBS operator would have to impose a high degree of monitoring. Proprietary rights are not an attribute of the text itself, but instead define a relationship among people concerning the work. Determining the status of proprietary rights in materials posted on a BBS thus would require further investigation. A BBS operator would have to determine in each case whether a subscriber copied or independently created a certain news text, poem or program. This places a heavy burden on BBS operators. Intellectual property involves a sophisticated body of law that is ambiguous with regard to digitized works. To understand this body of law requires a degree of expertise. Determining whether any particular work infringes copyright [also] requires some familiarity with the texts posted and the state of the art in that field.[61]

In the case of information of a technical character, the person with the expertise will often be the only one able to detect the erroneous nature of a piece of information and hence to remedy the situation – that is, to replace the potentially harmful data by accurate or appropriate data. That person's liability is then greater.

The Foreseeability of the Use of the Information and of the Damage

In a number of countries the notion of foreseeability is central to the establishment of norms of conduct, the reason being that the person referred to in provisions stating the rules governing liability is a 'reasonable and careful' person. The notion of foreseeability is there-fore not only at the centre of the law of liability, it is also present in non-contractual liability for an act of information.

The criteria for the estimation of due care will be the likelihood of injury, the seriousness of the damage foreseeable and the burden of adequate protective measures. If serious injury is fairly likely, and the cost of taking the relevant measures is low, it will more readily be found that an obligation existed.[62]

According to Tiano, the likelihood and seriousness of damage have to be analysed on a case-by-case basis. The more dependent the user is on the provider, and the less control the provider has over the content of the information he or she transmits, the greater the likeli-hood of damage. Such an analysis may assist in foreseeing whether serious damage could reasonably be anticipated as a probable result of the acts and omissions of an information provider:[63]

> A duty of accuracy should not impose liability in every instance where inaccurate information is provided. Rather ... where the probability and gravity of foreseeable harm are great, the error reasonably pre-ventable and the user's reliance on the information justified, a duty of accuracy should be imposed.[64]

The purpose of the information may also have a bearing on the foreseeability of damage. If the information can be used for only one purpose, the provider can foresee more exactly the damage that could result from that use. Spoor explains that:

> Much will depend on the kind of data and the ends which it may be expected to serve. A library catalogue is different from a database containing financial information, and still other standards should pre-vail for a medical database, the exactness of which may have a direct impact on patients' health and perhaps even their lives. ... The ques-tion whether data is sufficiently accurate or not cannot be answered without also considering what precision should reasonably be required, taking into account the expected use of the data.[65]

If the uses to which the information can be put are unlimited, the provider cannot foresee any damage which may result. In contrast, and to illustrate this point, it is reasonable to suppose that aeronautical information communicated to a pilot in a professional context is specific to a single use and a single type of user.[66]

The Role of the User

Liability for the transmission of erroneous information in a non-contractual situation is conditioned by the importance of the information to the recipient and the use that is likely to be made of it. Indeed, the liability of the persons implicated in the information chain is due largely to the fact that our society is increasingly dependent on information systems, and these systems, for their part, have a duty to be increasingly efficient.[67]

A user who is unfamiliar or unacquainted with the type of information communicated will be more inclined to rely on it and will have fewer reasons to check the veracity of the information conveyed.[68] Thus in *Fernand Nathan v. Gribinski*[69] (the hemlock case), the judge found that:

> No charge of negligence could be brought against the victim and her husband, both doctors of medicine but not specialists in botany, who had faith in the reliability of the X guide and could, without behaving irresponsibly, allow their daughter aged 14, an age of discretion, to use it. Nor could negligence be imputed to Mélanie Gribinski, who, on the basis of the statements in the guide, could have believed that the plant she was picking was harmless.

The more restricted the number of possible uses of a type of information, the more reasonable it is for the user to expect that information to be accurate (in so far as the information is used for the purposes for which it is supposed to be used).[70]

Despite the factor of reliance on the information communicated, it must also be noted that the role played by the user in the information transmission chain is not negligible. In this connection, Jérôme Huet says that:

> One may notice that often the role played by the user to whom the information is sent is often not at all neutral. The user is involved in the searches he does or, where he is a patient receiving long-term treatment, participates in the process by supplying data himself, so that it will often be a very delicate matter to untangle the original cause of the loss.[71]

It is therefore important to take into consideration even the way in which the user made the inquiry and/or made use of the information obtained.[72] The user is also responsible for making appropriate use of the information.[73]

The Status of the Information Provider

Since electronic environments present a vast number of cases and the roles played by the persons implicated in the electronic information chain are diverse, it is imperative to take into consideration the different communication contexts in which information circulates.

The way in which the law of liability views communication situations varies according to whether the message is distributed to the general public or merely exchanged between two parties. In most legal systems, the law treats private conversation differently from the communication of information to the public. Furthermore, a vast number of locations for the distribution and exchange of information are to be found on the Internet and in other electronic environments. The term applied to them, bulletin boards, is very apt: users connected to a network post information on them so that it becomes accessible to all other users.

In cyberspace, everyone who is connected to the system can become an information provider. It would be inconceivable to assess the liability of the user who has a homepage on the Web without differentiating it from the liability of a large commercial business whose primary purpose is to supply the public with information. It is for this reason, moreover, that the law of most Western countries deals with messages by classifying them according to the context in which they were sent.[74]

The Accessibility of the Information

As in a paper environment, the data that a user receives must often be crosschecked to see whether they make sense.[75] The more possibilities there are of checking the accuracy of the data (for example, by means of legal data banks), the less justified and reasonable will be the user's reliance on their accuracy.[76]

> The very existence of damage will be likely to be disputed, in a case of the information service being unavailable, if the user had the possibility of applying to another source. The negligence of the user will often be put forward, particularly if it appears that the user should have checked the quality of the information supplied.[77]

It will no doubt be agreed that, generally speaking, a serious error that is difficult to detect should more readily incur the liability of the intermediaries, whereas 'a slight error that is obvious and cannot escape detection by the user ... should not be sanctioned'.[78]

To summarize, the factors taken into account in the incurring of liability always concern the existence of real possibilities of preventing damage to one or other of the participants in electronic communication. The more a person involved is in a position to intervene and prevent or limit the harmful effects of the circulation of information, the more marked is the tendency to render that person liable.

REGULATION: HOW BEST TO APPORTION RESPONSIBILITY

Responsibility is a source of uncertainty: those who participate in communication in cyberspace do so more or less intensively according to whether they are or are not aware that they will have to assume responsibility for the information they send or help pass on. This conveys some idea of the importance of the mechanisms designed to apportion responsibility among the persons participating in cyberspace. The apportionment of responsibility among them, also the conditions under which they incur liability, are a consequence of the norms and regulations which apply in cyberspace and which constitute the source of the rights and duties of the persons participating in communication therein.

The different forms of regulation of electronic environments are in competition with one another.[79] Although national norms are currently the ones to which all those involved spontaneously refer, their legitimacy must not be taken for granted. Furthermore, despite the fact that alternative forms of regulation are increasingly gaining recognition, this does not necessarily signal that they will replace the national norms. According to Reidenberg, the hold of national governments is tending to weaken, but it will not cease to exist and should not be excluded as a matter of course:

> For global networks, governance should be seen as a complex mix of state, business, technical and citizen forces. Rules for network behaviour will come from each of these interest centres. Within this framework, the private sector must be a driving force in the development of the information society and governments must be involved to protect public interests. At the same time, policy-making cannot ignore technological concerns and technologically driven decision-making.[80]

Trotter Hardy, for his part, pointing out that the existing legal regime will continue to apply with regard to the issues it can deal with in electronic space, expressed the view that the issues specific to electronic environments would no doubt call for original solutions:

Of course, a specific statutory response is only one of many legal reactions. Case-by-case adjudication and its common law build-up of precedents can also be applied to cyberspace legal issues as well; an international convention can enact uniform model laws; citizens can create their own customs; service providers can specify behaviour in their 'part' of cyberspace through contracts; a modest degree of anarchy may even be desirable.[81]

Such norms and regulations are conveyed by different means. They are sometimes embodied in international texts designed for application in all countries. In domestic law, constitutional provisions may lay down guidelines and principles as to what state law can do in connection with communication environments. In the United States, for instance, the First Amendment to the Constitution prevents the state from making any law which abrogates the freedom of speech or of the press. Such principles are often endowed with a long life. Owing to their 'supralegality', constitutional principles represent more than a mere technique of governance; they define the scope of the other rules that the state can introduce. On this account, they must necessarily be taken into consideration in any analysis of the regulatory techniques conceivable in respect of an information and communication phenomenon such as cyberspace. Furthermore, international and national norms are supplemented by a wide range of forms of regulation. Contracts, self-regulation, customs and practices, and sometimes even technology, all constitute different means of regulating the various activities connected with electronic environments.

This process of apportioning responsibility may assume a contractual form, as demonstrated by the many stipulations declining responsibility to be found in the contracts proposed by the Internet access providers. The apportionment of responsibility may often be defined in relation to national regulations, in order either to forestall or to anticipate some of their effects. First and foremost in the rule-making process, however, are the rules based on personal ethics and social pressure.

Personal Ethics and Social Pressure

The rules that have emerged so far to regulate the circulation of information on the Internet rest on the personal ethics of the users and are perceptible in communities sharing common aims or interests. Until now, rule-making has taken the form of self-correction by the members of communities of users. For instance, a piece of information disseminated by a web site may be the subject of feedback from someone located at any point connected with that site.

Information communities may develop generally accepted rules of conduct without the intervention of the law or state regulation. Internauts have arrived at rules in the interests of harmony in their relations with one another. These rules reflect the characteristics of this electronic environment.

Such cases of the spontaneous emergence of norms generally occur when there is a prospect of continuity in relations. Relations may be regular in certain contexts, such as networks of university researchers; they are much less so in the case of networks set up around more evanescent or more transitory interests. For this reason, the viability of an approach based solely on the rules of conduct adopted by the persons involved under the social pressure of just one particular electronic environment is open to question. Such rules usually appear in the presence of certain conditions, such as the need felt by the participants to continue to belong to a site observing certain rules.

On the other hand, it would be a mistake to dismiss too quickly the regulatory role of social pressure. Reference is often made to the practice of 'flaming'. Users dissatisfied or displeased with the behaviour of a participant at a site may inundate that person with sometimes insulting messages of protest. These practices reek of public obloquy, and the prospect of them suffices to encourage integrity on the network.

The desire to remain in an electronic environment may be enough to incline a number of protagonists to observe the rules that prevail there. The factors that appear to determine the extent to which norms of conduct are obeyed seem bound up with the individual's interest in remaining in a continuing relationship or one likely to be followed up. Is it not the normal reaction of any trader to behave in such a way that customers will want to come back?

While the regulatory effect of social pressure seems undeniable, it is nevertheless limited. It cannot, in isolation, ensure an efficient system regulating responsibility for information circulating in cyberspace.

Contracts

As electronic environments are primarily places for interaction, it is assumed that the protagonists want to be in contact. Apart from situations involving unsolicited electronic mail, interaction seldom occurs without a consensual move on the part of each of the protagonists. This shows the importance of contracts in the issue of the regulation of electronic environments.

Information is communicated over the Internet by means of a connection made deliberately by the user. It is therefore easier to see the legal situation thus created as proceeding from a contractual relationship between transmitter and recipient. The fact that consent, or the option of withdrawing it, remain initiatives on the part of the user appears to be a key regulatory principle of the Internet. Nevertheless, while this contractual mechanism is appropriate for ensuring the protection of individual interests, it is not appropriate to the protection of necessary collective values.

Self-regulation

Self-regulation refers to norms that are voluntarily developed and accepted by those who take part in some activity. It is already widely practised in the sphere of the media and advertising. Use of the Internet reveals that several types of self-regulation are current.

For instance, webmasters may adopt policies in relation to access to the site, acceptable behaviour and prohibited acts. Most university institutions have established policies or rules defining the rights and prerogatives of those who make use of the institutions' information technology. These policies – sometimes made explicit in official documents or in the standard-form contract signed by the members or clients – relate to lines of conduct in matters such as the private character of e-mail, the conditions of use of the software available on the network, the obligation to use one's real name, the right to make public commercial announcements, the right to make use of the network's resources for personal purposes, and responsibility for the behaviour of subscribers or clients.

While the sanctions entailed by the non-observance of self-regulation are often only psychological, reproof may, in certain cases, be nevertheless very hard to endure. The Internet, in fact, gives wide publicity to unfavourable information: dissatisfied users can make people pay dearly for inappropriate behaviour.

National Law

Despite the obvious limitations to its effective application in some cases, national law may continue to apply in a great many situations resulting from the circulation of information on the Internet. A significant number of disputes implicate protagonists coming under the same national jurisdiction but, in disputes implicating protagonists coming under different national jurisdictions, the question of the application of the national law of a state arises in accordance with the principles of private international law. It is then a matter of determining which law is applicable and trying to obtain the sanction of the law appealed to. The problem of applicability and of effectiveness is the same here as any private international law situation. A more serious problem arises in situations with regard to which national legislations contain public policy or morality provisions – for instance, what is obscene in one country may be quite acceptable in another. Indeed, each legal system reflects a slightly different cultural background, and the differences which can exist in national legislations further complicate the process of determining an appropriate body of rules to govern cyberspace. This may well lead to self-censorship in line with the policies of those countries which have the most restrictive systems of liability.

Even though networks are interconnected regardless of national frontiers, there are many circumstances in which a network will be considered, under state legislation, to be located on a particular national territory, so that someone can be rendered liable for what circulates in the environment over which the network is supposed to exercise control. It is therefore through the rules in regard to responsibility and liability that the law catches up with the protagonists.

It is naive to imagine that increasingly significant interaction can be developed in cyberspace without anyone being answerable for what goes on. So in the different national territories it is the most high-profile, and above all the most solvent, protagonists who are likely to take the rap for any offences committed in the electronic environments over which they exercise some control or which they help make available on a particular national territory. This encourages self-regulation. It is, indeed, in the interests of solvent protagonists to lay down rules to prevent matters getting out of hand and to avoid incurring liability for damages. Cyberspace communities, in accordance with their priorities and conceptions of the world, will have to set about promoting the emergence of a coherent and equitable legal framework to define the responsibilities of the participants in electronic communication.

CONCLUSION

It would be fitting to summarize the developments of this study by proposing an analytical interpretation of the rules and other factors determining responsibility as well as of the norms providing for its apportionment among the participants in electronic communication.

Determining the criteria for the apportionment of responsibility is a procedure which concerns all the participants in electronic communication as much as the authorities entrusted with making provision for the rules of conduct that are bound to govern the relations established in cyberspace.

In the early years of the Internet explosion it was possible to be content with asserting, by way of analysis, that the space created by the environments of interconnected networks transcended frontiers and afforded opportunities for evading regulations. Nowadays, it is important to go further and to acquire the means of establishing a set of norms appropriate to this environment. For this purpose, it must be recognized that the characteristics of cyberspace make it necessary to depart from the national paradigms which often predominate in any consideration of standard-setting in general, and of law in particular. The categories of law, as we know them, seem inadequate to cover all the rules essential to the smooth working of something as global and virtual as cyberspace. On the other hand, the fact that the laws of states can no longer be regarded as possessing a monopoly of the regulation of behaviour in this virtual environment does not mean that they are irrelevant: they will continue to play a major role when it comes to determining who is liable for tortious information.

To ensure equitable apportionment of responsibility, comparisons, but also the necessary distinctions, must be made between roles and functions in familiar communication contexts and those in cyberspace. It is also important to identify ways in which the values and precepts often proclaimed in international instruments should prevail in the apportionment of responsibility in electronic environments.

In short, it is more essential than ever to make a comparative evaluation of all the regulatory techniques in order to identify those most appropriate for bringing about the balances sought. Cyberspace law lags behind, not so much in the absence of rules covering certain incidents which may occur there as in the legal community's persistently confining itself to exclusively national paradigms when posing problems and establishing a basis for rules of conduct.[82] Yet in environments transcending frontiers, such as the high seas or airspace, it has long been known that the laws of states are only one aspect of regulation.

All the participants in electronic communication have a role to play in determining the principles of apportionment of responsibility. The protagonists need not wait for rules to come from the state. It is incumbent on them to define equitable precepts proactively in order to apportion the responsibilities to be assumed by the various participants in cyberspace activities. These precepts ought not to lie beyond the scope of the universally recognized principles concerning respect for human dignity and equality, and also for freedom of expression.

In any case, state authorities do not escape the obligation to ensure that their national legislations take due account of the balance between different fundamental values and adequately apportion responsibility among the various protagonists while respecting fundamental rights. State authorities must ensure that the rules laid down by their legislation are adjusted to suit the new contexts of cyberspace.

NOTES

1   This study was carried out as part of a research project on the legal and regulatory framework of the new electronic environments undertaken by the Public Law Research Centre of the University of Montreal in 1995. This research was financed in the main by the Information Superhighway Fund of the Government of Quebec, with a supplementary subvention from the Social Sciences and Humanities Research Council of Canada. Fifteen researchers applied themselves to examining the principal legal aspects of cyberspace law and standard-setting with a view to making an initial summary of the law applicable to this sphere from a French-Canadian standpoint. The team, led by Pierre Trudel, comprised France Abran, Olfa Alani, Mylène Beaupré, Karin Benyekhlef, Athanasia Bitzkakidis, Luc Boucher, Sophie Hein, Fabienne Léonard, Eric Marcoux, Martin Michaud, François Quellette, Serge Parisien, Véronique Watiez-Larose and François Themens. An initial general study resulting from this research programme appeared in 1997 under the title, *Droit du Cyberspace*, Montreal, Editions Thémis, 1997. See http://www.droit.umontreal.ca/crdp/fr/texte/cyberspace/nv/nv001.html.
2   It is generally agreed that the word 'cyberspace' was coined by the author William Gibson in his novel, *Neuromancer*. Cyberspace, also called 'infosphere', is the virtual space of computers all linked up by means of networks explored by 'cybernauts' whose nervous systems are directly plugged in to the networks by means of 'plugs' fixed to their skulls. See G. Klein, 'De la cybernétique à la cyberculture', *Le Monde, Télévision, Radio, Multimédia*, 21–22 January 1996, p.28.
3   See J-C. Guédon, *La planète cyber Internet et cyberespace*, (Collection 'Découvertes', no. 280), Paris, Gallimard, 1996.
4   P. Lévy, *Cyberculture: Report to the Council of Europe*, Paris, Odile Jacob, 1997.
5   H.H. Perritt jr, 'Dispute Resolution in Electronic Networks Communities (The Congress, the Courts and Computer Based Communications Networks: Answering Questions about Access and Content Control)', *Villanova Law Review*, (38), 1993, pp.349ff. P. Trudel, F. Abran, K. Benyekhlef and S. Hein, *Droit du cyberespace*, Montreal, Editions Thémis, 1997, ch. 1. Also available at http://roma.crdp.umontreal.ca/crdp/chercheurs/trudelpar3/cyberspace/cnc/cnc010.html.
6   See P. Trudel and R. Gérin-Lajoie, 'La protection des droits et des valeurs dans la gestion des réseaux ouverts', in CRDP, *Les autoroutes électroniques: usages, droit et promesses*, Montreal, Editions Yvon Blais, 1995, pp.279ff at pp.306–7.
7   P. Trudel and R. Gérin-Lajoie, 'The Protection of Rights and Values in Open Network Management', in E. Mackay, D. Poulin and P. Trudel (eds), *The Electronic Superhighway: The Shape of Technology and Law to Come*, The Hague, Kluwer Law International, 1995, pp.159–92.
8   P. Trudel, 'Quel droit pour la cyberpresse? La régulation de l'information sur Internet', *Légipresse*, March 1996, pp.9–16; E. Schlachter, 'Cyberspace, the Free Market and the Free Marketplace of Ideas. Recognizing Legal Differences in Computer Bulletin Board Functions', *Hastings Community Enterprise Law Journal*, (16), 1993, pp.87ff. at p.100.
9   I. de Sola Pool, *Technologies of Freedom*, Cambridge, MA, Belknap Press, 1983,

p.2: 'America has had a trifurcated system of communications in which each mode, be it print, common carrier or broadcast, performed its specific function in ways unique to itself.'

10   T.A. Cutera, 'Computer Networks, Libel and the First Amendment', *Computer Law Journal*, (11), December 1992, pp.555ff. at p.581.

11   R.M. Neustadt, G.P. Skall and M. Hammer, 'The Regulation of Electronic Publishing', *Federal Communications Law Journal*, (33), Summer 1981, pp.331ff.

12   D.J. Loundy, *E-Law: Legal Issues Affecting Computer Information Systems and Systems Operator Liability*, 1995, http://www.leepfrog.com/E-Law/E-Law/Contents.html.

13   M.H. Ryan, *Canadian Telecommunications Law and Regulation*, Toronto, Carswell, 1995, p.416; L. Becker, 'Electronic Publishing; First Amendment Issues in the Twenty-First Century', *Fordham Urban Law Journal*, (13), 1984–85, pp.801ff. at p.857.

14   D.R. Johnson and K.A. Marks, 'Mapping Electronic Data Communications onto Existing Legal Metaphors: Should We Let Our Conscience (and Our Contracts) Be Our Guide?', *Villanova Law Review*, (38), 1993, pp.487ff. at p.495; Cutera, 'Computer Networks', op. cit., p.583. *Chastain* v. *British Columbia Hydro and Power Authority* [1973], 2 WWR 481; Law on telecommunications, LC 1993, c. 38, Article 36: 'Il est interdit à l'entreprise canadienne, sauf avec l'approbation du Conseil, de régir le contenu ou d'influencer le sens ou l'objet des télécommunications qu'elle achemine pour le public.'

15   T.C. May, 'Who is Responsible on the Net?', law.listserv.cyberia-l. Subject: Cyberspace is more like property, lease space, rent, etc. 7 February 1995. 12:31:21.

16   Ibid.

17   *Hellar* v. *Bianco*, 11 Cal. App. 2d 424, 244 P.2d 757, 28 ALR2d 451 (1952); *Scott* v. *Hull*, 22 Ohio App. 2d 141, 259 NE 2d 160 (1970); *Tackett* v. *General Motors Corporation*, 836 F. 2d 1042 (7th Cir. 1987); *Woodling* v. *Knickerbocker*, 17 NW 387 (Minn. 1883).

18   Schlachter, 'Cyberspace, the Free Market and the Free Marketplace of Ideas', op. cit., p.118.

19   J.R. McDaniel, 'Electronic Torts and Videotext – At the Junction of Commerce and Communications', *Rutgers Computer and Technology Law Journal*, (18), 1992, pp.773ff. at p.825.

20   L.E. Becker jr, 'The Liability of Computer Bulletin Board Operators for Defamation Posted by Others', *Connecticut Law Review*, (22), 1989, pp.203–39 at p.217.

21   T. Arnold-Moore, 'Legal Pitfalls in Cyberspace: Defamation on Computer Networks', *Journal of Law and Information Science*, 5 (2), 1994, pp.165ff. at p.178. Also available at http://www.kbs.citri.edu.au/law/defame.html.

22   Johnson and Marks, 'Mapping Electronic Data Communications', op. cit., p.492.

23   Index No. 31063/94, NY Sup. Ct, 24 May 1995.

24   D. Loundy, 'Holding the Line, On-line, Expands Liability', *Chicago Daily Law Bulletin*, 8 June 1995, p.6.

25   Ibid.

26   T. Hardy, 'The Proper Legal Regime for "Cyberspace"', *University of Pittsburgh Law Review*, (55), 1994, pp.993–1055 at p.1003. Johnson and Marks, 'Mapping Electronic Data Communications', op. cit., p.493.

27   *Balabanoff* v. *Fossani*, 81 NYS.2d 732, 733 (Sup. Ct. 1948). US legal doctrine goes so far as to consider that a law imposing strict liability on distributors – a librarian, for instance – for the content of the works they distributed would be unconstitutional, since it would indirectly have the effect of restricting the information transmitted to the public (the works available being only those inspected by the librarian). See *Smith* v. *California*, 361 US 147 (1959), reh'g denied, 361 US Trotter Hardy, ibid.

28 Johnson and Marks, 'Mapping Electronic Data Communications', op. cit., p.493.
29 *Cubby Inc. v. Compuserve Inc.*, 776 F.Supp. 135 (*SDNY*, 1991), p.140. Also available at http://www.jmls.edu/cyber/cases/cubby.txt; http://www.leepfrog.com/E-Law/Cases/Cubby_v_Compuserve.html; http://ww.cpsr.org/cpsr/free_speech/cubby_v_compuserve.
30 McDaniel, 'Electronic Torts and Videotext', op. cit., p.823.
31 H.H. Perritt, jr, 'Tort Liability, the First Amendment and Equal Access to Electronic Networks', *Harvard Journal of Law and Technology*, (5), 1992, pp.65ff. at pp.110–11.
32 Trudel, and Gérin-Lajoie, 'La protection des droits et des valeurs', op. cit., pp.324–5.
33 Schlachter, '*Cyberspace, the Free Market and the Free Marketplace of Ideas*', op. cit., pp.113ff.
34 Ibid.
35 S.D. Charkes. 'Editorial Discretion of State Public Broadcasting Licensees', *Columbia Law Review*, (82), 1982, pp.1161ff. at p.1172.
36 Ibid.
37 McDaniel, 'Electronic Torts and Videotext', op. cit., pp.817–18.
38 Johnson and Marks, 'Mapping Electronic Data Communications', op. cit., p.492; R. Beall, 'Notes: Developing a Coherent Approach to the Regulation of Computer Bulletin Boards', *Computer/Law Journal*, (7), pp.499ff. at p.505.
39 Johnson and Marks, 'Mapping Electronic Data Communications', op. cit.
40 Ibid.
41 F. Jongen. 'La liberté d'expression dans l'audiovisuel: liberté limitée, organisée et surveillée', *Revue trimestrielle des droits de l'homme*, 1993, pp.95ff; M. Dejeant-Pons, 'La jurisprudence en matière de liberté d'expression audiovisuelle dans le cadre de la Convention européenne des droits de l'homme', in C. Debbasch and C. Gueydan, *La régulation de la liberté de la communication audiovisuelle*, Paris, Economica, Presses Universitaires d'Aix-Marseille, 1991, p.285; A. Namurois, 'Aspects du droit de la radio et de la télévision dans le monde, en rapport avec la liberté d'expression', *Etudes de radio-télévision*, **27**(1), May 1980; M. Fallon, 'La radio et la télévision face au juge européen', *Annales de droit de Louvain*, (47), 1987, p.153; S.W. Head, *World Broadcasting Systems – A Comparative Analysis*, Belmont, Wadsworth, 1985, pp.377ff; D. R. Browne, *Comparing Broadcast Systems*, Ames, Iowa State University Press, 1989.
42 P. Trudel and F. Abran, *Droit de la radio et de la télévision*, Montreal, Editions Thémis, 1991, pp.153ff; A.C. Evans, 'An Examination of the Theories Justifying Content Regulation of the Electronic Media', *Syracuse Law Review*, (30), 1979, pp.871ff at p.884.
43 Ryan, *Canadian Telecommunications Law and Regulation*, op. cit., p.416. Becker, 'Electronic Publishing', op. cit., p.857.
44 Johnson and Marks, 'Mapping Electronic Data Communications', op. cit., p.495; Cutera, 'Computer Networks', op. cit., p.583; *Chastain v. British Columbia Hydro and Power Authority* [1973] 2 WWR 481; *Loi sur les télécommunications*, LC 1993, Ch. 38, Art. 36: 'Il est interdit à l'entreprise canadienne, sauf avec l'approbation du Conseil, de régir le contenu ou d'influencer le sens ou l'objet des télécommunications qu'elle achemine pour le public.'
45 F. Abrams and D. Ringle. 'Content Regulation (Symposium: Legal Issues in Electronic Publishing)', *Federal Communications Law Journal*, (36), September 1984, p.153.
46 Index No. 31063/94 NY Sup. Ct, 24 May 1995, http://www.customs.com/prodigy2.html.
47 N. Vallières and F. Sauvageau, *Droit et journalisme au Québec*, Quebec, Editions GRIC-FPJQ, 1981, pp.25–6.

48   M. Vivant (ed.), *Lamy droit de l'informatique: informatique, télématique et réseaux*, Paris, Lamy SA, 1996, p.1206, No. 1893.
49   Perritt, 'Tort Liability', op. cit., pp.110–11.
50   J-L. Baudouin, 'La responsabilité causée par les moyens d'information de masse', *Revue juridique, Thémis*, 1973, pp.201ff.
51   Becker, 'The Liability of Computer Bulletin Board Operators', op. cit., p.217.
52   Perritt, 'Tort Liability', op. cit., p.107.
53   907 F. Sup. 1361 (ND Cal. 1995).
54   'The Scientology Lawsuits and Lawyer Letters: The Problem Faced by On-line Services Who Get Notice of Users' Alleged Violations', *Legal Bytes*, 4(1), Spring 1996. Also available at http://www.gdf.com/1b4-1.htm.
55   H.H. Perritt jr, *Computer Crimes and Torts in the Global Information Infrastructure: Intermediaries and Jurisdiction*, 12 October 1995, http://www.law.vill.edu/chron/articles/oslo/oslo12.htm.
56   N. Vallières, *La presse et la diffamation*, Montreal, Wilson & Lafleur, 1985, p.20.
57   J.H. Spoor, 'Database Liability: Some General Remarks', *International Computer Law Adviser*, (3), April 1989, pp.4–6: 'It may well be argued that the producer will be liable if he publishes or fails to correct inaccurate data after he discovers they are unreliable, at least if he is aware of their potentially damaging nature … . On the other hand, liability may be limited because the defendant knew, or at least should have been aware, that the data were not reliable.'
58   W.H.O. Mueller, 'Responsibility of Contractors and Project Managers for the Defective Design of Building Components and Systems and Exclusion of Insurance Coverage for this Risk', *Connecticut Law Review*, 1986, pp.103ff.
59   T. Pritchard, 'The Information Specialist: A Malpractice Risk Analysis', *Online*, 13(3), 1989, pp.57ff; J.A. Gray, 'Personal Malpractice Liability of Reference Librarians and Information Brokers', *Journal of Library Administration*, 9(2), 1988, pp.71ff.
60   B.B. Sookman, 'The Liability of Information Providers in Negligence', *Computer Law and Practice*, 5, 1989, pp.141ff.
61   N. Elkin-Koren, 'Copyright Law and Social Dialogue on the Information Superhighway: The Case against Copyright Liability of Bulletin Board Operators', *Cardozo Arts and Entertainment Law Journal*, 13, 1995, pp.345ff. at p.405.
62   B.R. Bawden, 'Les dix commandements de l'informatisation: l'obligation de diligence face à l'usage de la technologie, *CA Magazine*, 126(34), August 1993, pp.34ff.
63   J.R. Tiano jr, 'The Liability of Computerized Information Providers: A Look Back and a Proposed Analysis for the Future', *University of Pittsburgh Law Review*, 56, 1995, pp.655ff. at p.687.
64   Ibid., p.676.
65   Spoor, 'Database Liability', op. cit., p.6.
66   Tiano, 'The Liability of Computerized Information Providers', op. cit., p.683.
67   J. Huet, 'Liability of Information Providers: Recent Developments in French Law Contrasted with Louisiana Civil Law of Liability and United States Common Law of Torts', *Tulane Civil Law Forum*, 5, 1990, pp.101ff. at p.127.
68   Tiano, 'The Liability of Computerized Information Providers', op. cit., p.684.
69   Paris Court of Major Jurisdiction, 29 May 1986, RTD civ. 1988, p.365.
70   Tiano, 'The Liability of Computerized Information Providers', op. cit., p.683.
71   J. Huet, 'Liability of Information Providers', op. cit., pp.108–09.
72   Vivant, *Lamy droit de l'informatique*, op. cit., p.460, No. 719. As faulty equipment may contribute to faulty data, users are also responsible for the correct functioning of their electronic equipment: B. Tarter, 'Information Liability. New Interpretations for the Electronic Age', *Computer/Law Journal*, 11, 1992, pp.481ff. at p.530.

73 Ibid., p.532.
74 Trudel and Gérin-Lajoie, 'La protection des droits et des valeurs', op. cit., p.317.
75 Tarter, 'Information Liability', op. cit., p.532.
76 Tiano, 'The Liability of Computerized Information Providers', op cit., p.684.
77 J. Huet and H. Maisl, *Droit de l'informatique et des télécommunications*, Paris, Litec, 1989, p.637, No. 579.
78 L. Sabater-Bono, 'Banques de données: la responsabilité des informations', *Expertises*, (98–99),1987, pp.309ff at p.316.
79 Trudel et al., *Droit du cyberespace*, op. cit., ch.3.
80 J. Reidenberg, 'Governing Networks and Cyberspace Rule-Making', *Symposium on Information, National Policies and International Infrastructure*, Harvard, 28–30 January 1996, at http://ksgwww.harvard.edu/~itbspp/reidpap2.htm. The author goes on to say: 'State governments can and should be involved in the establishment of norms for network activities, yet state governments cannot and should not attempt to expropriate all regulatory power from network communities.'
81 Hardy, 'The Proper Legal Regime for "Cyberspace"', op. cit., p.995.
82 Trudel et al., *Droit du cyberespace*, op. cit., pp.cnc 1 to cnc 8.

6 Developing Legal Systems and Good Morals for the Internet

CHRISTINA HULTMARK

INTRODUCTION

The latest forms of communication via the Internet are causing new problems for national legislative bodies. The powers of the national state are diminishing and, at the same time, we are aware of the need to promote good behaviour both in the international environment and in cyberspace. In this short chapter I shall describe some of the problems related to designing legal rules and outline the shortcomings of legislation as a tool for enhancing morals for cyberspace.

THE NOTION OF THE INTERNET AS A LAWLESS PARADISE

The Internet has been described by enthusiasts as being totally out of the national authorities' reach – a paradise where one can do and say whatever one likes without having to observe rules and regulations laid down by an oppressive governor. This is, of course, nonsense. Wrongdoing on the Internet is just as illegal as if it were committed to paper. Most legal rules apply irrespective of the medium being used. Yet the Internet may be compared to a lawless 'Wild West' in the sense that it is very difficult, in practice, to apply remedies to illegal acts due to its international character and the difficulty of identifying persons acting on it.

MORALITY AND THE PROCESS OF ANONYMIZATION

A number of institutions in society aim at overseeing the moral behaviour of its members. Schools, churches, sport clubs and the family all teach children the difference between right and wrong, and how to behave in order for society to function smoothly. Basic principles are taught, such as keeping promises and not stealing what belongs to others.

One of the underlying problems with the Internet is the initial conception of everything being allowed – in other words, the notion that there is no need to obey the conventions and traditions of the 'real world' when acting in cyberspace.

The Internet is a natural consequence of a long established process of anonymization of society. Formerly, we lived in tiny, close-knit communities with the strong social pressure exerted by people living closely together, entitled to observe one another's behaviour and instantly disapprove of misbehaviour. We then moved into bigger towns and even bigger cities with skyscrapers where the opportunity and willingness to control each other's behaviour was limited. The social pressure was reduced accordingly.

Anonymity is almost total on the Internet; we neither see nor hear each other when we communicate. Frequently we do not care *whom* it is we are communicating with because we want to have an *effect*, not a *relationship*. Without the social pressure, one of the principal incentives to keep promises and stand by our obligations is missing. We are distanced from the fear of disappointing those we care for or depend on. It could be said that morals have been eroded.

LEGAL NORMS AND THEIR INFLUENCE ON MORALITY

Legal rules and regulations are necessary to the support of morality. Theft calls for restitution or compensation. A promise not kept must be atoned for. In serious cases, misbehaviour can lead to a prison-sentence. Most conflicts or potential conflicts are resolved through the soft traditions and conventions of society. Only rarely is help needed from the national authorities upholding the legal rules which are a codification of the society's moral values. The remedies attached to those rules are an ultimate guarantor of desired behaviour.

Aristotle said that legal rules need the support of the citizens' sense of what is just and fair. Society works on the assumption that the citizens obey the rules of their own free will. After all, the system would break down if every conflict required the authorities to solve it. The main challenge for the legislature is not so much writing down a rule (quite a difficult task in itself), as persuading people that the rule is fair and deserves to be loyally and voluntarily adhered to.

It is next to impossible to create rules that effectively prevent the activities of ruthless crooks. A society having such control mechanisms would make everyday life unbearable for honest people. Although the legal rules apply to illegal acts committed by sophisticated crooks, one must accept that the practical means of control often fail to prevent their actions. This grim but unavoidable fact has to be taken into account when regulating both the Internet and the 'real world'. It is necessary to weigh the need for efficient legal rules against the need to have a smooth-running, but not overregulated, society. The judicial system is primarily formed for members of society who voluntarily obey the norms and wish to participate as members of the community. It often has insufficient resources and power to catch and prevent individuals who consciously plan to act against legal rules and are indifferent to their status as outcasts.

HOW CAN THE SENSE OF MORALITY BE ENHANCED ON THE INTERNET?

When the Internet becomes familiar and common to everybody, traditional institutions (school, church, club and family) will transfer their traditions and moral values there. In addition, companies selling goods and services on the Internet may contribute to creating a sense of morality by reducing the feeling of anonymity. Examples of such 'virtual intimacy' abound:

- Some Internet commerce creates a greater sense of loyalty and personal commitment than is felt in ordinary stores. I, myself, feel more closely acquainted with Laura, who took my book order at Amazon.com, than I do with the saleswoman at the cash desk in the bookstore across the street. I have this feeling although I suspect that Laura is just a computer producing automatic messages such as the warm greeting 'Hi, Christina'. This intimate relationship with Laura makes me more willing to purchase the book I ordered – in other words, to abide willingly by my promise to Amazon.com.
- On electronic malls (portals) visitors are often attracted by activities such as interviews with famous persons, chat groups, games and the like. This is a parallel to shopping malls in the 'real world' which attract customers by means of musical performances and other happenings. Someone who continually participates in the activities of the electronic mall will probably acquire an unconscious feeling of loyalty that spreads to the

companies selling goods and services via this means. Thereby the risk of customers denying their orders is reduced. Someone who feels loyal towards the seller is unlikely to deny that he has sent an order to buy the seller's products or services.

- Many organizations are involved in trying to establish ethics of Internet trade. The International Chamber of Commerce (ICC) guidelines for marketing on the Internet are one example. These are non-binding recommendations which create a strong pressure to behave in accordance with the guidelines not only among the ICC members but also among companies doing business with such members or wanting to be associated with serious business.
- Extensive educational work is being done on the Internet. Statements on web sites indicating what is or is not permitted with information accessible on the Internet are commonplace. Organizations are also checking whether certain artists' copyrights are being infringed and contacting infringing persons to inform them of their illegal behaviour. Many of the infringers are unaware of the fact that, for example, showing the text of their favourite song on a web site is not allowed. Surprisingly often, infringers adjust their behaviour once they are in possession of such information.
- Different kinds of filter may serve the function of 'restricted areas' on the Internet. Pornographic sites can be barred by filters, thereby signalling to persons acting on the Internet that the content of these sites is not in harmony with the general moral notions of society. This is an obvious parallel to the situation in the 'real world' where pornographic commerce is often located in certain streets that most decent members of society avoid.

THE LEGISLATURE'S ROLE IN IMPLEMENTING GOOD MORALS ON THE INTERNET

The judicial system is unable to function as an efficient or adequate supporter of good morals on the Internet because the legislature is very closely connected to the national state, and its powers do not extend to cyberspace. It is a question of knowing not only where to sue a person and what country's law is applicable, but also who and where the person acting illegally on the Internet actually is and how the national legal remedy can be practically applied.

Technology may help in securing evidence of the identity of the sender of an electronic message. The new techniques produce more cogent evidence, thereby making it possible to secure predictable and rapid judgements. To some extent, strong technical evidence replaces the social pressure on members of society to behave in accordance with the law. Despite this, the judiciary's role as supporter of good morals on the Internet is very limited.

CONCLUSION

What is important in legal design is not the hard rule itself, but rather the establishment of the soft notion of what constitutes proper behaviour. Considering the limited potential of legal rules to promote good morals on the Internet, the legislature ought to be very careful before introducing new rules specifically aimed at Internet transactions. Instead the legislature should use different means to support the availability of electronic evidence, quick conflict-resolving institutes and efficient ways of executing foreign awards, judgments and sentences. In the long term, the national legislature ought to strive towards international harmonization of legal rules and thereby reinforce the powers of the latter in the international community. Beside these active legislative actions, the governor ought to promote the use and development of systems and techniques that contribute to good morals (such as filters against child pornography).

The idea of legislation is one of codifying existing behaviour. It is not a question of change, but rather one of preservation. On the Internet we desperately need to preserve the moral values that have slowly developed in the 'real world' over the millennia. Legal rules play a limited role in the development of moral values – a most frustrating experience for any ruler of a state.

Legislative regulation involves complicated processes of identifying goals and implementing them. Both these steps have to be undertaken in collaboration with the members of society. Such processes are necessarily slow and seemingly inefficient. However, since it is the only feasible way, it is in fact more efficient than the alternative – that is, rapidly imposing the rule decided from above.

In the era of information technology and cyberspace we are witnessing a drastic reduction in the power of state governors (be it parliament or dictatorship). Previously their power was based on threats that are now not as forceful as they used to be. The State governor's threats of jail and economic sanctions have limited reach in the international environment of cyberspace. When a ruler cannot rely on the power of threats, he must take full account of the ideas of the members of society to whom the rules apply. Societies can no longer be governed by force from above, but must develop through the complex interactions of their members. This is an immense challenge to the international community which has the task of harmonizing legal rules to be applied without reference to individual legal jurisdictions.

Appendix: Report to the Director-General of UNESCO on the International Experts Meeting on Cyberspace Law

(Monte Carlo, Principality of Monaco, 29–30 September, 1998)

I. MANDATE AND COMPOSITION OF THE MEETING AND ORGANIZATION OF WORK

1. The International Experts Meeting on Cyberspace Law (category VI of the UNESCO regulation on the classification of meetings) was convened by the Director-General of UNESCO in conformity with Resolution 36 adopted by the General Conference at its 29th session in order to advise him on the establishment at the international level of an ethical and legal framework for cyberspace and on the promotion of multilingualism and cultural diversity in this new environment.

2. Twenty-two experts, designated by the Director-General, participated in an individual capacity. Eighteen observers from Member States or international organizations participated as well.

3. Mr Jérôme Huet, Professor at the University of Paris 2 (France) and director of the review '*Droit de l'informatique et des télécoms*', and Mr Suman Naresh, Professor at Tulane University School of Law (New Orleans, United States), were designated, respectively, Chairperson and Vice-Chairperson. Ms Longworth (New Zealand) and Ms Woo (Korea) were designated, respectively, Rapporteur and Vice-Rapporteur. Ms Teresa Fuentes, Division of Information and Informatics of UNESCO, acted as the Secretary of the Meeting.

4.   The experts met on 29 and 30 September 1998 at Monte-Carlo (Principality of Monaco). They were guided in their debates by the Working Document prepared by the Secretariat and referenced CII-98/CONF-601.2. At the close of the meeting, the experts adopted for consideration by the Director-General a set of principles to be promoted by UNESCO and a number of activities to be undertaken by the Organization.

II.   PRINCIPLES AND ACTIONS PROPOSED BY THE EXPERTS

The Experts Meeting on Cyberspace Law:

1.   Recognized the interest of UNESCO in the promotion of human rights and fundamental freedoms in cyberspace, particularly in the fields of education, science and culture;

2.   Recognized the mandate and the ethical and intellectual mission of UNESCO, its universal vocation and the transdisciplinary character of its fields of competence;

3.   Recognized that current international discussions concerning cyberspace activities and digital works tend to emphasize economic matters rather than social and cultural interests;

4.   Recognized that the global nature of the Internet raises issues of common concern for governments and peoples around the world;

5.   Recognized the need to work in cooperation with other international organizations concerned with matters of cyberspace law and the need for international efforts on harmonization and to resolve jurisdictional issues;

6.   Recognized the open and decentralized character of 'cyberspace' as well as its interactive and dynamic nature, system of electronic linkages, and the irrelevance of geographic and physical boundaries;

7.   Recognized that cyberspace offers benefits and opportunities as well as undesirable consequences that raise complex issues for humanity.

A.   Principles to be promoted by UNESCO

The Experts Meeting on Cyberspace Law proposes to the Director-General that UNESCO promote the following principles:

1. Communication Principle

- *The right of communication is a fundamental human right.*

2. Participation Principle

- *Every citizen should have the right to meaningful participation in the information society.*

The above key principles embody the concept of every person's right to access the new environment of cyberspace, in particular:

3. Universal Service Principle

- *States should promote universal services where, to the extent possible given the different national and regional circumstances and resources, the new media shall be accessible at community level by all individuals, on a non-discriminatory basis regardless of geographic location.*

4. Multiculturalism and Multilingualism Principle

- *States and users should promote cultural and linguistic diversity in cyberspace by the promotion of regional and local participation in Internet activities, information collections, and new information services.*

5. Ethics Principle

- *States and users should promote efforts, at the local and international levels, to develop ethical guidelines for participation in the new cyberspace environment.*

6. Education Principle

- *All persons should have a right to appropriate education in order to read, write and work in cyberspace. There should be specific initiatives to educate parents, children, teachers and other Internet users on the implications of their participation in cyberspace and on how to maximize the opportunities presented by the new media.*

7. Free Expression Principle

- *States should promote the right to free expression and the right to receive information regardless of frontiers.*

8. Privacy and Encryption Principles

- *The fundamental right of individuals to privacy, including secrecy of communication and protection of personal data, should be respected in national law and in the implementation and use of technical methods as well as private legal remedies and other self-regulatory measures.*

9.   Access to Information Principle

- *Public bodies should have an affirmative responsibility to make public information widely available on the Internet and to ensure the accuracy and timeliness of the information. This information could include government information, information concerning cultural heritage, and archival and historical information.*

- *The traditional balance between the rights of authors and limitations on these rights, including the free use of ideas in published works, should be maintained in cyberspace in the interests of the public and of the authors.*

- *States should preserve and expand the public domain in cyberspace.*

10.   Training Principle

- *Job training in electronic media should be encouraged to enable people to communicate in the new media and to create new opportunities in employment.*

11.   International Co-operation Principle

- *States shall co-operate at an international level and seek to harmonize national law to resolve jurisdictional or conflict-of-laws differences.*

B.   Activities to be undertaken by UNESCO

The Experts Meeting on Cyberspace Law Proposes to the Director-General that UNESCO undertake, *inter alia*, the following activities:

1.   Pursue the on-going publication of the collective work on the 'International Dimensions of Cyberspace Law'.

2.   Study the application to cyberspace of each article of the Universal Declaration of Human Rights.

3.   Conduct an empirical study of the realities, significance and consequences of all barriers to access, whether publicly or privately created, and in particular an investigation of barriers to access, such as:
- *The blocking of information and transactions due to practices of black-listing and barring from discussion groups.*
- *The use of filtering devices.*

- *The requirements of standardization which may preclude information in non-standardized forms.*

4. Assess the adequacy of translation software and take steps to increase the availability and development of improved versions.

5. Promote specific initiatives for the education of parents, children, teachers and other Internet users on reading, writing and working in cyberspace, on the implications of participation in cyberspace, and on the maximization of the positive benefits presented by the technologies.

6. Represent, in international debates on intellectual property law, all interests concerned with the need to expand the public domain.

7. Conduct an independent study of the actual economic cost of piracy on the Internet and the degree to which the resulting disincentive has reduced the supply of works desired by the public.

8. Study the significance of jurisdictional issues and conflicts of law and promote harmonization of national laws.

C.   Task forces and advisory committee to be established by UNESCO

Invites the Director-General, in order to undertake these activities, to:

9. Establish a small Group of Experts designated by the Director-General and acting on their own capacity, on the basis of two from each region and one from each international organization directly concerned, to propose and monitor the activities to be conducted by UNESCO in the area of cyberspace law.

10. Establish global and regional study groups or task forces to carry out or commission the studies in these recommendations.

LIST OF EXPERTS

Jaime R. ANGELES
Lawyer
DOMINICAN REPUBLIC

Kweku APPIAH
Africa Online
GHANA

Taik Sup AUH
President, Korean Cyber
Communication Society
Dean, Graduate School of
Journalism and Mass
Communication
Korea University
REPUBLIC OF KOREA

Anna Maria BALSANO
European Space Agency
ITALY

Ndiaw DIOUF
Professor, University of Dakar
Faculty of Law
SENEGAL

Félix FERNANDEZ-SHAW
Ambassador of Spain
SPAIN

Adeeb GHONAIMY
Professor of Computer Systems
Faculty of Engineering
Ain Shams University
ARAB REPUBLIC OF EGYPT

Jérôme HUET
Professor, University of Paris II
President, Informatics and
Telecommunications Law Revue
FRANCE

Christina HULTMARK
Professor, Department of Law
Göteborg University
SWEDEN

Dennis KARJALA
Professor of Law
Arizona State University
UNITED STATES OF AMERICA

Elizabeth LONGWORTH
Longworth Associates
NEW ZEALAND

André LUCAS
Professor, University of Nantes
FRANCE

Suman NARESH
Professor, Tulane Law School
UNITED STATES OF AMERICA

André NAYER
Director, Creations and
Multidisciplinary Research,
Professor, University of Brussels
BELGIUM

Michel PACHE
Chief, International Service of
Media, Federal Department of
Foreign Affairs
SWITZERLAND

Yves POULLET
Professor and Dean, Faculty of
Law
Director, Research Centre
Informatics and Law, University
Notre-Dame de la Paix, Namur
BELGIUM

Tomas de la QUADRA SALCEDO
Professor,
University Carlos III of Madrid
President, Telecommunications
and Informatics Law Spanish
Association
SPAIN

Marc ROTTENBERG
Director, Electronic Privacy
Information Centre
UNITED STATES OF AMERICA

Carlo SARZANA DI SANT'IPPOLITO
Co-president – Chamber of
Judges on Preliminary Enquiries
Penal Court of Rome
ITALY

Pierre TRUDEL
Professor, Public Law Research
Centre
Faculty of Law
University of Montreal
CANADA

Mark TURNER
Herbert Smith Law Firm
UNITED KINGDOM

Jisuk Clara WOO
Research Fellow
Korea Information Society
Development Institute
REPUBLIC OF KOREA

Index